NO MILK TODAY

Liz Gwinnell

Michael Terence
Publishing

First published in paperback by
Michael Terence Publishing in 2022
www.mtp.agency

ISBN 9781800943575

For Philip Gwinnell
who blazed like a comet and was gone too soon

Prologue

Morwenna

My mum was Nellie Morgan, the chat show host, the Page 3 girl, the photographer; an enigma, a shooting star who lit up the skies in the 1980s and then crashed and burned, leaving nothing of herself behind.

That was how I felt when I was growing up. I had no first hand memory of her; no photograph I could point to and say that was the day we did this or that was the time she said that. I couldn't remember her voice or the smell of her perfume. Sometimes it felt like she was my mother in genetic sequence only.

I wanted to find her for myself; to look beyond the news stories and the photographs and find out who Nellie Morgan really was. Whenever I tried to ask questions, Dad went quiet and Rhoswen looked awkward like she wished Nellie Morgan had never existed. The more silent they remained, the more my curiosity burned.

When I was nineteen, Auntie Polly gave me mum's unfinished autobiography, *Street Life*. Mum was writing it as part of her therapy when she was in The Suns of Life; going over the past to try and make sense of how she'd got to where she was. It brought me closer to her but there was still something missing. It was like she only existed through the written word and in photographs and when I tried to bring her alive in conversation, Auntie Polly went on about the Miners' Strike or Dad went on about the band.

To celebrate my nineteenth birthday, Auntie Polly, Uncle Vincent, my dad and Rhoswen took me out for dinner in an Italian restaurant in Llandudno. Nineteen years ago, Nellie Morgan had given birth to me in a London hospital and I wanted to bring her to the party.

"Who was with mum?" I said. "When she gave birth to me?"

Everyone went quiet and Rhoswen rolled her eyes as Auntie Polly reached across the table and laid her hand on mine.

"None of us were there *cariad*," she said. "Nellie was living in London and we – me and your dad – were in North Wales."

I looked from her to my dad.

"So when did you first see me then?" I said.

Dad rolled his eyes.

"Not this again," he said. "It's a long time ago Morwenna. A long time."

I stared at him.

"How old was I?" I persisted. "When you first saw me?"

"We're supposed to be celebrating your birthday," Rhoswen said. "Not going over the past."

"I wouldn't have a birthday if it wasn't for the past," I pointed out. "Wouldn't you want to know these things if it was you? The only person who's ever spoken to me about Nellie was Uncle Joe."

"She's got a point you know," Uncle Vincent said after a moment of awkward silence. "She's got a point."

Uncle Vincent. Always the peacemaker. Uncle Vincent who tactfully suggested that Auntie Polly and dad write down what they could remember from the moment Nellie Morgan walked into their lives.

"And then maybe," he said. "Maybe you could put it all together in a book. There's a big market for that sort of stuff these days. The story of her life through your lives."

I could have hugged Uncle Vincent.

Dad looked at me thoughtfully and sipped at his wine.

"Alright," he said. "If that's what you want but it might not be easy reading. It might not be easy at all."

"I just want the truth dad," I said. "I just want the truth."

PART ONE

1978-1979

Polly

I first met Nellie on Talacre beach in the Spring of 1978. I didn't see her at first because she was hidden by the curve of the dunes and the spiky Marram grass. I was on my way to see Nanny Gwynn, surfing the dunes on my bike, flying from one peak to another, when suddenly a girl with long brown hair sat up and shouted at me.

"Watch where you're going!"

"I'm sorry," I said, as I pulled on the brakes and came to a sudden halt. "I don't usually see anyone out here."

"Well you need to be more careful," she said in that funny accent the English have.

"What are you doing in the dunes?" I said, sitting astride my bike and looking down at her. "It's freezing."

She was about the same age as me, with pale skin and blue eyes and what struck me the most was what she was wearing. It was late Spring and a cold wind was blowing in from the sea. I could see the goosebumps on her bare arms.

"Why are you wearing a ballgown?" I said.

Instead of answering, she crept towards me on all fours, reached up and pulled at my left arm.

"Get down!" she hissed. "He'll see you!"

The bike tilted sideways, discharging me into the Marram grass and I landed in the fine white sand with a bump.

"My step dad," she said, as I sat there with the bike lying on its side, the wheels spinning up at the sky.

I rolled over on to my stomach and peered through the spiky grass like a sniper in a war film. A very tall man in a black top hat was leading a group of women in long dark cloaks across the sand towards the red and white lighthouse.

"The tide's coming in," I said. "They'll get stranded."

"He won't care about that," she said, crawling over to me on her elbows. "They're looking for ghosts. And I'm supposed to be locked in my room but I'm running away."

I turned my head and looked at her.

"Are you in trouble?"

"I'm always in trouble," she sighed. "Owen got cross because I swore but I don't see anything wrong with saying "fuck" do you? I was supposed to rinse my mouth out with soap and spend the day in my room. As if," she said, rolling her eyes to the skies.

"Oh," I said, not really knowing what else to say. I knew that "fuck" was a very bad word. Not even my brother Joe would dare say it in the house.

"What's your name?" she said, sitting back on her knees but keeping her eyes on her step dad.

"Polly," I said. "And you?"

"Nellie Norris May Morgan," she said. "But you can call me Nellie. Have you seen Saturday Night Fever?"

I had difficulty keeping up, even then.

"What's that?" I said.

Nellie rolled her eyes.

"Only the best film EVER," she said. "I've got the LP. You can come round and listen to it if you like."

"I don't think I'd be allowed to go to England," I said cautiously.

Nellie laughed.

"Not England silly," she said. "I don't live in England. I live over there, in that hotel."

She pointed at the black and white gabled hotel to our right, at the top of the beach road.

"You live there?" I said. "In the Castle Bay?"

Nellie shrugged.

"It's a dump," she said. "I've got three buckets in my room to catch the rain when the roof leaks. That's my room, there. The window on the first floor. I climb out of it when Owen locks me in."

I stared at it in awe. I couldn't imagine someone climbing out of it in a ball gown.

"Do you want to come round for tea tomorrow?" she continued. "My mum and Owen are going away tonight. We can listen to my Saturday Night Fever LP and I'll show you the dance if you like."

"Aren't you running away?" I said.

Nellie shivered and rubbed at her bare arms.

"No," she said. "I'll probably do that next week."

Nellie

Extract from her unfinished autobiography, Street Life

I was fifteen when we went to live in the Castle Bay Hotel in Talacre. I've never liked Wales that much and I couldn't care less if I never see it again. I'm not proud of it like Polly and Chimp are and I was pissed off that moving there ruined my plans for seeing *Saturday Night Fever* at the Pictures.

It was Easter 1978. North Wales was cold and gloomy and when I walked into a shop with my mum, they stopped speaking English and started jabbering on in Welsh.

My stepfather, Owen was Welsh. That's why we went to Wales. He wanted, he said, to go home. He was a strange man. We'd be sitting at the kitchen table and he'd suddenly stand up with his hands raised above his head, close his eyes and say in this great big booming voice:

"The spirits are with us Gillian! The spirits are with us!"

And when the spirits were with us, I had to go to my room and let them speak to them in private.

I spent a lot of time on my own in that hotel. Mum and Owen were either away or, when they were home, Owen was always sending me to my room for one misdemeanour or another. I stared out of the window at the sea. I taped the Top 20 off the radio on a Sunday evening and I lost myself in music.

Owen ran what they called psychic fairs They went all round the country and he put his hands on people and healed them. Mum got right into it. She could change just like that, mum, whatever the circumstances she found herself in, she changed colours like a chameleon.

"Owen's the best thing that ever happened to me," she said, as we stood amongst the boxes and crates ready to move to Talacre. "You'll love Wales Nellie. You will. You'll love it."

We lived in North Wales the longest we lived anywhere. We were always moving from one place to another and I was never at one school long enough to make any friends. But Polly, ah Polly. Polly was the first friend I ever had.

Polly

When Nellie invited me round for tea, I thought it would be a posh hotel tea with white tablecloths and a silver cake stand like the tea me and mam once had in the Alys Tea Rooms in Llandudno.

Instead I found plates of pickled eggs and burnt toast dumped haphazardly on the kitchen table.

"We only came here a few weeks ago," Nellie said as I nibbled at a piece of hard, cold toast. "On the first day, the staff walked out because Owen shouted at the chef and the guests left because the roof leaked and the cooker packed up. Mum hasn't stopped moaning since we got here."

"Can we look round?" I asked her.

Nellie shrugged.

"If you want," she said.

I had never been in the Castle Bay before but to me as a child, it had always looked magical, a black and white palace looking down on the beach. I used to imagine that a princess lived there or maybe even dragons until Mam poured cold water on my dreams.

"It's been empty for years," she'd say. "Nothing but woodworm and dry rot in there."

And now Nellie's parents had bought it and brought it back to life. I held my breath as we walked round. The stairs creaked and there was this air of hush about it, like it was waiting for something, like the air was touched by magic. It had twelve bedrooms and all of them had a view of the sea. We went into the honeymoon suite and looked out of the window. The red and white lighthouse was so close we could almost touch it.

"Have you seen the ghost?" I asked her as we knelt on the bed looking out. "It's supposed to be the old lighthouse keeper, walking around that balcony on the top, checking his light."

Nellie snorted and tossed her long dark hair back from her shoulders.

"No such thing as ghosts," she said.

After that day, we became proper friends and I spent a lot of time at the hotel. Despite there being no such thing as ghosts, we scared ourselves silly looking out of the bedroom windows hoping we might see one.

"You're spending a lot of time with that English girl," Mam said one evening, eyeing me suspiciously as she pummelled the ironing.

"I'm helping her with her Welsh homework," I said which wasn't true at all because when we weren't looking out of the window trying to see the lighthouse ghost, Nellie was busy teaching me the dances in *Saturday Night Fever.*

Mam wouldn't have approved of either.

Nellie

Extract from her unfinished biography, Street Life

The only good thing about school was that Polly and I went to the same one, St. Ages of the Sacred Heart in Talacre. The bad things were that it was a single sex school with no boys in sight and we had to learn Welsh. I tried to get out of it on the basis that I was English but that only got me detention.

"I'm not very good at it myself to be honest," Polly confessed one afternoon as we sat on the bank at school watching the girls play hockey. I had a forged note excusing me from PE and Polly had asthma. "I mean we speak it at home and that but it's Joe you want to talk to about writing it."

So about a week or so later, we caught the bus to Ffynnongroyw to meet her brother.

Talacre was a shabby seaside town and Ffynnongroyw was a mining village and both of them belong in the last century if you ask me. As we went along on the bus, Polly pointed out landmarks like I was a tourist or something.

"That's Point," she said, wiping at the condensation on the inside of the window. "That's the Mine where Da and my brother work."

"Oh," I said, pretending to be interested in the great looming winding wheel that rose high in the sky. It was like those wheels you see at a fun fair except it was grey. I had never seen anything so ugly.

"And those are the Clwydian mountains," she said. "And just over there to the left is Talacre Abbey, where the nuns live."

I yawned. I didn't really care about coal mines or mountains or nuns.

Polly's house was tiny, like a doll's house and the toilet was outside in this little shack sort of thing. The only word I can think of to describe it is *primitive.*

Polly's brother made up for it. Joe had thick black hair and was very turbulent looking. Turbulent! That's the word I wrote in my diary at the time. What sort of word is that for a fifteen year old girl to use?!

I knew he liked me from the way he kept looking at me when we were having tea. It was bacon and fried egg and beans. I hadn't had anything like that for years and it was all I could do not to wolf it down. Mum never cooked when she was home and mostly, I lived on pickled eggs and toast.

Joe made quite an effort to be nice to me.

"So you're living in the Castle Bay Hotel?" he said, watching me as I devoured my food.

"Yes," I said in my best English voice, being careful to swallow before I spoke. "A film star from America stayed last week."

"You never told me that," Polly interrupted but I ignored her and kept my eyes fixed on Joe.

Joe nodded thoughtfully and took a big swig of tea from his mug before answering.

"We used to go to the beach a lot when we was kids," he said. "Do you remember that day mam when you lost your purse and we spent hours on the beach searching for it. You said we couldn't go home until we found it and it got dark and then, when we got home, Da found it under the washing."

Polly and Joe laughed but their mum got up from the table and started clearing the dishes away.

"Your Da will be home from shift soon," she said. "Give him some room to have his tea."

The three of us went into their front room. That was tiny too but there was a big fire roaring in the fireplace. It was lovely to be warm. The Castle Bay was so cold I used to wear my coat indoors most of the time. Owen wouldn't let us put the heating on because it was oil and oil was very expensive.

Joe bounced down on the couch and patted the seat beside him. I went and sat next to him and Polly sat down opposite us by the fire.

"Right then," he said. "Let's have a look at that Welsh homework shall we or are you worried about being given the Welsh Not?"

I looked at him puzzled.

"She hasn't got time for a history lesson," Polly said. "The bus goes in half an hour."

Polly

Nellie became part of our lives from then on. I felt sorry for her in a way because her home life didn't seem that happy. I've lost count of the times she stayed over at ours after Owen locked her out or they had a big row.

Joe was smitten with her from the start. He used to wear his *Brut* aftershave when she came round to do her Welsh homework and he didn't mind having to sleep downstairs when she turned up on our doorstep late at night.

I shared a room with Joe. It was a small room divided by a curtain and he'd open the window at night so we could hear the owls hooting in the woods. Nellie always shut it when she stayed but I didn't say anything because I was so thrilled she was there.

"Has Joe got a girlfriend?" she asked me one night as we lay in the dark.

"No," I said. "Why?"

"Oh," she said. "I just wondered."

"He doesn't like English girls," I said.

It was a little unkind of me to say that and I honestly didn't know if he liked English girls or not but I felt a little jealous of the time they spent together at our house as Joe tried to teach her Welsh. As far as I could see, she couldn't even remember *Bore da*. She was my friend but she seemed to prefer Joe's company.

One Saturday afternoon, Nellie got herself locked into the second floor bathroom at the Castle Bay. I was on my way to Nanny Gwynn's and as I cycled past, Nellie was hanging out of an upstairs windows.

"I'm locked in the bathroom!" she shouted as I stopped on my bike and looked up at her. "Go and get someone to help me!"

I turned my bike around and pedalled back to Ffynnongroyw as fast as I could. If I hurried Joe would be coming off shift and he'd know what to do. In times of trouble, I always ran for Joe.

I was always amazed at how many men worked underground, how many poured out of that dark place at the end of a shift. As I approached the gate the men were clocking off and three of them walked towards me: Dai Jones, Bobby Twice and Richard Lightboy.

"Have you seen Joe?" I asked them as they came closer.

"In trouble is he?" Dai joked. "What's he done now?"

"Nothing," I said. "I just came to meet him."

Joe was the last to come out of the gate and when he saw me, he frowned.

"Is Mam alright?" he said.

"Mam's fine," I said. "It's Nellie. She's locked in the bathroom and can't get out."

"How did she do that then?" he said as we headed towards the bike shelter.

"I don't know," I sighed. "It's just Nellie."

Joe smiled and released his bike from the stand.

"Come on then," he said, swinging his leg over the saddle. "I'll race you."

Nellie

Extract from her unfinished biography, Street Life

I'd been in that bathroom for about an hour and a half by the time Joe got there. He put his shoulder to the door but the wood was so thick and heavy I don't think anyone could have got through without a battering ram. The handle on the bolt on the inside of the door had come off in my hand and I was locked in and well and truly stuck.

Joe went off to get a ladder and Polly went off to see her Nan. It seemed ages before I heard Joe shouting to open the window and then he and another man manoeuvred the ladder to rest against the window sill. The ladder shook as he climbed up it and shortly afterwards his face appeared in the open window.

"Rapunzel Rapunzel let down your hair," he grinned.

"It's not funny," I said. "Get me out of here."

I didn't feel like laughing. I wanted to cry. I wanted to get out of that miserable bathroom and go back to England. I hated that hotel and I hated Wales.

Joe climbed over the window sill, walked over to the door and put his shoulder against it but it refused to move.

"Stuck right and proper," he said.

I didn't mean to do it, really I didn't, but I was frightened and uptight from being locked in that bathroom and I started to cry.

"Aw…" he said. "Don't cry, don't. We'll get you out of here in no time."

Joe came towards me and I reached up and looped my arms around his neck. He was warm and I felt safe as his arms awkwardly flapped around for a minute and then settled on my shoulders where he held me away from him and looked down into my eyes.

"No need to cry now is there?" he said, wiping at my tears. "I've got many a cat down from a tree. Polly will tell you that."

I don't know how it happened but one minute we were standing there and the next we were kissing. It was a gentle kiss, no tongues or anything and I closed my eyes and sank into it. It was my first kiss but I wasn't telling him that.

"Sorry," he said, breaking away suddenly and looking embarrassed. "I shouldn't have done that what with you only being fifteen and all…"

"I'm nearly sixteen," I said which was stretching the truth a little.

"Even so," Joe said. "I don't want you thinking I'm taking advantage of you."

"I don't think you are," I said. "Why don't you kiss me again? I quite liked it."

And before he could answer, I stood on tiptoes and kissed him on the mouth.

Joe groaned.

"What are you doing to me?" he said. "I'm supposed to be getting you down a ladder not kissing your face off."

"Joe!" a voice called up from below. "What are you doing up there?"

Joe stuck his head out of the window.

"Sorry boyo," he shouted. "Technical hitch!"

Joe showed me how to reverse out of the window and feel for the ladder with my feet.

"I'll be right behind you," he said. "I won't let you go."

He disappeared out of the window, and I bit my lip, followed his movements and reversed out of the window.

"That's it, that's it," he said, as I felt his hands clamp around my waist. "Steady does it now, steady."

I followed his instructions not to look down and to keep three points of contact with the ladder: one foot, two hands.

I repeated it in my head as we made our slow descent. One foot, two hands. One foot, two hands.

"One more," he said. "One more and we're home."

At the bottom of the ladder, he held me around the waist for a moment and then he let me go.

"Thank you," I said.

"You'll be alright then?" he said as he and the other man brought the ladder down. "I could get Dave the Bins to have a look at that lock if you like."

"I'd better wait until Owen gets back," I said, turning to go up the hotel steps. "Thanks anyway."

And I left him standing there just like that. What else was I supposed to do? Marry him?

Polly

Joe got Nellie safely out of the bathroom although I was surprised that she'd climbed down a ladder.

"A natural she was," he said. "A natural."

I spent a lot of time on the beach at Talacre that summer of 1978. I liked having a best friend. I had never had one before. Nellie loved to lie in the sun, but I kept to the shade of the dunes because I always burned. The tourists from Liverpool invaded the town like they did every summer, staying in the caravans behind the Castle Bay and in the chalets further along the beach. We watched teenagers just a few years older than us lying on the sand with their transistor radios blaring and playing with brightly coloured beachballs and hula hoops. One day Nellie turned up in a red bikini she'd ordered from her mum's Kay's catalogue. She got a lot of looks from the boys when she ran into the sea and I was a little jealous because in my all-in-one black bathing suit, I was completely invisible.

"Can I have a bikini?" I asked mam one evening as she rubbed calomine lotion into my sunburned skin.

"No," she said. "You're too podgy for a bikini."

So that was that.

We've been going to Talacre beach as far back as I can remember. I was always fascinated by the red and white lighthouse which sometimes was surrounded by water and sometimes marooned on the sand. There is something about the light and the feel of North Wales, the vast skies, the long white beaches, which is like nowhere else on earth. When we were on that beach, Da used to breathe in great big lungfuls of air and say, "you know you're home when you smell that sea."

As a child, I don't think I appreciated how much it must have meant to him to spend time in the sea air. He spent all his life down the hot, dark mine and being able to breathe in the sea air and feel the cool breeze on his face must have felt like heaven.

As summer drifted into autumn, we left the beach behind and went back to school. That was the winter of the strikes and school was often closed because the lorry drivers wouldn't bring oil for the heating.

Nellie was pleased about that because she hated school.

"What do I want to go to school for anyway?" she'd say. "I'm going to be rich and famous, and they can't teach me that can they?"

Polly

One afternoon in November 1978, Nellie rang me and asked me to get her some cigarettes. I thought she had a bit of a cheek. I didn't hold with smoking and I didn't see why she couldn't go out and get them herself.

"I can't," she hissed down the phone. "I can't go out."

"Why not?" I asked her. "Are you ill?"

Nellie sighed.

"No," she said. "Please Polly. Please just go and get me some fags."

There was thick fog that day. We get it like that round here sometimes, it rolls in off the sea and covers the Clwydian hills in a big grey blanket. Joe used to say fog was old ghosts coming back.

Pimple Jones was working in the beach front newsagents that afternoon and made me promise to give him a kiss in return for selling a fifteen year old girl cigarettes. Pervert Jones we called him at school because he used to letch at us when we went in there to get our traffic light lollipops and sherbet dip dabs. I had to let him kiss me on the cheek and afterwards, I made him put the cigarettes in a paper bag so no one would see.

Outside the shop I rubbed vigorously at my face in case I'd caught something from his spotty skin and then I pedalled along the beach road to the hotel in the fog. The milk was still on the doorstep when I got there. Typical Nellie, I thought, adding it to my list of grievances for that day.

I leaned my bike against the wall, picked up the milk and went in through the back door, into the kitchen.

"You need to bring the milk in," I told her, banging it down on the table.

Nellie was sitting at the table in her coat and sunglasses. I didn't think much of it at first. Nellie was often dressed in something strange.

"I had to let Pimple Jones kiss me to get these," I said, throwing the paper bag on to the table. "Honestly Nellie the things you make me do."

She took off her sunglasses and all the niggles I had felt towards her disappeared.

Nellie's left eye was puffy and closed and her right eye was bloodshot in sympathy.

"What…" I said. "What's happened?"

"I could tell you I fell over," she said. "That's what mum says I should say. Or I could tell you the truth, that Owen slapped me across the face and I fell and hit my eye on the table."

"He *hit* you?"

Nellie nodded and shrugged and I could see she was trying not to cry.

"Oh don't, don't," I said, rushing over to her, crouching down and putting my arm around her shoulders. "Does it hurt?"

Nellie remained rigid. She didn't bend to emotion that much.

"No," she said. "It's just difficult to see."

Nellie pulled the cigarettes out of the bag and a leaflet floated out and landed on the floor.

"What's this?" she said, picking it up and squinting at it.

"Pimple Jones must have put it in there," I said. "Don't tell me. It's an advert for rubber underwear or blow up dolls. You know what he's like."

Nellie held up the leaflet and read it.

"It says two bands are playing at Ffynnongroyw church hall next Saturday night," she said.

I didn't care about the bands. I was shocked at her revelation. Da never laid a finger on us although I knew some kids round here got it quite bad at times. But a black eye? That was bad. That was very bad indeed.

"Shall we ring the police?" I said, concern for my friend replacing the irritation I had felt just twenty minutes earlier.

Nellie gave a little snort of laughter.

"The police?" she said. "What are they going to do? He's my step dad. It's not the first time and it probably won't be the last. Anyway," she said, unwinding the cellophane on the gold Benson and Hedges box and pulling out a cigarette. "They've gone off to Liverpool to see the cathedral and hopefully they won't be back for weeks. Thanks for these Poll. I needed a fag."

I looked around the kitchen. It was a mess. Nellie stood up and took a five pound note out of a drawer and put it in front of me.

I ran the tap in the hope of hot water so that I could at least try to wash up but the water ran cold and the washing up liquid bottle was empty so I sat down at the table instead.

"So," she said, exhaling the smoke from her cigarette and looking at the glowing tip. "Shall we go? To see the bands?"

She pushed the leaflet towards me. Her fingernails were painted bright red.

"I don't know," I said looking at it. "I've never been to see a band before."

"I've seen loads," she said, blowing smoke up at the ceiling. "You never know Poll, we might meet our fate."

I looked at her.

"You can't go with a black eye," I said.

Nellie shrugged.

"It will be gone by then," she said. "So shall we?"

I sighed.

"Ok," I said. "Ok."

Chimp

I didn't know where to start when Morwenna asked us to write it all down. So I decided to start with the music because that's what brought Nellie into my life.

We'd just formed *The Sons of Glendower* and I was the lead singer. The best way to describe us in those early days was punk. There were a lot of punk bands in London and we copied their style, particularly the Sex Pistols. I loved the Sex Pistols. I used to go on stage wearing one of dad's old string vests under my parka and put soap in my hair to make it stand up. Menace wore a pair of old man's pyjamas and Boots tore holes in his t-shirts and wore a bicycle chain looped around his jeans. Anything went really but I suppose we were a bit radical for North Wales at the time.

Somehow, despite that, we landed a gig in the church hall in Ffynnongroyw. We had a double bill with *Rock Shock* who came over from Rhyl. They were very different from us and played heavy rock. There was a lot of rivalry between rock and punk at the time but what did the Church secretary know? He was just trying to put on something for the young people, he said. He didn't have a clue about music.

We played to no more than ten people. There were some punks there, girls with plum lipstick dressed all in black but they were in the minority. Some of the locals came too, mild mannered men who would go to the church hall on a Saturday night for company and drink their black and tans whatever was going on on stage.

Anyway the sound system kept breaking down, the feedback was horrific and I got into a fight with the drummer from Rock Shock. The old caretaker put an end to it all by throwing a bucket of water over us and then there was a massive powercut.

I was sitting backstage in the dark, soaking wet and nursing a bloody nose when this pretty girl peered around the curtain. That was the first time I saw Nellie, all decked out in a long floaty gold dress and pearls. She looked like she'd got lost on the way to Paris.

I liked that, I liked it. I felt she was like me: in the wrong place at the wrong time, restless to move on from where we found ourselves.

Polly

We dressed up in some of Nellie's mum's clothes to go and see the bands. Nellie wore a gold kaftan and a string of pearls and I chose a pink ballgown and a sparkly necklace.

We caught the bus over to Ffynnongroyw early in the evening. We didn't wear coats because Nellie said you didn't wear coats when you went out for the night and I was freezing. The snow was coming down quite heavily as the bus navigated the narrow, winding lanes and the driver pulled over several times to wipe the windows. He kept giving Nellie the eye in the interior mirror and somehow she cadged a cigarette off him and smoked it on the way.

When we got off the bus, the street was full of black rubbish bags, piled up from the bus stop to the church hall. The dustbin men were on strike and we had to hold our noses because of the smell.

We went straight to the Ladies when we got to the church hall and put the hand dryers on to try to warm up and then Nellie produced a lemonade bottle from her clutch bag.

"Have some of this," she said, holding it out to me. "It's vodka and orange. It will warm you up a bit."

I wasn't sure I wanted to drink alcohol because Mam always said no good ever came of it but Nellie insisted and so I took a swig.

"Right then," she said, as she put on more lipstick. "Let's go and see what's going on shall we?"

Polly

I felt uncomfortable when we walked into the hall. There was a straggle of girls and boys huddled in the shadows at the back who stared at us as we walked in and some of them laughed. The girls wore black eyeliner that flicked out from the corner of their eyes and one of them had a safety pin right through her lip. I kept turning round to stare at them and Nellie kept elbowing me and telling me not to.

"They're punks," she whispered. "Don't stare."

The music was so loud it hurt my ears and I felt a bit sick from the vodka I'd drunk in the Ladies. At the back of the hall was a table set out with food and I was shocked when the punks started throwing sausage rolls at the stage and the band threw them back.

Chimp Davis was the lead singer of one of the bands and I was taken aback at all the swearing and spitting he did and how he got into a fight. I wished I was down the Welfare with Mam and Da and Joe because it all felt very strange and edgy.

"Isn't this fun?" Nellie said, as the punks cheered on the fight.

I didn't think it was fun. I'd never seen fighting before. And then Old Dai threw a bucket of water over them and announced that the evening was over and shortly after that there was a power cut. There were hundreds of them that winter.

"Come on girls," old Dai the caretaker said as he swept up around our chairs and the punks drifted off into the night. "Time to go home."

Nellie seemed reluctant to leave.

"I think I recognise that lead singer," she said.

"Chimp?" I said. "You know Chimp?"

She shrugged.

"I think so," she said, standing up. "I'll just go back stage and check."

I opened my mouth to say something because I didn't see how Nellie could possibly know Chimp and I wanted to go home but she had gone, leaving me sitting in the empty hall with old Dai sweeping up around me, retrieving sausage rolls from under the tables and muttering on in Welsh about young people and God.

When Nellie re- appeared, Chimp was swaggering along behind her. I dropped my eyes hoping he wouldn't remember the childish crush I'd had on him years ago.

"Polly," he said, nodding his head.

I smiled and was glad it was dark because my face was burning with embarrassment.

"Chimp's going to walk us home," Nellie said bending down to speak to me.

"But Joe's picking us up," I whispered. "In Bryn Thomas's car."

"Change of plan," she said quietly, as she turned to give Chimp her most bewitching smile. I stood up and didn't say anymore and followed them out of the hall into the cold, snowy night.

Nellie

Extract from her unfinished biography, Street Life

It was still snowing when we got outside the church hall. Joe was waiting for us in an old gold coloured Ford Cortina. The engine was running and pumping out clouds of smoke into the still, cold air.

"Get in then girls," he said, poking his head out of the driver's window.

I didn't want to get in the car. I know we'd had that kiss and a few more since but it wasn't anything serious and I wanted to walk home with Chimp.

"You're alright ta," Chimp said, stepping forward. "I'll walk Nellie back."

He said it like it was already decided and Joe glared up at him. I didn't know there was history between them, I only found that out later.

"To Talacre?" Joe said. "In this snow? She's not wearing a coat."

Chimp slipped his parka off and draped it around my shoulders.

"So she is now," he said, taking my elbow and steering me away. I looked back at Polly who remained standing by the car.

"I'll be fine," I called back at her over my shoulder. "Go home!"

As we turned the corner and reached the lanes, Chimp looked down at my feet.

"You might want to take those off," he said, nodding at my high heels.

So I took off my shoes and he gave me a piggyback across the fields. Chimp had a torch and it threw long shadows across the woods and the snow.

Chimp did most of the talking on the way home. He talked about his band and how he wanted to be a big rock star and how nothing was going to stop him. When we finally got to the Castle Bay, we stopped at the bottom of the steps and I slid off his back.

"I can't believe you live here," he said, looking up at the hotel in wonder.

There was magic in the air that night, I swear there was. I don't know if it was because of the special light that snow brings, the power cut or the feeling that it was just the two of us all alone in the dark world together. Chimp said later that he felt the magic too and that it had been the inspiration for ***Looking at the Stars.*** It never became as big as ***No Milk Today*** but it was still big and the best thing of all was that he wrote that song about me.

Snow falling, we're halfway home
Come over here babe, don't walk alone
There's no one else on the streets tonight
The world is ours, let's make it right.
We pull back the curtain, look up at the stars
And I wonder how soon we'll travel to Mars
I can smell moondust, it's in your hair
And I say look at The Plough babe, it's just over there.
It's our night, it's our first night
I want to take you there
To Mars and Venus and the Moon
With stardust in your hair

Years later, when people sang that song back to the band at concerts, I used to get a little thrill knowing it was about me and the night we first met. Sometimes, when it comes on the radio, it brings it all back to me: the snow, the cold and the magic of that night, even now, even after all that's happened. And sometimes it makes me sad that all that magic went, that all that magic turned into something else.

Inside the hotel, he stopped in the hall and looked up at the ceiling. The Castle Bay looked different without the lights on, different when I saw it through his eyes.

"We used to come here for scampi and chips when I was little," he said. "And then it closed down and was empty for years. I'm glad your dad's bought it."

"He isn't my dad," I said. "My real dad is a prince."

"Oh," he said.

"And they're away," I said. "My mum and step dad."

"Good," he grinned. "That means we've got it all to ourselves."

I thought he might kiss me but he didn't. Instead he started to explore the hotel and we ended up in the Star Room.

"Mum says you can see the Plough from the window," I said. "Whatever that is."

Chimp turned and stared at me.

"You don't know what the Plough is?"

I shook my head.

"No."

"Well then let see if it's true," he said, taking my hand and leading me over to the window. He pushed it open and the sound of the sea and the cold of the snow rushed into the room.

"We won't be able to see it tonight," he said. "There won't be any stars out in this weather. We'll have to catch snowflakes instead."

He poked out his tongue and let the snow fall on it and I copied him. In between we laughed because it seemed such a ridiculous thing to do but it was fun. Sometimes I forget we had fun, that it wasn't all about fighting.

Snow fell like glitter from the sky and he pulled me closer to him.

And then he kissed me.

Polly

After we saw the bands in the church hall, all Nellie talked about was Chimp Chimp Chimp.

I cycled over to Talacre the next morning to fetch my coat and make sure she'd got home safely.

"I don't know why you bother so much about that girl," Mam said. "She looks the sort who can look after herself."

Nellie was still in bed when I got there and she came down the stairs wearing this ridiculous dressing gown with pom poms dangling from the sleeves.

"I'm in love," she said, holding her arms up in the air and spinning around in the hall. "Beautiful beautiful love."

The milk was on the doorstep again and the kitchen was a mess but all Nellie wanted to know about was Chimp. So I told her how he used to march in the Colliery band when I was little, leaving out the bit about the big crush I'd had on him.

I stayed there for about an hour, washing up in cold water and trying to impose some order on the messy kitchen.

"So are you going to see him again?" I asked, before I left. "Chimp?"

"Maybe," she said, mysteriously. "Maybe."

When I got home, Mam was cooking the Sunday lunch.

"Where have you been?" she said. "I could have done with some help Polly but oh no you just go swanning off to see that English girl."

"She's got a name Mam," I said.

Mam ignored me and shoved a bunch of knives and forks into my hand.

"Lay the table," she said. "Your Da is starving."

Joe walked into the kitchen and took a can of beer from the side.

"Is she alright Polly?" he said. "Nellie? Did she get home alright?"

I looked at Joe and I knew he'd fallen for her.

"Oh Joe," I said softly, touching his arm. "Joe"

Joe shrugged and snapped the ring pull just as the lights went out.

Mam slammed the door of the oven in protest.

"Well isn't that just what we need," she said. "Another bloody powercut."

Nellie

Extract from her unfinished biography, Street Life

At Christmas 1978, mum and Owen gave me a camera and then, on Boxing Day, they packed up the van and disappeared off to Glasgow.

"There's a great need for spiritual sustenance at this time of year," Owen said. "A great need. You'd do well to seek some yourself Nellie."

I didn't reply. I'd had so many rows with Owen about my lack of morals and spiritual direction I didn't have any energy left.

"At least with a camera you might find some purpose in life," mum said as we sat round the kitchen table eating hard sprouts and rubbery turkey on Christmas Day. I wore my coat at the table because it was so cold.

"What," I said lightly. "Like you did?"

Owen glared at me.

"Don't speak to your mother like that," he said.

Owen had only been in our lives for about two years but he acted like he was God. Mum worshipped the ground he walked on. When she first met him, she bought this K-Tel LP *Sing with Wales* and we had to listen to the Welsh national anthem over and over again. Before Owen there was Gerald of the Brylcream bounce and before him there was a long list of men and heart breaks that ran right back to my dad although she has always refused to tell me his name.

After they left, I rang Polly. Sometimes we stayed on the phone for hours. I didn't care about the phonebills, they were Owen's responsibility.

"You can't be on your own at Christmas," Polly said. "I'll ask Joe to come over and fetch you. You can stay if you like."

So Joe came to get me in Bryn Thomas's old Ford Cortina which had a passenger door tied up with string. I felt awkward with Joe now I'd met Chimp. Several times he reached for my hand and I pulled it away and he drove on without mentioning it.

It was warm and cosy in Polly's house with a big roaring fire in the grate. They were wearing paper hats and watching *The Sound of Music* and as we walked in, Joe caught his mum's hands and pulled her up to dance and she laughed and protested but you could see she loved it really.

Polly's dad stood up and put a shovel full of coal on the fire and it sparked up and Joe released his mum's hands and flopped down beside me on the couch making me bounce up in the air.

"So what did you get for Christmas then Nellie?" he said, casually draping his arm along the back of the couch so that it trapped my hair. He leaned forward to reach for a can of beer on the table in front of us and he was so close to me I could smell beer and earth and coal tar soap.

"This," I said, holding out the camera I'd taken with me. "It's a Canon AE-1."

Polly's mum shot a look at me but I didn't take much notice of it.

"That looks expensive," Joe said, turning it over in his hands. "You can take the pictures on our wedding day can't you?"

I think he meant it as a joke but no one laughed and Polly's mum got up to fetch her knitting.

I liked Joe. I really did but after that night with Chimp, I didn't feel the same. He whispered in my ear that we should go outside but I shook my head and kept my eyes fixed on Julie Andrews and the nuns. A few minutes later, he got up and went into the kitchen and we heard the back door slam behind him.

Polly's mum looked up from her knitting and raised an eyebrow at me and I just shrugged and looked back at the TV. What Joe did was up to him. It was nothing to do with me.

Polly

She was two timing them for a while, I know she was. Joe and Chimp. Nellie couldn't help it but I didn't like her playing with my brother's emotions. Joe was sensitive despite all his joking around and bluster and I didn't want her teasing him like a cat with a mouse. Because that was what Nellie was like. She was the best friend I ever had, there was never a dull moment with Nellie around, but put her near a boy or a man and there was a chemical reaction. I don't know what it was but they were drawn to her, like a magnet. Even Da was soft on her.

As for Chimp and Joe, well they didn't get on. When they were at school they were always fighting in the playground. Over the years, that rivalry grew into something else, something that, in the end, caused so much anguish and sorrow it's almost too much to think about.

Nellie

Extract from her unfinished biography, Street Life

Snow started falling on New Year's Eve and it didn't stop. Chimp came round in the afternoon and insisted we went outside in it. I wanted to lounge around by the fire in a ball gown drinking Babycham like James Bond girls did but Chimp had other ideas. He made me put on a pair of Wellington boots and I found one of mum's old fur coats in the wardrobe and we went outside to build a snowman.

It wasn't my idea of romance but I went along with it because well, I was besotted.

The first picture I took on my new camera was of him and the snowman dressed in one of Owen's cloth caps and a scarf with two pieces of coal pushed into his face for eyes. I'd never made a snowman before. It wasn't something I'd ever done as a child.

"Let me take one of you," he said, taking the camera from me. Later he said it was one his favourite pictures: me standing in the snow in a moth eaten fur coat wearing big black oversized Wellington boots.

Finally we went in and sat by the fire. and then, just when I hoped we might start kissing and maybe I'd let him touch me OVER my dress, he started going on about the English taking all the Welsh houses away and how it shouldn't be allowed and how people were going to do something to stop it.

I didn't know it then but Chimp was someone who liked a cause. He took them up, he ran with them for a while and then he moved on. Maybe that's how he saw me to start with: a nearly sixteen year old girl all alone in a big hotel by the sea.

He stayed with me all evening and I was happy and hopeful and the world was different. With Chimp in it, it sparkled.

And then, just before eleven o'clock, he got up and fetched his parka.

"I'd best be off now," he said. "Thanks for a great day."

I was heartbroken but I tried not to show it as he waved at me from the bottom of the steps. I went back inside, drank some Babycham and listened to my Saturday Night Fever LP, full blast.

Chimp

I know Nellie wanted me to stay that night and there's some things – lots of things - she says in her autobiography that aren't completely true. I mean she paints me as some sort of cold hearted rogue in most of it.

Nellie was nothing if not obvious. Even when we were making that snowman her body, her eyes, were flashing all sorts of come and get me signals. I don't know if she realised how provocative she was. Or maybe she did. All I know was I had other things on my mind and having a permanent girlfriend wasn't one of them.

Nellie says she was my other love; that music came first and in a way that's true. Being the lead singer in a successful band was all I wanted and Nellie, at that time, was just someone to have a bit of fun with. That's how I thought of her in the early days.

I had dreams for 1979. It was going to be our time to shine, to make it big as a band. And it was the band and the music that was on my mind that New Year's Eve as I walked home in the dark to Ffynnongroyw, not Nellie.

Polly

We spent New Year's Eve 1978 at the Welfare. That is what we've always done on New Year's Eve as far back as I can remember. The Welfare was the club for the mining community and their families. All sorts went on there from union meetings to Beetle drives.

The hall was decked out with balloons and at midnight everyone joined hands in a circle and we sang *Auld Lang Syne* and after that we all drifted off home in the snow.

1978 was the last year of calm before the storm because the next year, Margaret Thatcher became Prime Minister and everything changed.

Chimp

In January 1979, the world was on strike, the Government was disintegrating, and Da continued to moan at me about getting a job.

"Or at least one that lasts more than a week," he said. "You need to start paying your way boy. You can't expect to live here for free."

It was true that I didn't stick at jobs for long but jobs didn't interest me. All I wanted to do was hang out with the band at George's and jam in his dad's shed.

"You should have gone down the pit like Joe Evans," Da said. "Same age as you he is and he isn't afraid to get his hands dirty."

Mam remained quiet throughout this exchange but then she was always quiet compared to Da. Mam found solace in knitting jumpers and going to Chapel whereas Da liked nothing better than to be out down the Welfare drinking with his mates.

They called him Tom Horse because he'd been the head ostler at Point before the mine was mechanised and the horses left. Auntie Marjory, his sister, says it broke his heart to see them go.

Da was the NUM Union rep at Point and when he got up on an orange crate at the Welfare and spouted on about the rights of the working man, everyone listened to him with a sort of awed reverence. He had a lot of respect down the pit but our relationship was always tense. I think he found me a disappointment and I found him dogmatic and unyielding.

I was pissed off that he'd mentioned Joe Evans. All my life it was Joe Evans this, Joe Evans that; Joe Evans getting picked for the school rugby team; Joe Evans marching in front of the Colliery Band on a Sunday morning holding the banner high in the air.

"Where are you going?" Mam said as I got up from the table and fetched my parka.

"Out," I said as I left, leaving my fried eggs and bacon half eaten on the table.

When I got to George's, the new guys were there, Boots, our lead guitarist and Menace, our bass guitarist. With George on drums and me the lead singer, that was our new line up for 1979.

"I think we should start playing more gigs," I told them, as we cracked open a few beers and messed about with chords and drum beats. "Village halls, youth clubs, universities, that sort of stuff.

"In Wales?" Menace asked.

"Well where else do you think we should play?" I asked him.

"Germany," he said. "There's lots of bands playing the German circuit."

Boots cuffed him round the head and we got on with our beer drinking and jamming. But later I thought about it and he was right. The trouble was we were struggling to get gigs anywhere and I didn't have a clue how to push us forward.

Nellie

Extract from her unfinished biography, Street Life

In early 1979, I established myself as official band photographer. That way I got to be with Chimp as often as I could. He wasn't as keen on me as I wanted him to be and so this was my way of stamping my presence on his life and making him see what was right under his nose.

I thought it was glamorous, being Chimp's sort of girlfriend and travelling round in George's dad's van even though it was an old orange transit with ***David's Ironmongers For All Your Hardware Needs*** written on the side. Sometimes it broke down on the way home and we had to pull in a layby so George could get underneath it and get it going again.

The Sons played in backwater villages and towns in those early days, mostly in youth clubs or church halls. I was always a bit apprehensive about the audiences who jumped up and down in this dance they called the pogo and who thought nothing of hurling missiles at the stage. George always kept an eye out for me, much more than Chimp ever did. Chimp was so focused on playing a gig he didn't notice anything else. I kept myself busy taking photographs. Some of those early ones are good, they capture a time long gone. The film was expensive but I used Owen's money to pay for it. He had a stash kept in a shoe in his wardrobe so I just helped myself whenever I needed to. He owed me that. He owed me that for bringing us to Wales and for all the times he raised his hand to me.

Polly

No one at our school thought about careers in those days. We left school, we got a job and that was it. Most of the girls went to work at the Hotpoint factory in Llandudno or became shop assistants in Woolworths.

I had a Saturday job at Mrs Murgatroyd's toy shop and in January 1979, she suggested I might like to work there full time when I left school in the summer. I couldn't wait to tell Nellie my good news but when I did, she just yawned.

"So what are you going to do then?" I asked her. "When you leave school? What are you going to do?"

Nellie shrugged and fiddled with her hair.

"I'm not going to work for anyone," she said. "I've got other plans."

Chimp

There were hundreds of girls like Nellie. Especially later on. I mean I could have had my pick of them but girls were not my reason for living. George used to give me a hard time sometimes for the way I treated Nellie but honestly she used to turn up dressed like she was going to a Ball instead of travelling to a village hall in a van!

When I look back at those days, I wonder sometimes how we kept going. Not me and Nellie: the band. But I had this blind determination to succeed and that ambition drove me on.

Richard Jones wasn't typical of the usual sort of person who came to our gigs. We were playing in a village hall on the outskirts of Wrexham and he stood out in the audience with his camel coat and jaunty scarf. I thought we were being scouted, that he might be a record producer from London but George dismissed him as just another weirdo. We got a lot of them at our gigs!

Afterwards, as we were packing up the van, he hung around at the back door of the hall.

"You want something mate or are you just waiting to rob us?" Menace asked him. "'Cos I tell you what, after we've paid for this shit hole we've got about fifty pence left."

Richard laughed and lit a cigarette.

"No," he said. "I'm not going to rob you. I was wondering if you'd play at my sister's birthday party next Saturday night."

Nellie

Extract from her unfinished biography, Street Life

Rhoswen Jones was all the things I wasn't. She was five years older than me and she had short cropped hair and wore baggy men's trousers.

The Sons were asked to play at her 21st birthday party and honestly, that party was the weirdest party ever. The band played in a shed in the back garden and people lay around on mattresses and old sofas placed on the grass, smoking joints and drinking home made cider. It was freezing cold but some of the girls had bare feet and were wearing floaty hippy clothes. I didn't know how they'd take to a punk band but in that state they probably didn't even notice.

After the band finished playing, Menace and George and Boots starting packing up the van.

"So where's he got to this time," Menace complained. "It's always us what gets left to pack up the van."

"I'll go and find him," I said, keen to locate Chimp who had been missing for about half an hour.

The cottage was dark with narrow stairs and dark corridors that twisted this way and that. In the end I stopped and listened for a moment and when I heard a woman laughing in one of the rooms upstairs, I went upstairs and opened the door.

Chimp and Rhoswen were sitting at a table in tiny little room stuffed with books and papers. They looked up at me like they'd been caught with their hands in the sweet jar. I wasn't particularly worried about Rhoswen at that time. She was so *masculine* with her short cropped hair and her men's shirt and baggy trousers that I dismissed her as a lesbian. Chimp would never fancy a woman like that.

"The band want to go," I said.

Chimp glared at me like I wasn't wanted, like I was intruding.

"So tell them I'll be there in a minute," he said.

"They'll said they'll go without you," I said which was a lie but I wanted him back with me, not sitting up here with this woman. He looked at Rhoswen and she rolled her eyes, like I was his kid sister telling him to come home for tea and it really pissed me off.

Chimp sighed, scraped his chair back and ran his hand through his hair as he looked at Rhoswen.

"Sorry about this," he said.

Rhoswen smiled as if she understood how tiresome it must be to have a nagging girlfriend and a band who wanted to go home and said something in Welsh that I didn't understand.

I glared at her as I left the room with Chimp following at a distance behind me.

Chimp didn't say anything on the way home. Not one word. I could tell he was pissed off. He got pissed off if he didn't get his own way and I could see he'd wanted to stay there a bit longer. It made me feel uneasy but also I just didn't think that a woman like Rhoswen Jones could be any threat to me. I mean she was a lesbian and I was a princess. It was as simple as that. Wasn't it?

Chimp

There were plenty of reasons to hate the English. My great grandfather had been made to wear the Welsh Not at school, a piece of wood suspended on a string and hung around the neck of any child heard speaking Welsh. And then there was Henry VIII who, in 1536, banned Welsh speakers from holding public office and declared English the official language of Wales. And in the late 1970s, the English owned a large number of holiday homes in North Wales, forcing up the price of houses so that local people couldn't afford to buy a home of their own.

And when I met Rhoswen at her 21st birthday party in early 1979, I discovered she hated the English too.

Rhoswen was a member of ***Meibion Glyndwr,*** the Welsh nationalist movement that was determined to make Wales Welsh again. After we finished playing, she took me up to her study and offered me some home made cider so we could talk some more about our mutual hatred of the English. We hadn't been in there long when Nellie came in and broke the spell. I was so pissed off I don't think I spoke all the way home.

Nellie

Extract from her unfinished biography, Street Life

I didn't think about Rhoswen after the party. If I'd know at that time what a threat she would become to me and Chimp I would have paid more attention and pulled out all the stops to make my world the one he wanted to be in. But I didn't know, not then.

Chimp used to disappear for days at a time but I knew better than to question him on his whereabouts. He hated being accountable. I reassured myself that it wasn't long to my sixteenth birthday when we'd go all the way.

I looked forward to that birthday like no other. I had it all planned. We'd sit at the table in the hotel like a grown up couple and eat the dinner I'd cooked for him. He'd admire my skills in the kitchen and then after dinner, we'd wander up the stairs to the bridal suite and I'd cross the threshold from girl to woman.

"But you can't cook," Polly said when I confided part of my dream to her. I left out the bit about sex. Polly was a bit old fashioned about things like that.

"I can make cheese on toast," I said.

"You can't give him cheese on toast," Polly said. "Why don't you just come with us to the Welfare? He probably won't even turn up."

It was true that Chimp had a habit of not turning up when I expected him to but he wouldn't let me down on my sixteenth birthday. My sixteenth birthday was going to be a night to remember.

Polly

In the end, Mrs Murgatroyd came to Nellie's rescue. She sent me home from the toy shop with a meat pie and I took it over to Nellie's, balanced on the handlebars of my bike.

"You'll be alright then?" I said, as she sat at the table in a blue dress she'd once again borrowed from her mum's wardrobe.

"Course," she said.

"If he doesn't turn up, just get the bus over to the Welfare," I said. "They've got a comedian on tonight."

Nellie rolled her eyes.

"Of course he'll turn up," she said. "It's my sixteenth birthday."

I wasn't so sure. Chimp wasn't the most reliable of people. He was always arranging to meet Nellie and letting her down. I don't know what she saw in him to be honest. Always dressed in that old Parka and never cutting his hair. Our mam used to say Top Cat had more dress sense which made Joe laugh.

So I left her sitting at the table in her blue dress with candles burning in a silver candelabra. I was quite sure I'd see her later down the Welfare. As far as I was concerned, the sooner she got over him the better.

Nellie

Extract from her unfinished biography, Street Life

Chimp was an hour late. By the time he came in the back door, I had drunk quite a bit of Babycham and listening to my *Saturday Night Fever LP.* I was so pleased to see him but he had this dark broody look on his face and he hardly looked at me.

"Sid Vicious is dead," he said, walking straight past me and slumping into a kitchen chair.

"Oh," I said. "Is he?"

I didn't care about Sid Vicious. Why would I? He was in the Sex Pistols and I wasn't interested in the Sex Pistols. I thought they were a dirty bunch of Londoners who swore a lot and couldn't sing.

Chimp looked up and glared at me.

"Don't you watch The News?"

"No," I said. "The telly's broken."

Chimp looked even more dishevelled than usual and he jumped up and started pacing around the kitchen, pushing his hands through his hair.

"I can't believe it," he said. "I just can't believe it."

"Did you know him then?" I said, not really knowing what else to say. I was more concerned about the pie in the oven and whether it was burning.

Chimp stopped, turned, and glared at me.

"Of course I didn't know him," he said gruffly. "Why do you always have to say such stupid things? Don't you understand the magnitude of this?"

I didn't. And I definitely didn't know what magnitude was.

"We could eat the pie," I suggested brightly. "It's nearly ready."

Chimp threw his head back and looked up at the ceiling with a snort of laughter.

"Oh yes," he said. "Yes. Let's eat a pie. That will make everything alright won't it?"

There was an awkward silence and I didn't know what to do.

"Shall I take the pie out of the oven?" I said.

Chimp gave a little snort of laughter and shook his head slowly from side to side.

"You're unbelievable," he said, walking to the back door. "UN believable."

"Where are you going?" I said. "The pie's ready."

He didn't speak. He just shook his head again and left, slamming the door behind him.

I thought about going after him but I told myself he'd be back in a few minutes so I turned off the oven and sat down at the table to wait.

He didn't come back so twenty minutes later, I blew out the candles, threw the pie in the bin, changed into my jeans and caught the bus to Ffynnongroyw.

I never forgave Sid Vicious for dying on my sixteenth birthday. I mean how bloody dare he?!

Polly

I knew what had happened as soon as she walked in.

Joe met her at the door of the Welfare and guided her over to our table. Mam rolled her eyes. She was used to Nellie landing on us in times of crisis.

"Stood you up again has he?" she said.

Nellie looked Mam straight in the eye.

"No," she said. "Something came up, that's all."

A bit later, I got her alone in the toilets.

"Have you been drinking?" I said.

Nellie shrugged.

"So what if I have," she said. "Chimp walked out on me."

"Well there's a surprise," I said.

"Don't be like that," she said. "Sid Vicious died. He was really upset."

"What's Sid Vicious got to do with anything?" I said. "Did you eat Mrs Murgatroyd's pie"?

She shook her head.

"No," she said "I threw it in the bin. I didn't fancy eating it on my own."

I was furious with Chimp but I still couldn't understand what she was going on about.

"What else did he say?" I said. "Did you have an argument?"

"No," she said, lighting a cigarette and blowing the smoke up at the ceiling. "He just said Sid Vicious had died and then he left. Do you think I should go and find him and say sorry?"

I stared at her.

"What have you got to be sorry for?"

Nellie shrugged.

"I don't know," she said. "Maybe I wasn't understanding enough. Do you think he's finished with me? Do you think it's over?"

I wanted to say I didn't know they'd even started. It seemed a very one sided relationship to me, if you could even call it a relationship. I mean Chimp snapped his fingers and Nellie ran. For a girl with so much fire, I didn't understand it.

"Maybe you should just tell him to get lost," I said. "I mean it's not a very nice thing to do to someone on their birthday is it?"

Nellie shrugged.

"Maybe it's my fault," she said. "Maybe I should have been more sympathetic."

Nellie's eyes were blue and wide and lost. That night was the first time I realised that underneath the attitude she put on, Nellie was fragile, deep deep down she was fragile only she never let anyone see it.

"Come on," I said, spitting on a tissue and dabbing at her cheek like I was her mam. "You've got mascara all down your face. Let's go and listen to the comedian. It's not every day you turn sixteen."

Nellie ran her cigarette under the tap, threw the butt into the sanitary disposal bin and took my arm as we went back into the hall.

Within half an hour she was laughing and dancing with Joe. Nellie had to have a man around. It was as simple as that. People can say what they like about her now, they can put labels on her, point to all the insane and outrageous things she did but if they knew her, if they'd seen what I'd seen in her eyes that night, they might not be so quick to judge. Nellie was damaged, fatally flawed. And that made her her own worst enemy. All she wanted was to be loved. It was as simple and as dangerous as that.

Chimp

Sid Vicious was like an icon to me and when he died, I was knocked sideways. I mean we were the same age. How could death happen at 21? Nellie had invited me round for dinner but I wasn't in the mood. I went though, give me credit, I went. Nellie was dressed up to the nines, waiting for me like we were some old married couple. She didn't understand how upset I was about Sid, she just wanted us to eat dinner like nothing had happened. I know, I know it was her birthday but that's just how it was with Nellie. Outside the boundaries of her world nothing else mattered.

Rhoswen, on the other hand, now she got it. She listened. When I arrived at her door an hour or so later, she let me talk and she put this glass of home made cider in front of me and that took the edge off a little. I liked being at Rhoswen and Richard's cottage. It felt like home. I began to spend a lot of time with her there but it wasn't what Nellie thought it was. Not at that time anyway. Rhoswen wasn't interested in relationships. Her passions lay with the Welsh Nationalist Movement and that made it easier to be close to her. I didn't feel like I had to live up to anything, that I had to be a specific someone when I was with her. Things changed a bit later on but at that time it was just a good friendship. Honest. That's all it was.

Nellie

Extract from her unfinished biography, Street Life

They were complete opposites, Chimp and Joe. Chimp was scruffy and absent minded and determined to make *The Sons* as big as Joy Division, the Buzzcocks or the Boomtown Rats.

Joe on the other hand was strong and dependable. He didn't want to make a hit record, he didn't want to kick the English out of Wales. He just lived a simple life.

"Wanker," he said, when I told him Chimp had walked out on me. "You're better off without him Nellie."

So we danced and we laughed at the comedian but spending a Saturday night down the Welfare wasn't what I wanted. Oh it was alright for the night but I wanted so much more and I think that was what drew me to Chimp time and time again. I think I saw Chimp as my ticket out of Wales and the narrow confines of the lives lived there. I was determined to live the sort of life I dreamed about and that didn't involve becoming a miner's wife.

Polly

The general election on 4th May 1979 changed our lives forever. I wasn't old enough to vote but it was all the people in the village and the mining community talked about. Suddenly, James Callaghan and Labour disappeared and we had a woman Prime Minister and a Tory government. The night after the election, we were down the Welfare and there was this heavy, quiet atmosphere hanging over the place as the future became more uncertain.

"What does a bloody woman know about running the country?"

"She hasn't got a clue about the miners."

"Those Tories want only one thing and that's revenge for Ted Heath's downfall in '73."

Three weeks after she became Prime Minister, the price of a pint of milk rose to 15p and Mam had a big argument with our milkman about it.

"See that up there? she said, pointing up at the sky. "That's daylight that is and this," - she waved the milk bill in his face - "is daylight robbery. I tell you what Eifion Roberts, you want to start thinking about trading in that milk float of yours and getting yourself a horse and some pistols instead!"

Poor old Eifion standing there in his Unigate dairy hat and white coat!

"It's not my fault," he protested. "If you want to blame someone blame that new woman prime minister of ours" and he picked up the empties and slammed them into a crate on the back of the float.

"*Mae'r ehog yn ffoi heb neb yn ei erud!*" she called after him as he beat a hasty retreat. *The guilty flee with no one chasing them.*

It wasn't just milk that went up. Bread, tins of soup, Harvest apple pies, everything got more expensive. Sometimes I had to put items back when I did Nanny Gwyn's shopping in Liptons because I didn't have enough money to pay for it all.

I mentioned it to Nellie but the last thing she was interested in was the rising price of milk and bread. She was too busy running all over the place with Chimp and his band. And then they'd have a fight and she'd go running to Joe and then they'd make up and she'd go running back to Chimp. It confused my brother no end. He thought he had a chance with her you see. I started inviting friends home for tea to try to turn his head, to find him a proper girlfriend instead of making a fool of himself over Nellie. Joe was a big tough man but he was as daft as a brush where she was concerned and I tried to change that, tried to distract him but none of the girls was her. Of course they weren't and my little plan failed to work.

Anyway life went on and I left school that summer and went to work full time in Mrs Murgatroyd's toy shop. Nellie officially left school too but as she hadn't been going, it didn't really make much difference.

Mrs Thatcher mowed on with her plans to shake up the country, like she was the new head mistress appointed to restore law and order and discipline and she made it quite clear that she wasn't going to stand for any nonsense – not from the IRA, not from the Unions and not from the miners. Da used to turn off the telly when she came on the News.

"Can't stand that bloody woman's voice," he'd say.

Chimp

When I first heard *I Don't Like Mondays,* it knocked me for six. I was delivering frozen fish when it came on the radio and I pulled over to listen to it. I didn't know what it was about at that time. I thought it might be about the Great British disease of not wanting to go to work on a Monday. I certainly knew how that felt! All I wanted to do was play music and I had to drive around in a van on a blazing hot summer's day delivering stinking old fish. So I sat there and I listened. It was the chords. It was the piano. It was the story. It was so different it took my breath away.

I got out the van and I rang Richard from a phone box. I can still remember the heat and frustration of that day, the wanting more and not knowing how to get it. Richard was out of breath – he'd run up from the cellar when the phone rang and had been bottling cider.

"Fuck the cider Richard! You've got to work full time on the band! "

Richard sighed down the phone. He hadn't been our manager for long but if he was going to be our manager, he had to pull out all the stops.

"OK ok," he said. "I've got plans, good plans. Where are you by the way?"

I looked around me and sighed.

"In some piss forsaken phone box with a van full of melting stinking fish," I said.

Nellie

Extract from her unfinished biography, Street Life

I couldn't understand why Chimp was spending so much time with Rhoswen and her brother. Well maybe I understood the thing with Richard because he'd become their manager and on the rare occasions I dared to ask him about it, he insisted that was the reason. Anyway, I had other things to distract me for a while. Like the beauty contest Mum and Owen decided to hold at the Castle Bay.

It was all about trying to attract business to the hotel. The only people who ever came to stay were eccentric bird watchers with binoculars and serious middle aged walkers. We didn't get any of the holiday trade from Liverpool. The young people wanted to stay in the beach chalets and caravans their parents had visited for years and who would want to stay in a leaky old hotel like ours anyway?

"They probably think we're still closed," Mum said on one of the rare occasions they were home. "So we need to make them aware we're very much open. It's all about getting publicity, about getting the word out there. There was an article about it in last month's *She* magazine."

Owen didn't like her reading *She* magazine. *She* magazine had articles about sex and encouraged women to be independent and follow careers. It talked about orgasms and sex positions and mam read it in the bath with the door locked and kept it hidden in the laundry basket where Polly and I would find it and gasp and giggle about some of the things written in there. *She* magazine was an education all of its own.

Mum threw herself into organising the contest. Somehow she got *Sunshine Shampoo the shampoo that makes you feel like summer* to offer a prize of £100 and a year's supply of *Sunshine* shampoo. It was to take place in early August, when the holidaymakers from Liverpool would be swarming all over Talacre. Liverpool on Sea the locals called it and it was true, there were more Scouse accents than Welsh during the summer. The girls would dress up in bathing costumes and parade around the garden (we didn't have a pool) and then change into evening gowns to walk down a catwalk erected in the bar. I'd never seen mum apply herself to anything other than a relationship and I was impressed with who she cajoled and press ganged into helping her. Carpenters came to put up the catwalk, gardeners came to cut down the nettles and tame the garden they had let run wild. I quite fancied one of them but Owen stalked around keeping an eye on everything and I couldn't even steal a kiss. Posters went up in the window of the chip shop and on lampposts along the sea front but despite all this effort, take up was slow and by the time Cynthia arrived, there were only two entrants.

Cynthia was the promotions manager for *Sunshine Shampoo.* She drove down from London in a red shiny sports car and from the moment she arrived I was bewitched. She was so sophisticated in her high heels and smart navy suit. I bet she didn't need to read *She* magazine in the bathroom. Cynthia had been given the bridal suite as mum wanted to impress her and most of the other rooms had leaking roofs or damp.

She followed me upstairs and when we got to the door she stopped and stared inside.

"It's a bit frilly," she said in a very plummy voice, sounding like Joanna Lumley in the *New Avengers* which I watched at Polly's because our TV was still broken. "Do you throw a husband in as well?"

That made us both laugh.

"It's horrid isn't it," I agreed. "But at least you haven't got mice like room 15."

Cynthia stared at me in horror.

"Only joking," I said, but I wasn't. It was just I knew mum would kill me if that got out.

"Oh!" she said. "Funny! I don't suppose you could get me a teensy weensy little drink from the bar could you dahling? I'm parched after that long journey. Holiday makers bumper to bumper all the way. Gin and tonic. Not too much ice."

I ran downstairs to fetch one and took it up to her.

"How long have you worked here?" she asked me as she lay on the bed with her shoes off. She was only staying for the weekend but I'd never seen so many clothes, spilling out on to the floor from her open suitcase in a colourful exotic mess. I passed her the drink.

"Oh I don't work here," I said. "My step dad's owns it."

Cynthia sipped her gin and tonic. I had put a slice of lemon in it to impress her.

"Is he the man with the terrible BO?"

I laughed.

"Yes," I said. "That's him. He doesn't believe in deodorant. He says it's a sin."

"To wear deodorant?"

"Yes," I said. "Lots of things are sins in Owen's eyes."

"Come and sit up here and tell me some more," she said. "I think I'm going to enjoy my little stay here."

Polly

It was Cynthia's idea Nellie enter the beauty contest although I didn't meet the legendary Cynthia until later on. Owen didn't approve but he couldn't really say much when Cynthia suggested it. After all, *Sunshine Shampoo* were paying him good money to hold their competition at the hotel or so I heard. I didn't understand why, out of all the hotels in Wales they could have chosen, they chose the Castle Bay. It had buckets in all the rooms to catch the rainwater and mouse traps in the kitchen although I suppose they covered all that up when the contest took place.

I was working at the toyshop that Saturday and I always visited Nanny Gwynn on a Saturday afternoon so I didn't go to the contest. I was more interested in earning a bit of money and making sure Nanny Gwynn was alright than watching girls parading around in their bathing costumes. And besides, they were charging £5 to get in which was a bit steep if you ask me.

Nellie

Extract from her unfinished biography, Street Life

Owen wasn't pleased when Cynthia suggested I enter the contest.

"You've only got four girls," she said, looking at the entry forms as she sat behind reception, looking like she owned the place. "Nellie could make it up to five."

"I can count you know," Owen said a little rudely and Cynthia's perfectly painted eyebrows shot up into surprised arches.

"Sorry," he said, mopping at his brow. "It's a hot day and my blood pressure's playing up."

"She hasn't got a swimsuit," mum said, her arms crossed defensively across her chest.

"Yes I have," I piped up. "I've got a red bikini."

Mam narrowed her eyes and scowled at me.

"Have you been ordering from my catalogue again? What did I tell you about ordering clothes from my catalogue? Do you think we're made of money?"

Cynthia cut smoothly into the family dispute.

"We've got less than four hours to go," she said. "So unless we get a sudden flurry of last minute entries four girls is going to look a little thin."

"What if she wins?" Mum said looking aghast.

Cynthia smiled sweetly as she gathered the forms into a neat pile in front of her.

"She can pay for the bikini can't she?"

Nellie

Extract from her unfinished biography, Street Life

Oh I loved that day! Flowers and ribbons decorated the streets because the beauty contest was part of National Seaside Week and for once, the weather in Wales was doing what it was supposed to do: it was doing summer.

Five of us, with numbers fastened to our wrists, paraded around the garden in our bathing costumes and once we'd done that, I changed into one of mum's evening gowns. It was white with a silver neckline.

"I wore that to the Starlight Ballroom in Blackpool," she said wistfully as I stood on the landing wearing it. "Me and Gerald won first prize for the Venetian Waltz that night."

So we glided up and down the catwalk while holidaymakers in shorts and t-shirts sat at the tables and drank cool drinks through straws and a local DJ spoke through a microphone telling the holidaymakers that I was Nellie Morgan, 36, 24, 36, from Talacre and worked in a hotel as a waitress. Well you have to have some poetic licence don't you?

"You were fabulous," Cynthia enthused as we lounged around Room 21 afterwards. We had to wait in there until the bonny baby competition was over and in the meantime, the tourists would keep drinking and eating chicken in the basket to maximise profits.

I didn't particularly want to stay in the room with the other four girls who all knew each other and sat in a corner giggling at their own jokes and talking in Liverpool accents about the boys in the chalet park. It was hot and they wouldn't open the window because they didn't want to ruin their hair and so I decided to go outside while we waited for the results.

Cynthia was busy with the baby competition, mum was behind the bar and Owen was making sure the chef, who'd come just for the day, didn't put too many chips on the plates with the chickens in the baskets. I wandered out into the garden where it was cool and fresh and the smell of cut grass lingered in the summer air. I felt a little like that girl in the *Timotei* advert who wanders through flower strewn fields with the sun in her hair. From the fields behind, where the holiday caravans were, I could hear Candi Staton's *Young Hearts Run Free* floating out of a transistor radio.

"Hello," a male voice said out of nowhere, startling me. "Getting some air are we?"

I turned to see the disc jockey from the contest standing behind me, smoking a cigarette, with a tumbler of amber liquid in his hand. He'd undone his tie and opened the top button of his white dress shirt. It wasn't the weather to be wearing a black dinner suit.

"You were the most beautiful girl in the room," he said. "And as for that red bikini, wow! Knockout! You're the winner, I'm sure of it."

I looked far older than sixteen, I knew I did and yes, sometimes I played on it, as I did then.

"Got any cigarettes?" I said.

"For a beautiful woman, I've got anything," he said, taking a packet of Benson & Hedges out of his pocket and offering them to me. I took one and he fired a Zippo into life and I bent my head as he lit it.

He was good looking. Dark hair. Blue eyes. A bit pirate bad boy, I thought. We were at the bottom of the garden which you couldn't see from the hotel. It was cooler there under the shade of the apple tree.

I don't know how it happened but one minute I was smoking and the next he came forward and hooked my hair behind my ear, looking intensely into my face.

"What are you doing later?" he said, his voice soft, his eyes drowsy as they drank in every detail of my face.

We were interrupted by a shout from the patio.

"Nellie!" mum shouted. "Nellie! I'm just about to announce the results! "

The moment was broken and he stepped back, smiling at me with regret.

"See you later beautiful," he said, tapping the side of his nose and winking at me.

Nellie

Extract from her unfinished biography, Street Life

I took my place at the back of the bar and Cynthia came sidling up next to me smoking a cigarette. Mum was on the stage holding the microphone in one hand and a card in the other. I felt nervous and excited. It was only a silly old seaside beauty competition but I was loving every minute of the attention and being all dressed up in beautiful clothes.

"In third place… Susan Edwards… in second place… Molly Michaels. And the winner, the Sunshine Queen of 1979… with a prize of £100 and a year's supply of Sunshine Shampoo is Nellie! Nellie Morgan! Nellie please come up to the stage and claim your prize!"

For a moment, the world stopped turning. I felt like I'd been crowned Miss World. Cynthia nudged me and pushed me forward. Everyone was clapping and cheering as I crossed the room and climbed the steps to the stage and I bent my head and mum slipped the white sash with the black writing over it.

"Don't let on you're family," she muttered under her breath. "We don't want people asking for their money back."

Nellie

Extract from her unfinished biography, Street Life

That night, Cynthia and I wandered down to the funfair set up on the seafront. I was still wearing my sash. I was so proud of it! It was dark and the lights were bright and giddy and people were wandering round eating candyfloss and hotdogs. They smiled when they saw the sash proclaiming me Miss Sunshine Queen 1979.

As we walked in, *Stayin' Alive* was booming out from the merry mixer ride.

"I wanted to see Saturday Night Fever," I told her. "But I couldn't because we came to Wales."

Cynthia was holding my arm as we walked.

"Come up to London sometime," she said. "And you can see it there."

The thought lit up inside me like a lightbulb and made feel fleetingly happy.

We wandered over to the hoopla stall where Cynthia had a go at winning a cuddly frog but missed and as we turned away, we bumped into Joe Evans and a bunch of his friends walking towards us.

"Enjoying the funfair Nellie?" he said. "I see you won then."

He nodded at the sash I was wearing.

"Of course she did," Cynthia purred, steering me away by the elbow. "She's the most beautiful girl in town."

Joe watched us go but he didn't say anything else.

"Who is he?" Cynthia hissed in my ear through gritted teeth. "He looks like a cave dweller."

I felt it a little unkind but I laughed all the same and we wandered away.

Cynthia didn't want to go on any of the rides and after a while she said she was tired and would go back to the hotel.

"Long drive tomorrow," she said.

I didn't want to go back just yet. I spent enough time in that hotel and on the night I had been crowned Miss Sunshine Queen, I didn't want to be shut inside my bedroom. I wanted to do something wild, stay out with the night. I couldn't go home just yet.

"I'll just stay awhile longer," I said.

"No doubt you'll be meeting your friends," she smiled.

I didn't have any friends except Polly but I wasn't going to tell her that.

"Yes," I said. "You go. See you in the morning."

Cynthia headed off and as I looked around at the big dipper and the waltzer a man came up beside me.

"Ah," he said. "Miss Sunshine Queen herself."

I turned and saw the DJ from the hotel.

"What are you doing all on your own?"

"Oh…"I said. "My friend… she's tired. She's gone back to the hotel. She didn't fancy going on any of the rides."

He smiled and looked at me.

"And you do?"

"Well… I like the waltzer."

"Then come Cinderella," he said, crooking his elbow and holding it out to me. "You shall go to the ball."

The waltzer spun us so fast it pushed me into a corner right up against him and he put his arm around me and the lights blurred and the music played as we spun round and round and round. After, when we got up, I was a little unsteady on my feet and he put his arm around me.

"Shall we go somewhere quieter?" he said.

I nodded. I liked him and I could tell he fancied me like mad. Alright so there was Chimp but Chimp didn't seem to notice me most of the time and I wanted to have some fun.

We walked away from the lights towards the car park.

"We can sit in my car and talk for a while," he said. "Get away from all the noise and the crowds."

He opened the passenger door of a car and I got in.

He got in the driver's side and for a moment he just talked and then he turned in his seat and put his hand on my knee. I was still wearing the white dress although why I wore that to a fair I don't know and he started to push the material up my thigh.

"We could get to know each other better," he said, watching my face. "In fact I think I could show you quite a good time Miss Sunshine Queen."

I laughed because I wasn't sure what he meant although I should have known. I should have known that getting into a car with a man who was probably at least 7 years older than me was going to end in one thing and one thing only but I didn't know. I thought I was sophisticated and grown up but I wasn't. I was still a child.

"I'm not sure if we should be doing this," I said as his hand moved up further. "Maybe we should do some more talking first."

He caught my chin between his forefinger and thumb and leaned over and suddenly his mouth was on mine and his hands were all over my body. Somehow he managed to manoeuvre over the gear stick to lie on top of me where he started to push up the hem of my dress.

"Now," he said, his voice low and husky. "Now I'll show you what a good time is."

I knew at that point that this was not what I wanted but he was stronger and heavier than me and pinning me down. I beat my hands against his chest but that only seemed to encourage him more. I moved my head from left to right to avoid his kisses and all the time I was telling him to stop, telling him no.

And then suddenly, the passenger door was yanked open and because of the way I was shoved right up against it, I fell out on to the grass. The man looked up in surprise and the next moment Joe Evans punched him in the mouth.

"What did you do that for?" he said looking up in surprise.

Joe was standing above me breathing heavily.

"Because you're a cunt mate, that's why," he said, reaching down and helping me to my feet.

Joe slammed the door on the puzzled man who had blood coming out of his nose and looked at me.

"Are you ok?"

I wasn't sure what had just happened.

"Yes," I said. "Yes I think so."

"What the fuck are you doing?" he said. Joe sounded angry and I didn't know why.

"There's no need to be like that," I said a little huffily. "He's the DJ from the beauty contest."

"And you got in a car with him?"

"I thought we were going to talk."

Joe rolled his eyes and sighed.

"Don't you know anything?"

I looked up at him, puzzled. There was a soft light in his eyes and the fire went out in him.

"Come on," he said more gently. "I'll walk you back."

He took my hand as he strode across the car park and I had to run to keep up with him. The Castle Bay was all lit up and at the bottom of the steps Joe stopped and turned to look at me.

"Ok?" he said.

I nodded.

"Right then in you go."

I stared at him.

"What if I don't want to go home?" I said petulantly.

Joe stared at me.

"Be careful Nellie," he said. "Men aren't always what you think they are."

And then he walked away. I didn't want to go in and decided I might sit out in the garden for a while and think about what had just happened. I walked round to the side of the hotel where the beer barrels were stacked up against the side of the hotel waiting for collection. It was dark and shadowy and smelt of stale beer and suddenly I heard a noise and stopped, holding my breath Someone was in there. As my eyes got used to the darkness, I saw where the noise was coming from. One of the contestants was standing with her back against the wall with a man pushing up against her.

Owen.

Nellie

Extract from her unfinished biography, Street Life

Cynthia left early for London the next morning and I stood at the bottom of the steps in my dressing gown to see her off.

"Give me a ring if you're ever in London," she said, scribbling her phone number onto the back of a cigarette packet. "And enjoy the year's supply of shampoo!"

And that was it, she was off, her red sportscar roaring away down the sea road. I put her number in my pocket and watched until she was a dot on the horizon. I felt sad that she'd gone.

Mum and Owen were rushing around tidying up the hotel and getting ready to go off to another psychic fair. Owen's black van was parked outside with its back doors open and as I climbed back up the steps, Owen came out of the front door.

"You shouldn't be out here in your dressing gown," he said. "It will give the hotel a bad name."

"So will kissing girls in the barrel store," I said, and glided right past him.

Chimp

When I formed *The Sons*, I thought I'd write a hit record on Sunday afternoon and be famous by Thursday morning. What did I know? It was six years before we had a hit record with ***No Milk Today*** and that song has followed me all my life.

In September or October of 1979 Richard got us gigs in Liverpool, Manchester and Birmingham but when I was home, I went to the *Meibion Glyndwr* meetings at Rhoswen and Richard's cottage near Wrexham on a Tuesday night. Everyone at the group spoke Welsh and English was banned.

"Why don't you stay tonight," Rhoswen said after one of the meetings. "I've got somewhere I'd like to show you tomorrow."

I stayed on the couch, honestly, that's what I did, and the next morning, Rhoswen drove us out to Castell y Bere in the Dysynni Valley, in her bright yellow 2CV. I was impressed by how she did that, how she didn't expect me, as the man, to drive.

"It's my favourite place in the whole wide world," she said as we hiked up the hill to the ruins of the castle.

Rhoswen refused to go near any of the castles built by the English and there are so many of them in Wales. But Castell y Bere is truly Welsh, built by Llywelyn the Great in the 1220s. It was the last castle to fall to the English during Edwards I's campaign to capture Wales in 1283.

I was fascinated by Rhoswen, by her lively bright mind, by the things she knew, by the things she held dear and lived by. She could be completely practical and down to earth one minute and then mystical and connected to other worlds the next. She knew so much about Welsh history, she taught me so much.

"What do you think about the campaign then?" she said as we rested on a rocky wall. "About the fires?"

Ever since it was announced at the meeting the night before I'd had my doubts.

"I'm not sure," I said truthfully. "Do you honestly think setting fire to holiday homes is going to do anything? It could end up in a prison sentence but apart from that I'm not sure what it's going to achieve."

Rhoswen stared at me.

"Achieve?" she said. "It's not going to *achieve* anything. What it does is send a message to the English government that we won't tolerate absentee English landlords owning homes in Wales. Do you know how many there are here in Gwynedd?"

I wasn't so sure about fire. I mean getting Wales back for the Welsh was one thing but fire? On the other hand it was such a passion of Rhoswen's and I had so much respect for her I didn't want us to fall out.

"You're right," I said. "You're right."

"Of course I'm right," Rhoswen said, looking out over the hills. "No one's going to get hurt. They're empty aren't they?"

At that time, the News was dominated by the miners, by Mrs Thatcher, by the increase in the price of milk and by the IRA who had just killed Airey Neave and Lord Mountbatten. The Welsh nationalist movement didn't get a look in.

Until the fires started that December.

Polly

One night, Joe came home in quite a state and it took me ages to help him get his arms out of his donkey jacket and stand up straight. I didn't want Mam seeing him like that and so I made coffee and sat him down at the kitchen table. Da was down the Welfare and Mam was out at the Bingo. It was like that in Ffynnongroyw, before the Strike. Women lived in each other's kitchens, kids played together and Da went drinking with the other miners down the Welfare.

Anyway, Joe wasn't making sense. All he kept saying was "I'll have him Polly, I will, I'll call him out straight man to man."

I didn't realise until later that Joe had gone round to see Nellie and found Chimp walking out of the kitchen pulling on his trousers.

Nellie

Extract from her unfinished biography, Street Life

I was pissed off when Chimp said I couldn't go to gigs with the band anymore. They were going to play in England and there was a lot of travelling involved. We were standing in the kitchen when he told me and I went to push past him and walk out but he grabbed my hands and pulled me towards him and kissed me in a way I can only describe as *hungrily*. That's another word I wrote in my diary at the time. I am not sure where I got these expressions from. Some raunchy Jackie Collins novel mum was reading probably.

I hadn't expected the first time to be like that. I'd dreamed of it, tried to engineer it, and then it happened when I was completely off guard. Having sex on the kitchen floor wasn't quite how I'd imagined it would be but that's what happened. That's where I left my virginity. For days afterwards, when I watched Owen eating his tea at the kitchen table, it made me smile to think that we'd done it right there on the floor, right there at his feet and he didn't have a clue what had gone on in his kitchen.

It wasn't my fault Joe decided to come round that afternoon with a bunch of flowers just as Chimp was pulling on his trousers and I was looking for my blouse. Why he bought me flowers I don't know. It was quite an old fashioned thing to do. The front door was open, it was always open, it was a hotel, and he just looked at me and turned and walked back out again. Polly had a go at me about it later but I didn't see it was any of her business. All I'd done was kissed Joe a few times and he must have known how I felt about Chimp.

Chimp hung around that night to watch *Sapphire and Steel.* Owen had rented a new telly from Radio Rentals in Llandudno to replace our broken one. He seemed quite keen to keep me sweet after what I'd seen in the barrel store. As I lay on the couch with my feet on Chimp's lap, it felt like we had turned a corner and that things would be different from now on. At nine o'clock he got up to change the channel so he could watch the News on BBC1.

"What did you do that for?" I asked. I didn't want to watch the News. It was boring.

"Shh…" he said as the music faded and the newsreader announced that there had been a spate of house fires in Gwynedd.

Chimp stared at the screen for a few minutes and then he leapt up from the couch and started punching the air.

"Yes!" he shouted. "Yes! *Cymru am Byth! Cymru am Byth!*"

As he jumped, something fell out of his trouser pocket and I stretched across to pick it up from the floor.

"When did you go to Castell y Bere?" I asked him looking at the ticket.

Chimp's jubilation died away and he stopped leaping and turned to look at me.

"Why do you need to know?" he said.

"Well," I said. "I thought you were too busy to do anything else but play in the band."

Chimp sat back down next to me and took my hand.

"There's things I can't tell you Nellie," he said. "You have to trust me."

I looked at him. None of it made sense: Chimp jumping up and down while houses burned and a strange day trip to a Welsh castle.

"You do trust me don't you?" he said, leaning forward to stroke my hair. "I mean think about what we did this afternoon," he said. "That was special wasn't it?"

I melted. I always melted.

"Yes," I said, remembering the expression on Chimp's face as he reached the peak of ecstasy. "We could do it again if you like."

Chimp

To start with, *Meibion Glyndwr* targeted holiday homes in Pembrokeshire and Gwynedd, houses we knew were empty and which belonged to absentee English landlords. Rhoswen wrote anonymous letters to the police afterwards and signed them from Rhys Gethin and the police thought he was a real person. They didn't realise he'd died hundreds of years ago, that he was one of Owen Glyndwr's most devoted men.

I used to go out in the night and start some of those fires. All dressed up in black like the Milk Tray man I was. Except I wasn't delivering chocolates. I was delivering a message to those landowners on behalf of the people of Wales. And the message to the white settlers – that's what we called the non Welsh speakers – was *get out.*

There is something about a fire that lights up the whole sky. Something primaeval, something out of control, something that still frightens all of us despite our sophistications and progress. The trouble was that there were too many other things going on at the time for the fires to have much impact on the government. After all, it was happening in Wales, and if it happened in Wales, it didn't really matter did it?

PART TWO

The 1980s

1981

Polly

In February 1981, the News came on at twenty to six, just after *Tom and Jerry*. We always had it on when we ate our tea. Da was fixated with the News and his eyes never left the telly.

As the rallying theme music died away the news reader, Richard Baker, looked very serious as he announced the headlines. Margaret Thatcher's conservative government would be closing 23 pits across the UK.

"She can't do that!" Joe said, holding his knife and fork upright in clenched fists. "That's a breach of the Plan for Coal!"

"They won't close the pits," Da said calmly. "They wouldn't dare. This country needs coal and Thatcher won't want a repeat of 1973 when the miners brought down Ted Heath's government."

"But they just said it Da!" Joe said, getting angry with frustration and disbelief. "They just said 23 pits are to close! They wouldn't say that for a joke!"

The announcement sent ripples, waves, through the mining communities across Wales and Northern England. A ballot was held and nearly 88% of miners voted in favour of strike action if the Government breached the plan. Some of them went out on official strike but not the miners at Point.

"I don't understand them," Joe said. "If we stand united they'll have to back down."

Da sighed.

"Strikes don't work boy," he said. "And this isn't 1973 when the world was in the middle of an oil crisis and we had the upper hand. If we go out on strike now we're just playing into their hands. Gormley's right. No national strike."

Joe stared at him.

"Gormley's wrong," he said. "We need someone like Mick McGahey. Joe Gormley's had his day."

I knew far more about the politics of the miners than the average 18 year old. I learned all I ever knew at that tea table and Point was our life. It put bread on our table and food in our bellies and it kept our community tightly knit and stuck together. I had a distant memory of the power cuts in 1973 when the government introduced a three day working week during the oil crisis. I was only ten but I still remember having a bath in front of the fire in the dark. I also remember chanting *Mrs Thatcher Milk Snatcher* in the playground but none of us really knew what it meant.

In the end, Joe Gormley, the head of the National Union of Miners, told those who had gone out on strike to get back to work and negotiated a 9.3% payrise with the Thatcher government. In return, the government backed down and confirmed that no pits would close.

"It's better than a slap in the face," Da said.

Joe wasn't so sure.

"I wouldn't trust that woman if you put a halo round her head and called her Mary," he said.

Alot of miners, including Joe, were disgruntled by the deal, preferring the more militant attitude of the vice president, Mick McGahey, who didn't believe any of the promises the government had made. Joe Gormley, they felt, was too meek and mild, too much in the government's pocket.

By April 1981, unemployment had risen to 70% and 2,500,000 people were out of work. Riots broke out on the streets of Liverpool, Brixton, Leeds and Manchester. On the radio, the Specials sang ***Ghost Town*** and Prince Charles got engaged to Lady Diana Spencer.

"Well that's alright then," Joe said. "Nothing else matters if Prince Charles is getting married."

And from the way the engagement was splashed all over the newspapers, eclipsing everything else, you might just believe it.

Nellie

Extract from her unfinished biography, Street Life

One Spring morning in 1981, Owen and I had a massive argument in the kitchen. He had received the phone bill which was over £300, Mum had a final demand from Kay's catalogue and he had discovered a lot of cash was missing from the stash he kept in his wardrobe.

"Well it's not my fault!" I said when he flapped the bills in my face. "What do you expect me do when you're not here?"

"I don't expect you to steal from me!" he said. "I have done nothing but be a good father to you! I have been patient, kind, generous and this is how you repay me!"

I wasn't going to take that portrait he painted of himself. It was massively skewed.

"What about all the times you hit me?" I said. "Was that being a good father? Was it?"

At that moment Mum came into the room.

"Don't speak to your step father like that," she said, her face dark and angry.

"Oh you!" I said, turning on her. "You think he's so perfect don't you? Well he's not! He's not! Why don't you ask him about the girl he shagged in the barrel store the night of the beauty contest? Well go on! Ask him!"

The words were out and I couldn't take them back. They hung in the air for a moment, changing everything and then mum stepped forward and slapped me across the face.

"You nasty little liar!" she said, despite the fact that I was nearly eighteen. "How dare you say such things!"

I touched my face and stared at her.

Owen dropped his chin to his chest and stared at the floor.

"I think you should leave," he said in a low, controlled voice.

I half laughed, not sure what he meant.

"Yes," mum said. "I think so too. There's no place here for you anymore. I can't believe a daughter of mine would turn out to be such a… a… thief and a liar!"

I felt my stomach churning. I hadn't meant it to go this far.

"Leave?" I said.

"You heard us," Owen said. "Pack your bags and go."

I looked from one to the other but they looked away from me.

"Where am I supposed to go?" I said.

"You should have thought about that before you stepped onto the path of hellfire and damnation," Owen said. "I want you gone within the hour."

I turned to mum but she wouldn't look at me and she turned and walked out of the kitchen, slamming the door behind her. Owen left by the back door leaving me standing there wondering what had just happened. Moments later, as I was still reeling from what had happened, Mum came back in, dumped a cardboard suitcase at my feet and left again.

I went up to my room with the case. I couldn't go to Polly's because it was pit shutdown and they were staying with family in South Wales. I felt like crying and then the injustice of all they had ever done to me rose up inside and I found my strength and started throwing things in my case. As I packed, I thought about Cynthia and I pulled open my dressing table drawer where I had put her number and shoved it into the pocket of my jeans. Ten minutes later I left by the front door and walked down the road to the phone box on the sea front where I dialled her number and shoved a ten pence piece into the slot when she answered.

"Cynthia?" I said. "It's Nellie from Talacre. I don't know if you remember me but I've just been kicked out and I've got nowhere to go. Is there any chance I could come and stay with you for a while?"

Chimp

1981. We were still touring round the place in George's dad's old van and George's dad's old van was still breaking down in the most unlikely of places leaving us stranded in laybys in the middle of the night.

1981 was also the year Nellie left Wales. She didn't say goodbye or anything, she just wasn't there anymore. I went round to the hotel and her mum gave me the frosty cold shouldered treatment. All she said was that she had gone and she didn't know where she was. I thought that was a bit odd, not knowing where your eighteen year old daughter was but they *were* odd. Very odd. I've met Gillian three times in my life and at that first meeting, she struck me as a cold, strange sort of woman. It was no wonder Nellie turned out like she did.

Anyway, the band carried on getting nowhere. We were living in a world where unemployment and strikes were every day headlines. Da went on and on about what the government was doing to the mines and why the NUM didn't support strike action.

Music was my escape. Living in that world made me even more determined to make something of my life, to rise above the chaos and uncertainty. If I'd been living in a world that was more settled, in a United Kingdom that didn't have these divisions and flashpoints, maybe I wouldn't have been so driven.

Polly

We were away when Nellie left Talacre, down in South Wales staying with our Auntie Alison and Uncle Frank during pit shut down. We'd had a day out in The Gower and I spent ages looking in the shops for a present for Nellie. I didn't think she'd like Welsh love spoons or traditional dolls so I chose a pale pink plastic heart filled with *In Love* talcum powder.

"It's not very Welsh is it?" Mam said.

When we got home, I rang the hotel, keen to tell her all about our holiday and go round there with the pink heart. No one answered and so the next day, me and Joe cycled over to the hotel. We banged on the door and looked in the windows but no one was there and the front door was locked.

"Do you think we should call the police?" I said.

"No," Joe said. "They've probably gone on holiday."

"They never go on holiday," I said.

We went for a walk on the beach, looking up at the windows of the Castle Bay in the hope that Nellie might appear in one of them. It was early Spring and a cold wind blew in from the sea and the old lighthouse looked forlorn and shabby.

Joe had this theory that they'd locked her in the hotel and were going to sacrifice her to the dark arts.

"All that bloody mumbo jumbo going on in there," he said. "I mean we don't know what they're like Polly do we? We don't know. Anything could have happened to her. They could be doing witchcraft. She could be tied to a wall and forced to drink fox's blood."

I don't know where the fox's blood came from but she rang about a week later while me and Joe were watching the Grand National. I went out into the hall to answer it

"Where are you?" I asked, holding my hand against my free ear to shut out the noise of Joe shouting at the telly and the commentator whipping himself up into a frenzy.

"London," she said. "Don't worry Poll. Everything's fine."

"Nellie's in London," I told Joe afterwards.

"What the blazing armpits is she doing down there?" he said, his eyes glued to the telly. "I suppose I'll have to go and get her will I?"

"No," I said. "She's fine. She's living with a girl called Cynthia and working in a club."

Joe didn't say anymore. Instead he reached for another beer and kept his eyes fixed on the Grand National.

Nellie

Extract from her unfinished biography, Street Life

When I told Cynthia I'd been kicked out, she said I was to get up to London immediately and telephone her when I got to Paddington. I had no money for a ticket so I hid in the toilet of the train. I tried to ring Chimp before I left but no one answered. He'd told me his mum never answered the phone because she was convinced germs could get down the line.

At Paddington station, Cynthia picked me up in her red sports car and drove like a mad thing to South Kensington where she lived in a big house owned by her dad.

"Stroke of luck the lodger's just moved out," she said. "You can stay here as long as you like. The rent is £55 a week."

Cynthia had left her job with *Sunshine Shampoo* and was working as a Rothmans' promotions girl. I joined her on the front line as they called it and I loved the navy dress and white gloves we had to wear.

We handed out cigarettes in shopping centres and hotel lobbies and ate olives and Italian bread for lunch. Living with Cynthia was exciting. I loved being in London. It was busy and exhilarating and there was always a party to go to. There were no mountains, no pits and no people mumbling on in Welsh. I was free!

Cynthia knew everyone in London and after Rothmans sacked me for smoking too many free fags, she got me a job working tables at the Cafe de Paris in the West End. I had to wear this short black dress which I thought made me look very sophisticated. I loved seeing all the famous people come in and the first time Rod Stewart asked me for a bottle of Bollinger, I nearly wet myself! Oh the clothes, the music, the lights, it was so so glamorous!

It was busy work, hot and hectic but we were treated well and I longed to be a part of the rich, exclusive world that ebbed and flowed just out of my reach.

One night, I found a leather wallet lying on the floor by the bar. There was at least a hundred quid in it and no one would have known if I'd taken it but when I saw the photograph of three beaming children inside, I handed it in to the office. The next day a huge bunch of flowers arrived for me and a few nights later, the owner of the wallet came over and thanked me as I was waiting tables.

"You do know who he is," one of the other girls said as we watched him walk away. "That's Tom Wainwright, one of the top producers at Thames TV."

I was always thinking about Chimp and whether he was missing me and I wrote him letters which Cynthia posted for me on her way to work. I waited eagerly for a reply but he never wrote back.

"He's probably met someone else," she said. "Now come on dahling. You don't need him! You're in London now!"

1982

Nellie

Extract from her unfinished biography, Street Life

One afternoon, after too much white wine at lunchtime, Celia suggested I could make quite a bit of money by posing as a centrefold for *Penthouse* magazine.

"Don't you have to take your clothes off for that?" I said.

Cynthia was reclining on the couch flicking through a magazine and she looked up and laughed,

"Oh you are funny," she said. "Of course you do. Have you ever seen a centrefold fully dressed?"

I had never seen a centrefold. I didn't make a habit of looking at magazines full of naked women.

"Oh yes," I lied. "I was thinking about something else."

Cynthia, who was four years older than me and so much more worldly wise, reached for her cigarettes and lighter.

"*Penthouse* is a top magazine," she said, flicking her lighter and looking at me over the flame. "Top."

"I'm not sure about taking my clothes off," I said.

"Don't be a prude dahling," she said, blowing cigarette smoke up at the ceiling. "It doesn't suit you. Money is money and centrefolds make quite a bit of cash."

So she rang one of her contacts and I arranged to meet a photographer in a warehouse in Tobacco Wharf. Cynthia made me take a pair of nail scissors in my handbag.

"It's the East End dahling," she said. "You just never know."

Nellie

Extract from her unfinished biography, Street Life

According to my 1982 diary, I got three wolf whistles on my way to Tobacco Wharf.

1980s London was teetering between the old and the new. In the East End, the docks were empty and great big cranes towered over silent and abandoned warehouses and wharfs. As I walked, I looked at the signs above the doors: rope makers, fish merchants, ships chandlers. My high heels made a terrible clanging racket as I headed for the old tobacco warehouse.

As I pushed open this massive heavy door, a handwritten sign which said PENTHOUSE THIS WAY directed me down the metal stairs.

My high heels clanged all the way down and that Kraftwerk song, *The Model* was playing so I adapted the speed of my descent to go with the beat.

Nick Butler was the photographer and he looked like a rock star. He was wearing a pale blue denim shirt unbuttoned to his navel from which his chest hair escaped like it belonged to a wild, untameable beast. His cream trousers were so tight they left nothing to the imagination. He had these sparkling deep blue eyes and his hair was black and feathered to his collar. He put me at ease instantly and he made me feel reckless and naughty, like I shouldn't be taking my clothes off in an old tobacco warehouse in the East End of London.

He had this idea that I should do a sort of Mandy Rice Davis shot. You know, sitting on a turned around chair so that no one could see the essential parts. *Penthouse* prided themselves on being a bit classier than other men's magazines. People can say what they like about them now but I don't think they exploited women. I didn't feel exploited. No one had dragged me in there kicking and screaming.

That shot was classic. Well I think so anyway. It was the first in a series of four and they were all shot in black and white. One by one they became more explicit, a sort of gradual tempting of the tastebuds I suppose until in the fourth one, I was lying on the chaise longue with my arms above my head surrounded by piles of soft fluffy fur throws. I think I look like I was in an opium den. I certainly look exotic, dazed and sleepy and of course seductive. Nick had his own method for getting his models to look like that. A sort of post coital look if you like. I won't give away his secret but let's just say it was a very interesting afternoon!

When I left the warehouse it was getting dark and a light rain was falling. The street lights were on and the world had this soft orange glow about it.

Two weeks after my centrefold in *Penthouse* was published, I got a call from *The Sun* newspaper asking me if I'd consider posing as a Page Three girl! Cynthia nearly wet herself when I told her and of course encouraged me all the way.

When they published the photo on page three of *The Sun*, the title above it was *Welsh Rarebit!* I didn't correct them about my heritage. All I cared about was fame and fortune and they could say I was Chinese for all I cared.

Polly

I went up to see Nellie in July 1982. Mam saw me off on the early train to Liverpool with a packet of cheese sandwiches and a pair of flat shoes. The railwaymen were on strike and lots of trains got cancelled and it took all day to get to Euston Station.

London was overwhelming. I got lost on the Underground and by the time I found Nellie's house, it was getting dark.

She was living in quite a nice house in South Kensington. I was pleased about that because I'd imagined her living in some dreadful place with drop outs. Instead, the house was bright, yellow and sunny and Nellie came to the front door in Levis and a white shirt and smothered me with an enormous hug.

"You'll love Cynthia," she said as she showed me up to her room where there were two single beds. "And London is fantastic. I don't know how I stayed in Wales so long."

Everything was Cynthia, Cynthia, Cynthia and when the mythical Cynthia appeared, she was all auburn hair and green eyes and long legs. The two of them made me feel quite frumpy!

Cynthia was very posh, very English. She was a South Kensington girl and she said "yah" a lot and peppered her sentences with lots of "absolutelys" and "darlings". I don't know how Nellie could stand it to be honest. It would have driven me mad.

We sat around the table in the kitchen while the two of them laughed and swapped stories and jokes and I felt a bit left out. They were drinking white wine and smoking cigarettes and I was starving and wondered if we would ever have anything to eat. I was also dying to ask Nellie something. A woman from Talacre had come into the toyshop one day and told me Nellie had posed for a pornographic magazine and Page Three of *The Sun* without her clothes on.

"Disgusting if you ask me," she had said, shoving an airfix kit into her shopping bag. "Mind you, she always thought she was better than the rest of us."

Cynthia put bowls of olives and peanuts on the table in front of us.

"You must be starving after your journey," she said.

I was and I kept hoping for something else but nothing came. Cynthia and Nellie seemed quite happy to pick at the dishes and smoke and drink. I was burning to ask her the question and when Cynthia disappeared to use the loo, I took my chance.

"So did you?" I asked, leaning across the table and confronting Nellie with a hard stare. "Did you take all your clothes off for *Penthouse and The Sun?*"

Nellie laughed, blew smoke at the ceiling and looked at me with amused surprise.

"Of course I did," she said. "What's wrong with that? Oh don't tell me. I've been banned from Wales for life."

"It's not funny," I said. "Someone sprayed "tart" on the front door of the Castle Bay last week."

Nellie snorted with laughter.

"Did they?" she said. "How funny. Well I suppose it gives them something to talk about other than the mines and Mrs Thatcher."

"That's not funny," I said, feeling a little cross that she was talking about the miners like that.

"Sorry Poll," she said, leaning forward and touching my forearm. "I didn't mean to upset you."

Cynthia came back into the kitchen.

"Anyone for ice cream?" she said.

"I think I'll just go to bed if you don't mind," I said, feeling overwhelmed suddenly by the long day.

Nellie came up with me and sat on the edge of one of the beds as I opened Mam's zipped holdall and pulled out my washbag and my nightie.

"Have you seen Chimp?" she said. "I've written him letters and tried to ring but he hasn't answered."

So, despite her glamourous life in London, Nellie was still thinking about him.

"He's in Berlin," I said. "With the band."

Nellie stared at me.

"Berlin?"

I shrugged.

"That's what Mam said. Tom Horse told Da."

Nellie looked thoughtful for a moment and then she stood up and shrugged.

"Oh well," she said. "I suppose that's why he hasn't contacted me. What do you want to do tomorrow?"

Mam had said I had to see the Changing of the Guard at Buckingham Palace.

"I'd like to see the Changing of the Guard," I said because I didn't have a clue what else might be on offer in London.

"Ok," Nellie said. "Changing of the Guard it is. Sleep well."

Polly

The next morning, we got on the Underground and I bought keyrings on London Bridge for Mrs Murgatroyd's sons, Ahmad and Kaspar. They were red double decker buses dangling from chains and as I paid my money, the chimes of Big Ben struck ten o'clock. It's funny what you remember but every detail of that day is etched into my mind.

Anyway Nellie started complaining about doing so much walking and that her feet hurt.

"Let's just go to Regents Park," she said. "It's too nice to walk about the streets and there's a zoo there. We could get an ice cream."

It was a shame about not seeing the Changing of the Guard but it was a lovely summer's day and it didn't really matter. We got on a double decker bus and sat on the top deck. Below us, London looked all green and leafy and people were out enjoying the sun.

A brass band was playing in the bandstand as we got off the bus and walked into Regent's Park. I remember thinking how mam would have loved it. We sat down on this bench near the rose garden and listened to the band.

"We'll go and get an ice cream in a minute," Nellie said, leaning back and tilting her face to the sun.

At first I thought it was thunder. Thunder like I'd never heard thunder before but to be honest, I didn't know what it was.

What I know now is that it was the bomb going off but at the time I just remember the bench vibrating and the ground shaking and flying up into the air and my breath going out of me as I hit the ground followed by complete silence. Even the birds stopped singing. And then slowly, noises. They were vague at first and I didn't recognise them but then the noises increased and I could hear people shouting and screaming and I opened my eyes and saw Nellie lying beside me on the ground and she had all these leaves and twigs in her hair and dirt on her face and I remember wondering why she had leaves and twigs in her hair and dirt on her face. My thoughts were all jumbled up and scrambled as I tried to work out what was going on and Nellie reached out her hand and touched my arm and whispered

"I think it's the end of the world Poll. I think this is nuclear war."

I didn't know why we were lying on the ground. We had been sitting on the bench as far as I could remember, but the bench had disappeared. The world had, quite literally, turned upside down. I won't tell you all I saw. It's too horrific, the people lying on the grass, a soldier's hat, an arm hanging from a tree. I remember trying to move but my legs felt heavy and didn't want to budge and then I started to feel sort of panicky and Nellie told me to lie still and closed her eyes again. I could see blood on her face now and I thought she might be dead and so I said

"Nellie are you dead?" and she opened her eyes and said

"Don't be daft Poll, I'm just having a rest. My feet hurt."

I remember looking at her feet and her shoes had gone and I became quite obsessed about why she wasn't wearing her shoes.

It seemed like we were lying there for ages. I knew I should get up, because we were going to get an ice cream and go to the zoo but my body wasn't obeying my commands. It felt strange: my brain knowing I needed to move and my body disobeying its orders. I remember seeing the keyrings I'd bought for Ahmad and Kaspa lying on the grass and trying to stretch my arm out to reach them but I couldn't. I didn't even have the strength to do that.

Images of feet. Feet in shiny black boots running past us. We were on the grass by the trees and I don't think anyone saw us at first but then this man crouched down in front of us and asked if we were hurt and I stared at him because why would we be hurt? We were in London and we were going to the zoo. Nothing made sense. I tried to stay awake but I felt so tired.

Images dip in and out. I remember smelling fresh grass like it had just been cut. Even now I can't stand that smell, takes me right back there it does. My next memory is lying in an ambulance and realising Nellie wasn't with me. They told me later that I kept trying to get up, that I kept asking for Nellie and saying we needed to find her shoes. I remember flashing blue lights, men's voices that were low and urgent, women's voices that were gentle, sirens, shouting, chaos really and all on a summer's day. I've never liked summer since which is hard to live with really when the rest of the world worships it. It's got better over the years but it never really goes away.

Nellie

Extract from her unfinished biography, Street Life

That day is a blur. I sat down on a bench on a bright summer's day and the next thing I remember is being in hospital. My brain couldn't bridge the gap at first or understand why I was there. Later, memories came back in flashes, never the whole sequence. Other people have filled in the gaps.

I never expected to be part of an IRA bombing. It was what happened to other people. We were nothing to do with Ireland. Nothing to do with any of it.

We were lucky. In total, eleven soldiers and seven horses were killed that day in the two bomb attacks in Hyde Park and Regents Park. We were statistics, two of the fifty civilians injured. The first bomb was a nail bomb, detonated from a parked car near Hyde Park. "Our" bomb was placed under the bandstand in Regent's Park and killed seven of the bandsmen from the Royal Green Jackets. I often think how we must have heard the last notes of the last music they ever played. Some of them were so young.

I don't know what the IRA thought they'd achieve. I didn't think I'd ever get caught up in it. It was not our war. It wasn't anyone's war.

Years later when I heard a rumour that Chimp might be involved in setting fire to holiday homes in North Wales, I remember thinking well at least they didn't try to kill anyone. The Welsh wanted similar things and maybe they had more to complain about than the Irish, I don't know, but at least they didn't do bombs. Politics isn't my thing. All I know is that I was alive and very glad to be alive and even though Polly thought I should leave London, I didn't feel that way especially after the visit I received from Tom Wainwright at the hospital.

I was hardly looking my best when he walked into the visitors waiting room.

"Nellie?"

I was sitting looking out of the window in a bored sort of way. I was fed up being on the ward and I wanted to wash my hair and they wouldn't let me. I even got told off for putting on makeup and smoking in the laundry room.

I didn't recognise him at first and my brain scrambled to put a name to his face.

"Tom Wainwright," he said. "You found my wallet at the Cafe de Paris."

He was wearing a suit and carrying a bunch of pink and white flowers while I was wearing a purple velour dressing gown they'd given me from lost property and conscious I wasn't looking my best.

"There's a load of photographers outside," he said. "I told the security guard I was your brother."

He held out the flowers to me.

"You're from Thames TV," I remembered. "Don't tell me. You want to make a documentary about the bombing. Well I can't help you. I can't remember anything about it."

"No," he said. "Not a documentary. I saw your name in the papers and I wanted to bring you these. You saved my life finding my wallet that day," he said. "Bringing you flowers is the least I could do."

"Oh," I said. "I was hoping you'd say you'd help me escape."

Tom grinned.

"Were you badly hurt?"

"No," I said. "Just bruised and scratched but they still won't let me go home and I'm dying for a fag."

Tom reached in his pocket and brought out a packet of Rothmans.

"Have one," he said. "If anyone comes in, I'll say it's mine."

I took a cigarette and he lit it for me with this expensive looking silver Zippo.

"You know Nellie," he said as I smoked greedily. "Ever since that day I saw you in the Club I kept thinking how you'd be good on TV. You've got more to offer than just taking your clothes off for *The Sun* and *Penthouse*."

"You disapprove," I said, eyeing him through the smoke.

"Disapprove? Good Lord, no. This is 1982 not 1882. I admire your nerve to be honest. Ok, I'll come right out with it. How do you fancy coming to work at Thames TV? It would just be a background role to start with although I'd like to try you in front of the cameras at some stage. What do you think? My hunches are usually right. I think you're made for TV."

I think I stared at him with my mouth open for a while.

"I haven't washed my hair," I said.

Tom handed me his business card and stood up to leave.

"Give me a ring when you're out of hospital. Oh and Nellie?"

I looked up as I ground out my cigarette.

"Don't wear the purple dressing gown."

Polly

We had to stay in hospital for three days. We weren't badly injured, more shocked and concussed than anything. We were lucky. How we weren't killed I don't know. After that I felt less safe in the world and I couldn't wait to get back to Wales. London seemed a frightening, unstable place and I wanted to go home.

When Joe heard what had happened, he dropped everything and drove up to London in Bryn Thomas's old Morris Minor. Mam wanted to come but I didn't want it turning into a family outing and so he came on his own.

Joe booked into a bed and breakfast near the hospital. I will never forget the look on his face when he walked in and saw me and Nellie lying next to each other in our hospital beds. He had this huge Liptons carrier bag filled with Mr Kipling cakes and *She* magazine (which Nellie nabbed) and bottles of Robinsons Barley Water and bars of Frys Chocolate Cream and a big card signed by all the men at Point. I think everyone in Ffynnongroyw sent something.

What did Owen and Gillian send? Nothing. Joe said the hotel was boarded up and they'd gone away but no one knew where.

So we sat up in bed and we shared everything with the other people on our ward. We made quite a few friends during those three days including Mary Williams from Yorkshire who became a lifelong friend of mine. She and her husband had travelled to London to celebrate their fortieth wedding anniversary in London. The next day they were walking in the park when the bomb went off. Her husband was ok but her legs were quite badly cut and bruised.

She used to come and sit in a chair by my bed and bring the newspaper with her. Nellie was usually off somewhere, prowling about in that ridiculous purple dressing gown she'd got from lost property and smoking sneaky fags in the toilet.

One afternoon, Mary brought the paper over and on the front page was a photograph of the horses killed in the Hyde Park bombing. The sight of those horses lying covered in blankets at the side of the road still haunts me. Their names were:

Cedric, Epaulette, Falcon, Rochester, Waterford, Yeastvite and Zara.

I think it's important to remember them.

Sefton was the horse who survived and became famous. His rider, Michael Pedersen also survived but years later, he shot and killed his children before turning the gun on himself.

I think it's important to remember that, too.

Nellie

Extract from her unfinished biography, Street Life

Joe always appeared at random times in my life and there he was again, walking into the hospital ward in his donkey jacket looking uneasy against the backdrop of drips and trolleys and nurses in dark blue uniforms.

Anyway he sat awkwardly on the side of the bed and delved into this great big carrier bag and handed out all these things the people in Ffynnongroyw had sent. There was a big padded card with a cat on the front signed by everyone from the pit. Really these things were sent to Polly, not to me, but at least they had the grace to address the card to both of us.

We were allowed to go home the day after Joe came. Polly wanted to go straight back to Wales but Joe and I persuaded her to stay at mine for one more night because it was nearly eight o'clock in the evening by the time we got discharged. We didn't have any clothes. There wasn't much left of the ones we'd been wearing in Regents Park and I was annoyed they'd cut me out of my Falmers jeans. They cost a fortune!

We were discharged wearing clothes from lost property and plastic clogs they wore in the operating theatre. They let us out of a side door to avoid the photographers and Press who were camping out at the front, hoping to get a photo of me. I was glad it was dark and no one could see what a mess I looked.

When we got back to the house, Cynthia was out. Polly checked all the doors and windows and went up to bed. Joe promised they'd leave for Wales at the crack of dawn because Polly didn't want to stay in London a moment longer than she had to.

I found a bottle of vodka in the kitchen cupboard and me and Joe stayed up to have a drink. One drink led to another and well, let's just say Joe got out of my bed about ten minutes before he had to drive Polly back to Wales the next morning.

He was very gentle, Joe, and it was just the sort of night I needed. I didn't want to be alone.

I honestly didn't know Joe was so in love with me. I honestly didn't know but that night he made his feelings clear as we lay in bed with the street light shining through a chink in the curtains.

"Nellie," he said "Why don't you come back to Wales and let me look after you. We could have a good life, you and me."

I was only nineteen but I definitely didn't see myself as the sort of girl who needed looking after. I had only slept with him. It didn't mean much more than that.

"I'm sorry Joe," I said. "I really like you and everything but it's not what I want at the moment."

"Is it Chimp?" he asked.

He looked so dark and strong and moody lying there, his head propped up against his elbow as he stroked my hair but it was too much, too much and he knew, he knew.

"I haven't heard from him for ages," I said, as if it didn't matter.

"So what do you say?" he persisted.

"I'm not sure I'm ready for commitment," I said. It was all I could think of to say. I didn't want to hurt him.

Joe smiled, kissed my cheek and turned away, pulling the sheets up over his shoulders.

"I love you Nellie," he said. "I've always loved you."

There was this song out at that time, ***All Of My Heart*** by ABC. I played it over and over again the next day until Cynthia shouted at me and told me to turn it off.

Chimp

I had a head full of everything in 1982.

Richard had got us some gigs in Berlin supporting acts like The Buzzcocks and The Stranglers. The people in the audience used to chuck stuff at us because we weren't the band they'd come to see! But we played on and ignored them because we were on stage and that was all that mattered. We were getting our music out there.

Rhoswen was in England, in Newbury, wherever that is. She'd marched with a group of women from Cardiff to England in August 1981. The rest of the world had their heads turned by Prince Charles marrying Lady Di but these women – and Rhoswen - had other things to think about, like protesting about the Americans storing nuclear weapons on British soil. They started off holding meetings in a little kitchen in Ammanford and those meetings grew into the Peace Women Movement and in September 1982, a big group of them crossed the old Severn Bridge with banners and pushchairs and peace signs, set up camp at Newbury and became known as the Greenham Common Women. Rhoswen was one of them.

I collected Rhoswen's letters from the post office in Frederikstrasse and they sometimes contained clippings she'd cut out of the newspapers. The Press made the Greenham Peace Women out to be a dirty bunch of lesbian troublemakers and the police were always arresting them, dragging them away from the railings of the old airforce base by their hair.

And then I forgot all about the peace women because Nellie turned up in Berlin.

Nellie

Extract from her unfinished biography, Street Life

I was asked, by a journalist from the *News of the World,* if I'd like to do an interview about the bombing.

"Something like, *The Welsh Rarebit girl gets toasted,*" he said.

"It's not very tactful," I said to Cynthia later.

"But it's money dahling," she said. "Money."

So about a week later, a journalist and photographer came to the house and interviewed me and took pictures of me for a feature they were going to run in the Sunday papers.

Since the bombing, Chimp had been on my mind and maybe I wished it had been him, instead of Joe, who had said those words to me in the dark. I won't go as far as to say that what had happened in Regent's Park was the first time I realised I wouldn't live for ever but it was probably close to it.

"You should fly out to Berlin," Cynthia said when I told her. "Go and see him. After a shock like that, you need to be with the man you love."

"But what if he doesn't want to see me?" I said. "He's never answered any of my letters."

"Oh I'm sure he'd love to see you," she said. "Who could resist you Nellie Morgan? I mean you're gorgeous, beautiful, aren't you?"

I stared at her.

"And what about that job Tom Wainwright's offered me at Thames TV?"

Cynthia rolled her eyes.

"I don't think you should work for Thames TV," she said. "I've heard dreadful stories about how they treat their staff."

"You have?" I said, wide eyed.

"Tell you what dahling," she said, leaning forward to stub out her cigarette.

"Book a flight and I'll drop you off at the airport," she said. "It will do you good to get away and you could make a weekend of it. And don't worry," she said. "I'll keep the *News of the World* for you."

I rang Polly and managed to persuade her to speak to Chimp's dad and find out where Chimp was staying. I wrote it down on a piece of paper. It was a hotel in Schoneberg, the district in Berlin where David Bowie had lived in the 1970s.

On the plane, I kept imagining how it would be in Berlin. It would be like a love scene out of an old 1940s film, a love scene where I fell into his arms in the snow.

It wasn't. For a start, when I landed at the airport I felt like I'd arrived in a third world country. Berlin was grey and cold and Chimp was pissed off that I turned up so unexpectedly.

"What the fuck are you doing here?" were his first words.

It was hardly the romantic scene I'd dreamed of.

Chimp

Rhoswen was elusive. You could never pin her down. But Nellie, she was so obvious you could trip over her. Like the way she turned up in Berlin wearing a ballgown.

"Just tell her it's over," Menace said. "She's a pain in the ass that one."

Why didn't I? Why didn't I tell her there was no future? I don't know. I did have some feelings for Nellie. I know the Press said a lot of things later on about the way I treated her during the custody case but not all of it is true.

At the time, there was so much more I wanted to do than settle down with a woman at the age of 24. I was conflicted about Nellie – I saw how other men looked at her when we were out and the sex was always out of this world. So what was I supposed to do when she landed on my doorstep in Berlin? Make her sleep on the pavement? She hadn't even thought about where she'd stay. She just presumed – and that was Nellie I'm afraid – that she'd stay with me in the hotel.

I kept pestering Richard to send a demo tape to Island Music and we enjoyed a couple of weeks of excited anticipation before they rejected it outright. We played every stage there was in Berlin and when we weren't working, I constantly worked on my song writing.

"What defines a hit record?" I asked Richard one day. "Is it the song that makes you happy or the song that makes the audience happy? "

"It's the song that makes the most money," Richard said. "Simple."

I was beginning to realise that was all he cared about – money – oh and stuffing a load of coke up his nostrils. On the other hand, he provided the discipline the band needed. Without Richard, Boots would have ended up in a coma and George would have gorged himself to death on pizza. He was a slave driver – that's what we called him behind his back – and so by the time Nellie landed in Berlin, we were pretty exhausted and going nowhere fast.

Polly

After the bombing in Regent's Park, I turned in on myself. Everything felt fragile. The world felt unsafe. I was happy to be back home in Wales, happy to go to work in the Toy Shop every day, happy with my own little world and its familiar boundaries and I didn't want to step outside that.

One day, Joe brought home a cat from the pit. He was half blind and had no tail and needed something more than the working life of a mice catcher.

"I thought he could keep you company," Joe said, holding him close to his chest and stroking his head. "Cats are good for making people feel better."

His name was Sidney and as soon as I held him, he started purring and I felt this great feeling of warmth inside me. Mam moaned a bit when she got home and found a cat in the house but soon she was picking up KiteKat for him with the weekly shopping. Sidney did help me to feel better. Having responsibility for something else stopped me focusing so much on me.

I kept in touch with Mary Williams. We used to write letters to each other and I remember in one she wrote:

"I don't even like leaving the house to go out for a loaf of bread anymore. Paul is struggling to understand where his independent, outgoing wife has gone. Do you feel different Polly? Do you feel different deep down inside yourself?"

I did but not everyone understood. I mean look at Nellie. She had a completely different reaction to what happened to us. She spoke to the papers and she featured in a Sunday magazine and she talked about getting a job in television. Oh and then she flew off to Berlin. She didn't seem to be affected by the bomb or understand how it affected me. But Mary did and it helped to know that there was someone out there who understood.

Da and Joe were fixated on other issues. Arthur Scargill had been elected President of the NUM and he was busy locking horns with Margaret Thatcher's government over the future of the coal mines. Arthur Scargill was militant, passionate, and brought a breath of fresh air to the battlefield but some miners, including Da, thought he was doing more harm than good.

"He's turning us into a bunch of Trotskyites that's what he's doing," he'd say, when he came on the telly. "All that tub thumping and war talk I mean that's not going to do any good is it?"

I couldn't care less about Arthur Scargill but I was concerned about Joe. There was something different about him since the Regent's Park bombing. I wasn't sure if it was because me and Nellie had come so close to being killed or whether he was worried about his job. Whatever it was he was spending more and more time down the Welfare and coming home completely plastered. I used to lie in bed at night and hear him crashing into the furniture and stumbling up the stairs and falling into the bedroom we shared.

No one talked about these things in broad daylight: the fact that Joe was drinking more or I had withdrawn into myself. Oh our parents were kind and we never went without and we, like good adult working children, contributed as much as we could to the housekeeping. On the surface, everything looked fine but underneath it was a different story. As long as there were no ripples on the surface, everything was fine.

Anyway, one night at the tea table that autumn, Joe announced he was going to South Wales to work down the mine in Merthyr Vale.

Mam dropped her knife and fork and stared at him with her mouth open.

"Don't be so daft," she said when she'd recovered herself. "Whatever do you want to go to the Valleys for? They're a funny lot down there."

Joe stared at her, holding his knife and fork upright like they were weapons.

"I've been speaking to Uncle Frank and the boys," he said. "Because down there, they speak my language. Down there, they won't let a bunch of Tories walk all over them."

Da stared at Joe, and for a moment there was a frozen silence.

"I tell you what language they speak," Da said. "A load of rubbish that's what. And I tell you something else Joe Evans," he added, pointing his fork at Joe. "Go along with Scargill and the pits will close within a year."

"So what do you suggest we do then?" Joe countered. "Let the government walk all over us? The men at Point just carry on day in day out believing that nothing's going to happen, that the pit will be there for ever. It's no good doing that Da. We need to take action, stand up against Margaret Thatcher and her cronies. They want to close the mines Da, that's what Scargill says and I believe him. We have to do something to stop them."

Da was breathing heavily. I could see it was an effort for him not to shout. He wouldn't shout if me and our mam were there. He wouldn't shout in front of a woman.

"No one's going to close the mines boy," he said. "You've had your head turned by that Marxist Yorkshire terrier."

Joe wouldn't let it rest. He had the blood up and the wind up and his sails were flying.

"Striking is the only way forward," he said. "And the way I see it is the men at Point don't get it, they don't get it at all. But the men in the Valleys, they get it. They see it the way I do."

Da and Joe glared at each other across the table.

"So what is it you're saying?" Da said. "That we're not good enough for you anymore? Striking will kill the pits you mark my words. Is that what you want? Is that what you want?"

Joe held his gaze and they stared at each other across the table in silent deadlock.

Da broke it. He left the table, walked off into the living room and slammed the door behind him. Moments later Joe stood up and went out the back door. I knew that he'd gone down the Welfare, and that hours later, I'd hear him crashing into the furniture and stumbling up the stairs.

"Eat your tea," Mam said, putting a teatowel over Da's plate. "Eat your tea Polly."

Nellie

Extract from her unfinished biography, Street Life

On my second night in Berlin, we ate dinner in the hotel dining room where the staff loitered round the edge of the room looking like they were plotting to kill us. Maybe I'd watched too many war films but it was edgy that place, edgy. When I look back on it, I see Berlin as *grey*. The food was grey, the people were grey, the rain was grey, the buildings were grey. I remember it as a dingy place full of horrible old grey buildings in the rain.

That day, I'd gone out with my camera and wandered around taking photographs. I didn't know it was all divided up and that there were places that were *verboten*. I soon found out when a soldier ran at me with a machine gun waving his arms and shouting ***No photo! No photo!*** He was so handsome but even I wouldn't flirt with a man holding a gun.

So there we were in the hotel dining room eating steak and chips. It was like some sort of work's canteen the way it was laid out with neon strip lights overhead that were so bright they made me think of search lights. It was hardly romantic. There were a few other diners in there but the place was so quiet, as if no one dared to make a noise. All I could hear was the chink of cutlery on plates.

"I took some photos today," I said, in an attempt to break the silence.

Chimp looked up at me in surprise, as if my voice had startled him, as if he'd forgotten I was there.

"Is that what you're doing with your life?" he said. "Wandering round all day taking photographs?"

His words stung.

"I'm doing other things too," I said, wondering where the man of the night before had gone. We had drunk German champagne until the early hours, staggered up the stairs and had wonderful, electric, magnetic sex. And now he was someone else. Chimp could change, just like that.

"I'm living in London now. Didn't you read my letters?"

Chimp stared at me.

"What letters?" he said. "I didn't receive any letters."

"I wrote to you," I said. "Lots of times. Cynthia – my house mate – she posted them for me."

"Well I didn't get them," he said.

"Anyway," I bubbled on brightly. "I've got a job at Thames TV."

It wasn't strictly true but all's fair in love and war.

Chimp raised a cynical eyebrow.

"Doing what?" he said. "Taking your clothes off or making the tea.?"

"Are you going to be staying long?" he said when I didn't answer. "It's just I've got a lot on with the band at the moment and I haven't really got time for this."

"For what?" I said, my heart beginning to pound.

Chimp put his knife and fork down and sighed.

"Look Nellie," he said. "I don't know what you think this… it's just… just… well, I'm not ready for anything serious and you seem to think we've got something going on."

I swallowed. I felt a little sick.

"Well haven't we?" I said. "What about last night? What about those times we spent together in Ffynnongroyw?"

He sighed again.

"Those were just good times," he said. "You shouldn't read so much into everything. I mean look at this, coming out to Berlin. You've put me in an awkward position with the band."

I stared at him, not really understanding what he was saying.

"Awkward?"

"All I want to do is make music," he said. "That's what we're doing out here, trying to establish ourselves. I'm sorry if you thought we were something else but the truth is I don't really want a relationship right now."

It was already deathly quiet in that place but when he'd finished, it seemed to freeze.

I hadn't planned to tip my plate of chips over his head but that's what I did. I stood up, tipped them over his head and I walked out. My high heels were the only sound in that place as I click clacked my exit across the marble floor. I wished I'd turned around to see the look on his face but it was enough to imagine it.

I went straight up to our room, threw my things into a bag and rang a taxi to the airport. I slept in the departure lounge that night, despite the security guard pacing up and down with his gun. I couldn't wait to get out of that country, couldn't wait to leave Berlin.

Twelve hours later, Cynthia picked me up from Heathrow.

"So how was Berlin?"

"Oh fabulous," I said, adopting one of her favourite words. "Fabulous."

When we got home, there were five copies of the *News of the World* Sunday supplement stacked on the table waiting for me. Inside was my story: how a page 3 girl, a little country girl from Wales, had been caught up in the Regent's Park bombing. There were some good shots of me too looking glossy and glamorous.

"Did you post those letters?" I said. "The ones I wrote to Chimp?"

Cynthia took a gold compact out of her handbag and started to apply more lipstick.

"Of course I did dahling," she said. "Of course I did."

"Well Chimp didn't get them," I said, watching her.

"You know how the postal service is," she breezed, snapping her compact shut. "And Berlin is practically third world isn't it?"

"He wasn't in Berlin when I wrote those letters," I said.

Cynthia looked at me.

"Wasn't he?" she said.

Later that afternoon, I rang Tom Wainwright at Thames TV. I'd show Chimp. I'd show them all.

1983

Polly

Nellie rang me on New Year's Eve. We were all ready to go out to the party at the Welfare and I was wearing a new red dress because Vincent Peters was going to be there.

"Tell her to ring back tomorrow," Mam hissed. "We won't get a table if we don't go now."

Da rolled his eyes.

"Don't be on the phone all night," he said. "I'm not made of money."

Nellie never rang just for a chat. She always rang when she wanted something or there was a crisis. We'd drifted apart a bit since Regent's Park – I didn't want to go to London and she didn't want to come to Wales and her phonecalls were few and far between.

So I was just about to give her an earful about not being in touch and being too caught up in her London life when she got in first and dropped the bombshell.

"I'm pregnant, Poll," she said. "I'm pregnant."

And not just pregnant, four months pregnant.

Polly

I'd liked Vincent Peters ever since Da invited him round for tea a few months before.

Vincent was a miner at Point and after tea, they sat at the kitchen table with books spread out in front of them.

"We're working on a project that turns coal into petrol and diesel," Vincent said. "If it works out, the government are going to fund a production line at Point."

"It's not really something for women to understand," Da said. "Put the kettle on Polly love and make us some tea, there's a good girl."

Da went out to use the toilet in the yard and Vincent helped me make the tea. He had bright red hair and blue eyes and he smelt of aftershave which wasn't something I smelt very often in our house.

Sidney wound himself around his legs and Vincent bent down to stroke him.

"He came from the pit," I said. "My brother Joe brought him home."

Vincent lived in Mostyn with his mam. There were just the two of them because his dad had been killed in a mining accident at Bersham when he was three years old. It was a fear that hung over every mining family. Our great grandad had been lost the same way.

Anyway I liked the way he'd tried to explain the fuel thing to me and the way he helped me make the tea. In our house, women made the tea. Da didn't even know what a teabag was.

After that night, Vincent became a regular guest at our tea table and Sidney always jumped up on his lap. After Joe went off to South Wales, the house felt empty and I missed him dreadfully but now I looked forward to Thursday nights when Vincent Peters came to tea. It was Shepherds Pie on Thursday nights and mam always gave him extra.

"You could do a lot worse than Vincent Peters," she said to me that New Year's Eve as we headed off to the Welfare in the cold. I had Nellie's secret on my mind and I felt all grown up and glamorous in my new red dress.

"Oh mam give it a rest," I said, but secretly I was pleased because I liked Vincent Peters, I really did.

Nellie

Extract from her unfinished biography, Street Life

Cynthia thought pregnancy was the end of the world. Cynthia said it would ruin my life, my figure and my sleep.

"Why don't you get rid of it dahling," she said, blowing a smoke ring up at the ceiling. "I know someone who could fix you up in South London for about a hundred quid."

Polly, on the other hand, sent brown paper parcels of hand knitted baby clothes made by the women of Ffynnongroyw and that touched me because I was hardly part of their world was I?

When Cynthia realised I wasn't going to get rid of the baby, she changed. She wasn't sure she wanted a baby in the house crying all night. It would cramp her style, stop the partying, make everything smell of sick.

"Maybe it's time to go our separate ways," she said.

I felt sad but what choice did I have? I didn't want the option she suggested, that was out of the question. So I looked through the small ads in the Evening Standard and found a room to rent in a house in Kennington, south of the river.

"South of the river?" Cynthia said when I told her. "Oh dear."

I didn't know about north and south of the river at that time. I was pregnant and I had to find somewhere to live. Polly suggested I go back to Wales but no way was I going back *there*. The other reason I wanted to stay in London was because of ***Let's Talk!*** Tom Wainwright had proved as good as his word and I was working on his Thames TV chat show. I hadn't told him of course, about the baby. I was slim enough at that stage to get away with it.

Let's Talk! interviewed celebrities who were usually promoting a film or a book or a record. My job was to run around the studio with a clip board, getting people into the right dressing rooms and meeting the demands of some of the more eccentric guests. When I wasn't doing that, I drank it all in from the sidelines, watching what everyone did to make a TV show happen.

The host at that time was Pamela Powell. She was a bit past her prime and liked to have a drink or two before we went on air. Sometimes she was late, sometimes her shoes didn't match, sometimes she called the guests by the wrong name and worst of all, she wore that dreadful *Poison* perfume which hung in the air like witches' brew and its sweet sickly smell made me nauseous.

One Friday night, Pamela arrived at the studio so drunk she could hardly stand up. We had about an hour to go before the show went out live on air and the makeup artists were frantically walking her around her dressing room and pouring coffee down her throat.

Tom appeared from behind a curtain where I was discussing shots with Bob the cameraman. Bob was such a great bloke. I wonder what happened to him.

"Bloody woman," he said, looking flustered and stressed. "I told Mark Baker she wasn't right for this show. I told him."

I swallowed and what I did next still amazes me. It was either crazy or brave, depending how you look at it.

"I could do it," I said. "I could interview the guests."

Tom stared at me.

"You?" he said. "Don't be daft. You've only been here five minutes."

"But I know how it all works," I said. "It's just about getting people talking isn't it? And it can't be that difficult because most people like talking about themselves."

Tom's eyes twinkled. He enjoyed my take on things.

"You've got balls, I'll give you that," he said. "And as much as I want to try you out Nellie I wanted it to be in the longer term."

"She knows the show inside out," Bob the cameraman interrupted. "Sometimes she suggests shots even I didn't think about."

This wasn't strictly true but I loved him for it.

Tom hesitated.

"I don't know, I don't know…"

"I won't let you down," I said. "I can do this."

God! Where did I get my nerve from!

Tom nodded

"Ok," he said. "Although I will probably live to regret this and look back on it as the moment when a very promising career in television ended."

I touched his arm.

"Trust me," I said.

Tom walked away shaking his head leaving a trail of Eau Savage behind him. I think he probably went and lay down in a darkened room for half an hour with a very large whisky but as for me, well, this bubble of excitement rose up inside me and I looked at Bob and burst out laughing.

"Way to go Nell," he grinned. "Way to go."

Polly

I don't know how she did it. All I know is that one night, Nellie was on the TV presenting the chat show ***Let's Talk!***

"Mam!" I shouted. "Mam! Nellie's on the telly!"

It was nine o'clock in the evening and Mam came in from the kitchen wiping at a plate with a tea towel and frowned at the television screen.

"That's never Nellie Morgan," she said. "Whatever has she done to her hair?"

"Never mind her hair!" I said. "She's hosting the show. Nellie's hosting the show!"

Mam snorted and screwed up her face.

"Looks a bit podgy to me," she said.

I glared at her.

"She's not podgy mam, she's pregnant."

"She still looks podgy," mam said, going back to the kitchen.

The ***Let's Talk!*** studio was all decked out like a jungle ready for the appearance of Chloe Demetria from the rock group *Bow Wow Wow.* They'd released that slightly mad song ***Go Wild in the Country*** not long before and Nellie was poised on a pink sofa wearing a ridiculous leopard print jumpsuit with a big pink bow tied in her hair.

Chloe Demetria wore an outfit that was just as outrageous although I forget what it was now. What I do remember is that show had an edge and was much better with her presenting it than it was with the previous host, what was her name, Pamela something, who was very old school and quite prim and proper. Not Nellie though. She had Chloe Demetria, the lead singer, climbing all over the couch and wrestling with this massive plastic snake.

"Disgusting," Mam said, coming back into the room and staring at the television as Chloe lay on the couch with the snake on top of her. "I don't know how they can put such filth on the telly."

"It's not filth Mam," I countered, wishing she'd be quiet. "It's just a bit of fun."

"Well," she said. "In my day we called it something else."

The back door slammed and Mam dashed across the room and turned the telly off.

"What did you do that for?" I said, staring at her in disbelief.

"Your Da won't want to see that," she said. "He doesn't pay the TV licence for you to watch rubbish."

I wanted to say that it wasn't rubbish and that it was Thames TV and so it had nothing to do with the TV licence but I didn't. Instead I sat there feeling hot and frustrated and I didn't dare turn the telly back on. Instead I went up to bed, comforting myself with the thought that I'd seen her, I'd seen Nellie. I'd seen Nellie make her debut on the telly.

Nellie

Extract from her unfinished biography, Street Life

23 Black Prince Road, Kennington wasn't like the sunny house I shared with Cynthia.

It was a cold afternoon in March 1983 and I pulled my coat around me and looked up at the terraced house that had seen better days. The baby was beginning to show but I hoped if I wore a big coat, the landlady wouldn't notice. People could be funny about renting rooms to pregnant women, at least that's what Cynthia told me.

"It's about the room," I said when the landlady opened the front door. "The one advertised in the newspaper? I rang you yesterday about it."

Just then, a big black man with long dreadlocks spilling out of his hat loped past the front gate.

"Afternoon Mrs B!" he called, raising his arm in greeting.

"Hello Derek!" she called past.

"He's a Rastafarian you know," she said, in a conspiratorial whisper. "They live in a squat around the corner."

I followed her inside and up a a narrow flight of stairs.

The bedsit was tiny. The single bed was in the same room as the cooker and the kitchen but it had a big window and was clean and bright.

"You can see The Oval on a sunny day," she said, crossing the room to open the window.

I looked out over her shoulder. I couldn't see the cricket ground she was referring to but I could see a gasometer squatting like an grey urban warrior in the distance.

"I only let my rooms to women," she said. "Less trouble, you know. When's the baby due?"

I swallowed.

"May," I said. "Do you mind? About the baby?"

"Mind?" she said, a surprised look on her face. "Oh no dear. Why would I mind. Got a nice man to look after you when it comes have you?"

"Yes," I stumbled. "Yes of course."

"The rent is £32 a week," she said. "There's an electric meter in the cupboard which takes 50p pieces and the one in the bathroom takes 10p pieces. So dear. Do you like it?"

She was so kind to me, Mrs Bennett. Sometimes, after Morwenna was born, I didn't know what to do but she did. I used to wander downstairs at three o'clock in the morning unable to get the baby to settle and she'd just take her from me and let me go and get some sleep.

Anyway, I moved in five days after first seeing the flat. Tom Wainwright stepped up, taking me across London in his red Toyota Celica with my possessions - mostly clothes of course! - stashed in black bin liners on the back seat.

"We'll talk more after you've had the baby," he said. "I think you've got a good future on Let's Talk!"

"You mean you know? About the baby?"

"Of course I know," he said as we stopped outside number 23 Black Prince Road. "I've got two of my own. Why would a baby change anything? Women juggle everything these days. That show you did with Chloe Demetria went down a storm and the powers that be are impressed. Pamela Powell it seems, is history and there's a new girl on the block. And her name," he said, smiling across at me, "is Nellie Morgan."

His words were magic to my ears and that night I opened the window and breathed in cricket grounds and gasometers and my shiny, sparkly future.

Nellie

Extract from her unfinished biography, Street Life

It was Derek and Mrs Bennett who got me to Guy's Hospital when my waters broke.

Derek drove through London at breakneck speed in this old car that reminded me of the one Joe used to borrow from Bryn Thomas. The passenger door was tied up with string and he had to keep the engine revved up at red traffic lights. Mrs Bennett sat next to me in the back and kept a calming hand on my arm but after she leaned forward and whispered in Derek's ear, the car suddenly leapt forward and from then on all road signs and traffic lights were ignored.

"Where's your mother dear?" Mrs Bennett shouted above the noise of the backfiring engine as we raced through the empty lamplit streets. "Do you need me to ring her?"

My mother was the last person, ever, I wanted to see or hear from. I shook my head. I had knives in my belly and I couldn't think about her now.

"The father then? Would you like me to telephone the father when we get there?"

She was switched on Mrs Bennett because when I looked at her, she could read in my eyes that there was no one, anywhere.

"Oh I see dear," she said, patting my arm. "Just us is it? Well let's see what we can do shall we?"

Mrs Bennett was probably the most law abiding woman you'd ever wish to meet but that day she encouraged Derek to commit a whole string of traffic violations and refused to leave my side when we got to the hospital; not exactly saying she was my mother but not exactly denying it either.

"It hurts," I complained to her as they wheeled me into the delivery room with an oxygen mask over my face and Mrs Bennett held my hand and walked beside me.

"Well of course it does dear. But when it's all over, you won't remember any of this. All you'll remember is the most wonderful day of your life when you became a mother."

I thought I saw tears in her eyes but they were rushing me along so quickly I couldn't be sure. The world was all misty and vague and I couldn't be sure of anything except the pain in my body.

Twelve hours later, with Derek pacing up and down the corridor and Mrs Bennett still by my side, the world stopped spinning and became a quieter, calmer place.

And I looked down at the tiny little wrinkled thing in my arms and I looked up at Mrs Bennett and she smiled and squeezed my arm and I felt overwhelmed with this feeling, this great surge of love towards this tiny little baby girl sleeping against my chest. Suddenly I realised what love was and that it had a name. And the name of love was Daughter.

Morwenna

I didn't have a name for the first three months of my life. Mum and dad couldn't agree on anything, let alone what to call me. Mum wanted to call me Kitten or Snow or Kveya or Flame or Delight. I don't know what my mum was on half the time. Or maybe she wasn't on anything because her history has been spread out all over the papers and I don't know what to believe. All those cobwebs and dark corners. Anyway, Dad favoured the more traditional names like Meredith or Ffion or Angharad who was, apparently, the 12th century wife of the King of Gwynedd.

In the end it was Granpy and Nanna who banged their heads together to make them reach a decision.

"You can't have a child without a name. It's not right. She needs to know her place in the world, she needs to know who she is."

Well, that's how Granpy told it.

So they called me Morwenna. It's Cornish and it means waves of the sea.

I came into this world on 3rd May 1983. Spandau Ballet were number 1 in the UK Charts with *True* and the new pound coin had just come into circulation. Mum kept one from that year because it was the year I was born. It was with her things and I treasure it. She kept so many souvenirs.

I share a birthday with James Brown and Bing Crosby and my birthday was a Tuesday. In her diary, mum says Tuesday's child is full of grace. Grace is another story, a name that has its own connotations in our history and so I won't say anymore about her at this point.

Dad didn't know Mum was pregnant. He found out by accident after George told him. He has told me other bits and pieces, snatches and insights. There's a lot he hasn't told me but gradually I'm piecing it all together. One thing I learned quite early on was that my parents were special because people were always taking photographs of them. I was photographed a lot as a child. I'd be down the park or something and some man would jump out from behind a tree and a flash bulb would go off in my face. I used to think it was normal until I realised it didn't happen to other kids.

Chimp

In early 1983, George inherited Hope Cottage in The Gower from some ancient, distant aunt.

When I wrote to Rhoswen and mentioned it, she wrote a letter back full of capital letters, underscored words and exclamation marks, accusing George of being just another English landlord and accusing me of abandoning *Meibion Glyndwr* and losing sight of my priorities.

It pissed me off. All I was doing was trying to make it with the band and who was she to say these things when she was in England and miles away from *Meibion Glyndwr* herself? She was still at Greenham Common and her letter was full of drama; how many hours she stayed padlocked to the perimeter fence; how the police had dragged them away; how she had spent two weeks in Holloway prison. I didn't write back.

The band was my focus. After Berlin, we went on to play gigs in other parts of Germany and France and then we flew to England where we drifted around the University circuit for a while and ended up in Scotland. George went off to Wales for a few days to see his family and sign some paperwork for the cottage and when he came back to Edinburgh, he dropped some earth shattering news at my feet.

"Nellie Morgan's had a baby," he said. "Apparently she's living in London and she's got a job on the telly."

"Who's the father?" I said.

"You tell me," George said and then there was no time to talk about it anymore because we had to run on stage. Later, in the dressing room, I asked him about it again. It had been on my mind as we played. I could see Nellie in my mind, particularly when I sang *Looking at the Stars.*

"How old is the baby?" I said. "Nellie's baby?"

George shrugged. It was a stupid question really. Men never know how old babies are, do they? They're just babies and then they're teenagers as far as we're concerned.

"Quite young I think," he said. "Mam sent some baby clothes over to Polly's."

George could be infuriating at times. He spoke in riddles unless he was behind a drum kit because that was the only way he could properly express himself.

I rang Polly. She wasn't particularly friendly. Our fathers might have been best friends but that bond hadn't extended down the generations. The furthest we'd got was when she had that crush on me when we were kids but now she was Nellie's best friend and cagey.

"She had the baby in May if you must know," she said. "Although I don't see how it's any business of yours."

"Mam wants to send her a card," I lied. "Can you give me her address?"

"Your mam?" she said. "Why doesn't she just ask my mam?"

"I don't know," I said. "Just give it to me will you Polly? This call is costing me a fortune."

I was surprised that she fell for it but she did and so, a few days later when we had a break in our schedule, I caught the train to London.

I had never been to London and I arrived there like an alien who didn't have a clue how to navigate a foreign planet.

In the end, with some help from bus drivers and random strangers, I found the house in Kennington. And I found Nellie, Nellie with cropped peroxide hair trying to get a pram out of the front door on a sunny Sunday morning in early June. It was the most un-Nellie like scene I'd ever seen and it's stayed with me. Because despite all that happened later on, I honestly think that's the day I realised I loved her.

I'd also done some calculations on my fingers. And if she'd had that baby in May, that meant she'd got pregnant in August. And where was she in August 1982?

In Berlin. With me.

Nellie

Extract from her unfinished biography, Street Life

1983 was a long hot summer and *The Style Council* sang about it everywhere you went.

I was happy with my life but I couldn't have done it all without Mrs Bennett. When I worked, she had the baby. When I came home, she had the baby. I was working until late at night and sometimes there were parties too but when I got home, there was always something in the oven with Morwenna fast asleep in bed.

I learned years later that Mrs Bennett's only son had been killed when he was fifteen years old. He'd been fishing by the canal when his line got caught in the electricity cables overhead. I don't know how you get over something like that. Anyway she had all this love to give and she gave it to me and the baby. I don't know why, no one had ever done that before. It was completely new to me.

My first instinct, when Chimp turned up at the house, was to tell him to piss off. I mean I hadn't heard from him since Berlin and we hadn't exactly parted on good terms. I had my own life now. I had a job I loved and a baby I adored and focusing on them had helped shove him to the back of my mind.

But he was still there, somewhere.

Polly

I wanted to go and see the baby, really I did but I couldn't. I couldn't get on the train, I couldn't go to London. Nellie sent me a framed photograph of the two of them wrapped up in a big white blanket. I've still got it somewhere. Nellie looked so different with her short blonde hair. It suited her though.

Joe came home to Ffynnongroyw one weekend and offered to drive me to London to see Nellie and the baby. It wasn't getting to London that was the problem, it was *being* in London. I couldn't do it. Joe was very interested in Nellie, of course he was. He used to sit looking at that photograph for hours. I had hoped that South Wales might have knocked it out of him; that he might have met some nice girl from the Valleys and settled down with her. But from what I could gather he wasn't doing much but working hard and drinking. I hoped he had stopped drinking so much but during the week he stayed with us, when the pits were on shut down, I soon realised he hadn't. One night he got into a fight at the Welfare when someone accused him of deserting his own and that night he came home crashing into the furniture and stumbling up the stairs just like he used to.

Nellie had moved to a bedsit in another part of London and the landlady sounded like she was an absolute angel always looking after the baby and making Nellie soup! That's what her real mother should have been doing but Gillian, well, she didn't even know she was a grandmother. Nellie didn't want her to know and anyway, the Castle Bay was all boarded up and she and Owen had gone away and no one knew where they'd gone. They weren't part of our community anyway. They were drifters, outsiders.

Nellie and I spoke on the phone a lot and it worried me that she still hadn't given the baby a name. I mean she was six weeks old and she was still calling her baby.

"I can't decide what to call her," she said. "What do you think about Kitten?"

I thought she was joking at first but when she went on to suggest Treasure, Delight and Innocence, I realised that she wasn't.

"You can't call a baby that sort of name!" I said. "Why don't you give her a good solid name like Susan or Elizabeth or something?"

She snorted down the phone when I said that. No baby of Nellie's was ever going to be a Susan or an Elizabeth. Far too traditional.

Years later Chimp would throw it all back at her as evidence she wasn't fit to be a mother: how she hadn't named Morwenna until she was three months old; how she left her in the care of a stranger for most of the time while she pursued her television career. It wasn't true, none of it was true, it was all taken out of context. But who was the more believable? Chimp or Nellie? Who was the more grounded in the end? Well Mr Emyr Davis of course. The great rockstar with the world in his hands and a conscience that spanned continents.

Joe had a word he used to use a lot at that time so excuse me if I borrow it for a moment: Bollocks.

Nellie

Extract from her unfinished biography, Street Life

I think Chimp was more interested in my role on ***Let's Talk!*** than the baby. Well, to start with anyway because when I told him I'd interviewed Gary Numan he turned green with envy.

"Could you get us on the show Nell?" he said as I rocked the pram. "I mean we're doing pretty well now and we could do with the publicity."

Were they? The Sons were hardly a household name. Later on, people would bite your arm off to get an interview with them but at that time, they were just one of many.

I don't know why I let him in. I don't know why I let him into the world I'd created for myself but I did. I had a blindspot for Chimp which is why, later that night, he was sharing my bed.

It must have taken him hours to drum up the courage to ask me but it was then, in the shadows of a summer night that he did.

"Is she mine?" he said. "The baby? Is she mine?"

I got up and lit a cigarette and paced around the bedroom a bit.

"Sorry…" he said. "It's just that the boys, you know…"

I turned around and stared at him.

"The boys what?"

"You know. You know how they are. They're saying you probably don't even know who the father is."

The words stung. I had thought that the band were friends of mine. I mean we'd travelled around in the van, we'd slept in laybys, we'd sort of all pitched in together for a while and they talked about me like this?

"Fuck them," I said, turning away. "What's it got to do with them anyway?"

Chimp got out of bed, took hold of my hands and pulled me into him. I'd always loved the way he did that.

"I don't care what they say," he said. "She's mine isn't she? That night in Berlin?"

I don't know why I cried but I did. Perhaps it was the hormones.

"You ignored me," I said. "I came all that way to see you and you just ignored me."

"And you threw chips over my head," he said, a smile playing on his lips. "I'm sorry Nellie," he said. "I know I haven't treated you well but now… now… well, we could have a fresh start couldn't we? With the baby?"

I searched his face. Was this Chimp or was I dreaming?

"She's mine isn't she?"

"Yes," I whispered. "Yes she is."

I didn't know if she was or she wasn't. I'd slept with him and Joe in August but I wasn't going to mention it. I wasn't daft but I did feel confused and emotional. So I let him lead me back to bed and we lay there in the darkness holding hands and being quiet.

"Shall we get married?" he said, breaking the silence.

"Yes," I said. "Yes."

Chimp

I don't know why I did it. It was something about the light, about Nellie standing there in front of the window with the light fading and the fact that she'd given birth to my baby and that baby was sleeping downstairs. It was purely on impulse that I did it, that I proposed. I surprised myself because quite honestly, I'd been pretty pissed off with her after she caused that scene in Berlin.

Maybe I'd spent so long on the road that something inside me longed to settle for a while, to just opt out and live a normal life. By that time I think I was pretty much burned out. We'd been touring non stop for 18 months, taking uppers to keep us going and dope to bring us down again. Boots was always in demand – with us and with the other bands we played with. No matter where we were Boots always managed to score. He certainly deserved his name. He had more pharmaceuticals than a chemist.

So, I put what the boys had said out of my mind. I didn't believe Menace when he said she'd had a bit of a thing with Joe Evans. Nellie would never look at Joe Evans let alone have a thing with him. He wasn't her type. The boys weren't great fans of Nellie's at the best of times. They remembered how precious she'd been on the road, how she spent hours getting ready and always made us late. Things like that. So they were bound to come out with crap like that.

And so, on that June night in 1983, I honestly thought I was in love with her. I think I was in love with the idea of love. Of having a family. Of living in a little house somewhere with tea on the table every night. As if Nellie was ever going to deliver that! I was also impressed with how she had re-invented herself, how she'd got in with the television people and become the chat show host on ***Let's Talk!*** Nellie had found her purpose. Nellie had grown up.

Nellie

Extract from her unfinished biography, Street Life

We dropped the baby off with Chimp's parents and flew to Las Vegas in September 1983. We couldn't get married earlier than that because of *The Sons'* commitments.

It was a crazy ceremony performed by an Elvis impersonator but that is what I wanted, something whacky and out there. I thought, when I was growing up, that I'd have a winter wedding with snow on the ground and lanterns lighting up a winding path leading to an old stone church. But now that I was grown up, Las Vegas was what I wanted. I loved the glitter and the glamour and the bling!

I'd never been on a jumbo jet before. Oh I'd flown to Berlin but that was in a clapped out old plane that had probably been in the war. My flying outfit was a white lacy dress that fell to my ankles and I wore it with a pair of Doc Martens. Chimp wore his old Parka and as we waited in the departure lounge, he slept on the chair next to me. We were just sitting there waiting for our flight to be called when a very smart British Airways air hostess came over to us and crouched down next to me.

"We saw your name on the passenger list Miss Morgan," she said. "And I'm pleased to tell you we've upgraded you to First Class with the compliments of the airline. Are you going to Las Vegas for a special occasion?"

I looked at Chimp who had woken up and was staring at the air hostess.

"We're getting married," I said, using my best British TV presenter voice.

"How wonderful!" she said. "Are you ready to priority board? LOVED that interview with Gary Numan by the way."

I don't know why Chimp was so pissed off about it. I mean First Class! Maybe it was because I'd been recognised and he hadn't. Anyway as soon as we'd boarded and the red warning light went off, he lit up a cigarette and chain smoked through most of the flight. At one point he went to the toilet and was gone for ages because they'd refused to let him back into First Class! It was that old Parka that did it. Sometimes he looked like Top Cat, like he'd spent the night in a dustbin. What did he expect?

Nellie

Extract from her unfinished biography, Street Life

It was a beautiful ceremony even though it only took fifteen minutes. That is all the time it takes to get married in Las Vegas. Fifteen minutes to stand there with glitter in my hair in my very own fairytale and agree to handing over the rest of my life to Chimp.

The song I chose to walk into was one I'd played a lot when we first met. All those ups and downs, a song about love that can lift you up or knock you down. I was such a romantic!

It was Bette Midler's, *The Rose.*

Some say love, it is a river, that drowns the tender reed
Some say love, it is a razor, that leaves your soul to bleed
Some say love, it is a hunger, an endless aching need
I say love, it is a flower, and you, its only seed

It's the heart afraid of breaking, that never learns to dance
It's the dream afraid of waking, that never takes the chance
It's the one who won't be taken, who cannot seem to give
And the soul afraid of dying, that never learns to live

Afterwards, we had our wedding breakfast in a room full of other people who'd just got married. It was surreal and we made our excuses and spent the afternoon in bed.

You see those were the times, those were the times that made me believe in us. We could have moments that moved me beyond the realms of time, moments when I truly thought my heart would overflow with love for him. That was what kept pulling me back, time and time again. And now of course, I was his wife and officially the happiest woman in the world. Officially.

Nellie

Extract from her unfinished biography, Street Life

We spent our honeymoon, if you can call three days in Wales a honeymoon, on The Gower peninsula. George had inherited this old house in Laugharne, overlooking the estuary. Chimp loved its location because there was some old Welsh castle in the area where Dylan Thomas used to spent time writing in the garden. I didn't give a monkey's about Dylan Thomas and I wasn't keen on honeymooning in Wales either. What was wrong with Jamaica or Barbados? But Chimp had said we didn't have that sort of money and it was Wales or nothing. So we dropped Morwenna off with Chimp's parents and stole some time for ourselves.

Hope Cottage was a little white house crouched by the estuary as if it was apologising for being there. It was so old fashioned it didn't even have central heating. But despite its primitiveness, it was a peaceful time for us. Perhaps it was the only peaceful time we ever had together. The rest certainly always seemed to be fireworks and fighting.

We walked on the beach. We gathered driftwood and we lit fires. We sat up late talking by the fire and we talked, really talked; perhaps it was the first time we'd ever done that too. When I look back, I think I was happy. I used to wake up in the morning not quite believing that it had all turned around like it had. That I was Chimp's wife. That I was a mother.

A week later, we drove up to Ffynnongroyw to collect Morwenna from Tom and Sarah's. She was four months old by then and his mum kept going on about giving her a name. The trouble was, Chimp and I couldn't agree on one. He wanted something traditional and I wanted something modern. His mum and dad said we weren't leaving until we'd decided on a name. I was desperate to get out of there and so I probably would have agreed to Ermintrude. Luckily we agreed on Morwenna. It was different enough for me. It was traditional enough for Chimp even though it has its origins in Cornwall rather than Wales.

I didn't realise it at the time but you have to register and name a baby within 42 days of its birth and I got fined for not naming my own baby! They brought that up in Court later, of course they did. It was one more example of what a bad mother I was.

After Wales, Chimp had to re-join the band and I went back to London with Morwenna. Mrs Bennett was thrilled to hear the baby had finally been given a name. She said Morwenna made her sound magical, like a princess. She was a lovely woman Mrs Bennett. I still get upset when I think about what happened later, when the custody battle was going on. But at that time, my world felt perfect. Absolutely one hundred per cent perfect. I had Morwenna, I was Mrs Emyr Davis and I had a job I loved. I never heard from Cynthia. I tried to phone her a few times but she never answered.

"You've got new friends now," Mrs Bennett said when I told her about it. "New friends."

That winter, I published my first book on glamour for mothers. It was an instant hit, full of photographs of me and tips on how to look good despite having children.

How perfect was my life?

Polly

Of all the crazy things Nellie ever did, marrying Chimp was the craziest of them all. One minute he was ignoring her and the next they were getting married in Las Vegas.

She called in when they were in Wales for their honeymoon. Morwenna was still "baby" because they hadn't decided on a name. Nellie couldn't stop talking about Las Vegas and Chimp went on about the band and so you could see naming her wasn't one of their top priorities.

"I'm interviewing Simon Le Bon next Friday," she said, as we sat at the kitchen table having a cup of tea.

"Oh," I said, not really sure who Simon le Bon was.

I didn't dwell on it because I loved the fact that just for a short while it was me and Nellie and the baby and a cup of tea. We didn't have many simple moments in our friendship anymore but that afternoon, the autumn sun streamed through the kitchen window and the world felt settled and right and just how it should be. I wanted to tell her I was going steady with Vincent Peters but I didn't get the chance. It didn't matter. I was always happy to hear about Nellie and her life. It was so much more exciting than mine!

I watched every ***Let's Talk!*** that she did. She was good. She had this way of getting away with questions other presenters didn't ask, of flirting so innocently with her guests and getting secrets out of them which the viewers loved to hear. I laughed out loud when Simon Le Bon told her he always wore green socks in bed! That's the sort of thing the public wanted and it was no surprise when ***Let's Talk!*** was voted the number one show on TV that winter.

Mam was more cynical.

"Getting a bit above themselves those two," she said, knitting furiously in her armchair. "They'd do well to remember where they came from."

I ignored her. It was something she often said about people who left Wales and made something of their lives.

Da didn't have much to say about it. Nellie and Chimp and the baby didn't mean much to him. He had more important things to think about, like how Margaret Thatcher had won her second general election in June

1983. Even though it was autumn, he was still going on about it.

"Flabbergasted I am," he'd say. "I mean how can you have all this unemployment, all these strikes, and re-elect the government that caused it all? It's the Falklands that's done it. I tell you the British people care more about booting the Argies off some remote island no one has ever heard of than saving the mines."

It was probably true. I mean outside of Wales the country was a vivid shade of Tory blue and to many, Margaret Thatcher was a saviour. It just depended on where you were standing at the time.

In November 1983, the NUM introduced an overtime ban in response to the National Coal Board's offer of a 5.2% pay rise which was rejected outright by the miners. Da thought they should accept it. Joe didn't and there were rumbles about going out on strike in protest.

I tried to keep out of it. I had Joe in my ear ranting down the phone and Da sounding off at the tea table so I just kept my head down and stayed somewhere in between.

That year, Culture Club released their song ***Victims*** which came out at Christmas. When I watched the video on Top of the Pops I cried because you could almost believe in the concept of the heaven Boy George created and forget the darkness of the real world.

Almost.

Chimp

Once I was back on the road, I started to wonder what I'd done. The boys couldn't believe that I'd married Nellie.

"It's not exactly rock n roll is it?" Menace said. "And she is a Page Three girl."

I nearly punched him for that but I managed to control myself. Instead I told myself that being married and having a baby didn't change anything. I still had that burning ambition to succeed; to write that one hit song that would propel us into the hall of fame and secure our place in it forever. Richard pushed us harder and to cope with it all I used more uppers, more downers, we all did. Maybe I was also trying to block out what I'd done, the responsibilities I'd taken on. I don't know.

Nellie used to write me long scrawly letters when I was away. I don't know what planet she lived on half the time.

"*I dream about this big house where we'll live and be a proper little family. My star is really rising Chimp and life is so exciting! My book on glamour for mothers has hit the list of top ten best sellers and the publishers are talking about a coffee table edition of some of my photographs! What a golden couple we are! What a perfect family!*"

I only kept one of her letters and Morwenna has scolded me about throwing the rest away. Maybe a part of me felt resentful, jealous, of how well she was doing in TV and publishing whereas I seemed to be getting nowhere fast and had been getting nowhere fast for years.

And then, out of the blue, Rhoswen turned up.

Polly

I'd fancied Vincent Peters ever since New Year's Eve when he'd pulled me under the mistletoe at the Welfare and kissed me. After that, our courtship was slow because Vincent and I were both quite shy and I was still adapting to the changes in my world: how I felt after the Regent's Park bombing and not having Joe at home. Vincent was busy down the mine with his job and with the liquidation plant and what was the hurry anyway?

We didn't become an official couple until the autumn of 1983, when he called into the toy shop one Saturday morning and asked me if I'd like to go for a walk when I finished work.

"I've got to go over to Talacre to see Nanny Gwyn," I said, as if he'd know who Nanny Gwyn was!

"So I'll come with you," he said. "We can walk on the beach afterwards. Get some chips if you like."

A solution! That's what I loved - and still love – about Vincent. He never makes a drama out of a crisis and always finds the solution. So that afternoon when I finished work, we cycled over to Talacre. Nanny Gwyn was my Dad's mum and she lived in a bungalow on the beach. It didn't have running water or electricity and Nanny Gwyn was still convinced we were at war with Germany.

"Get home safely before the blackout," she always said as I left the bungalow. There was no point trying to tell her we weren't at war and so I just went along with it.

Vincent was very kind to her that afternoon. He made her tea, fetched her glasses and looked out the window to see if there were any Spitfires flying around.

Afterwards, we were walking through the sand dunes when he said

"So what do you do for you?"

I didn't know what he meant at first.

"What do you mean?" I said.

"You seem to spend your life doing things for everyone else. What do you do for you?"

I couldn't think of anything at first so I listed the jobs I did for Nanny

Gwyn and Mam and Granpy Penri and Nanny Grace and how I worked at the toyshop and took the sheets to the launderette on a Monday… and… and then he pulled me into him, right there in the sand dunes, right there in the Marram grass and he took my words away with the biggest kiss I've ever had.

Afterwards I looked up at him in astonishment.

"What did you do that for?" I said.

"I did it for you," he said. "That kiss was for you."

After that we went for lots of walks.

We walked in the fields at Garth Mill and in the woods at Coed y Garth where the fallen leaves were crisp and brown and golden under our feet and we leaned over little rickety wooden bridges and listened as the streams rushed by under our feet. As the seasons turned, we wrapped up in hats and scarves and walked to the Estuary to see the oystercatchers but our favourite was always the beach at Talacre. You have to walk on that beach to understand the vastness of it. I like it best in winter when the tourists have gone. It stretches out for ever and it's there you can really see the sky with all its moods and temperaments.

Vincent used to stop sometimes and breathe in deep lungfuls of air. He loved being out in the open air after the darkness of the pit.

"It's a treat for my eyes," he'd say. "A treat for my eyes. When I come out of the mine into the daylight, it's like I'm born again, every time. I see things more vividly, all the colours, the shades, everything."

One afternoon just before Christmas 1983, we were walking on the beach at Talacre as the fog rolled in from the sea. The old lighthouse looked even more forlorn than usual and there were no lights on in the Castle Bay hotel.

"How's Joe getting on in South Wales?" he said.

I sighed.

"Drinking, fighting, talking about going out on strike," I said. "Apparently they weren't too impressed by the offer of the payrise. Do you think the miners will strike? Da goes on about it all the time."

Vincent walked on, a thoughtful look on his face.

"Not at Point they won't," he said. "The men are too loyal. South

Wales and Yorkshire… well, they're different. They think Arthur Scargill is god."

"Do you?" I said.

Vincent stopped and took hold of my hands.

"Well," he said, his blue eyes twinkling. "I'm supposed to say that us men with red hair should stick together but he's a bit too hot headed for me. Now," he said. "How about getting some chips and going to see that new film at the Pictures?"

Nellie

Extract from her unfinished biography, Street Life

I loved being famous! People used to stop me in the street and ask for my autograph. Mrs Bennett said I was a trend setter, a fashionista and it's true, I think I was.

I used to experiment. I'd go on the telly wearing a pink PVC mini skirt and a ripped up black top and Doc Martens boots. And a week later, that look would be copied in Jackie magazine or Fab 208. I was 19 years old and I was different: I was a young, trendy mother who worked on the TV. I was an example to young girls that you could be anything and everything you wanted to be. Polly said her teenage cousins used to watch ***Let's Talk!*** every Friday night just to see what I was wearing. And then they'd go off and put something together that looked like what I'd worn.

My role models were Madonna and Margaret Thatcher. Madonna broke rules and boundaries, with her clothes, her music, her videos. And Margaret Thatcher, our prime minister, well, she made you feel you could achieve anything you wanted to achieve. They might have been total opposites those two women but they were the influencers of their time: for women like me anyway.

Anyway when I look back, the weather forecast was mixed. One minute I'm having my outfits and my look copied by all these teenage girls and Morwenna is cutting her first teeth and saying her first word and the next, Chimp doesn't ring or write for months. He brought clouds to my sunny sky, there's no doubt about it. But in those moments when I felt a bit low and downcast about it, Mrs Bennett would point to my wedding ring and say

"He's your husband isn't he? He married you. There's some perfectly good reason why he hasn't contacted you. Maybe there's no phone. You know how it is with that one down the road. Sometimes it's working, sometimes it isn't. I don't think you've got anything to worry about dear, really I don't."

Chimp

I didn't expect Rhoswen to be mad. I didn't expect her to turn up in Lincoln either. But she was and she did and she paced around my hotel room chain smoking and asking me a hundred questions about Nellie and why I'd gone and married her.

"I thought you had your own stuff going on," I said. "Richard said you'd hooked up with a girl."

"That girl has a name," she said. "That girl is called Gift and that girl has more integrity that you'll ever have. And anyway, at least I didn't MARRY her in LAS VEGAS!"

What was this? Out of the blue at midnight. Rhoswen mad, Rhoswen conflicted. Rhoswen slagging me off for marrying Nellie whilst openly admitting she was in a same sex relationship. I wrote the song ***Radical Love*** about it all. It wasn't our biggest hit but I think it started to puncture that glass ceiling we were always pushing against.

"You've lost track," she said "You've lost track of all we were working for."

"By marrying Nellie?"

"Yes by marrying Nellie but also by compromising your spirit, your free will. When was the last time you went to a Meibion Glyndwr meeting? When was the last time you took up the cause?"

So now it was about that. I was confused. Rhoswen's mind was flitting from one thing to another. She had changed too, she was more angry, she was more radical. Perhaps that what's happened when you lived in a peace camp with hundreds of other women and constantly fought the authorities. I always knew how to calm Nellie down when she got upset. Nellie was easy. You put your arms around her and she'd melt. That didn't work with Rhoswen. Her name might have meant white rose but she was a rose with thorns all the way up the stem. She smashed a few glasses and then she walked out of the hotel room cursing me in Welsh. I ran after her before she woke up the rest of the band and before the management came and kicked us out.

She was still kicking and punching me when I laid her down on the bed. My first instinct had been to quieten her down, to stop her making so much noise and I was holding on to her wrists to stop her clawing my face and it just sort of happened. All that anger melted into something else.

And before I knew it she was tearing off my shirt and tugging at the zip on my jeans and I was yanking her t-shirt over her head.

And you might not believe it but honestly that was the first time. The first time Rhoswen and I ever slept together.

Nellie

Extract from her unfinished biography, Street Life

At Christmas 1983, I bumped into Cynthia at a party in The Chenin Blanc Hotel in the West End. It was quite a swanky hotel. At the door they took your coat and called you madam and the champagne flowed. It wasn't until I was inside that I realised it was a fancy dress party and there were people dressed up as Ronald Reagan and Marilyn Monroe.

Cynthia sidled up to me carrying a cigarette in a long holder and wearing a blue 1920s flapper dress and beaded headband.

"Dahling!" she said. "Don't YOU look fabulous?!" as if it surprised her, as if after having a baby, I would be wearing sackcloth and ashes. "Love the hair darling. Love the hair."

I told her I'd got married and had a baby girl called Morwenna.

"And you're doing so well on that talk show," she said lifting another glass of champagne from a passing tray. "I see you in the papers all the time. It must be difficult juggling it all though dahling. Is it? Is it difficult?"

"No," I said. "I leave her at home with the landlady most of the time. Like tonight," I said. "So it doesn't really interfere with my lifestyle."

"The landlady?" she repeated. "Are you and your husband in digs? I thought you'd be living in some fancy house in St. John's Wood or somewhere."

"It's complicated," I sighed, thinking of our domestic arrangements. It was a strange set up and her words made me think of Chimp. He was always away and sometimes, despite the ring on my finger reminding me, it didn't feel like we were married.

"Well of course it is," she said. "Isn't life always? Now do you fancy a little joint or are you all prim and proper these days?"

"No way," I laughed. "Being married and having a baby doesn't turn you into a nun."

We drifted outside onto the terrace where miniature Box trees were decorated with white fairy lights and there was this lovely Christmassy atmosphere about the place. Behind us light and laughter spilled out of the French windows and silently I congratulated myself on how far I'd come.

After the joint we went back in and the party really got going. I danced with a man called Toby who was dressed as one of the Blues Brothers.

"Who have you come as?" he shouted over the music.

"Myself," I said. "I'm Nellie Morgan. I don't need to be anyone else."

This made him throw his head back and laugh.

"Love it!" he said. "Love it! Tell me," he said, steering me off the dancefloor into a darker corner. "Is Nellie Morgan as wild as she makes out on TV?"

He had deep blue eyes that twinkled and I felt a frisson of excitement inside me. I hadn't done this for years. I'd worked and been a mother and got married and I'd missed the random wildness of life after dark.

"I might be," I said.

"Fancy going for a drive?" he said.

Cynthia came over and air kissed my cheek.

"I'm off dahling," she said. "We must meet up for lunch soon, really we must."

We never did.

Toby was drunk but no one cared about drink driving in those days. We drove down Pall Mall on the wrong side of the road with me shouting Merry Christmas!! out of the sunroof and we had drunken sex against a lamp post. I stumbled home in the early hours and tiptoed up the stairs carrying my shoes in my hand.

I didn't think about that night again until years later. It was just like any other night, or the sort of nights I was living then. Parties, home at dawn, sometimes a man in my bed, sometimes not. But later, it came back to haunt me. Later both Cynthia and Toby gave statements in the custody case. Cynthia's said how I frequently left Morwenna in the care of a woman I didn't know and how I went to parties, took drugs and picked up strangers. Everything she said screamed bad mother. I don't know how much Chimp paid her because I'm sure he did. He would do anything, at that time, to get what he wanted and Cynthia would do anything for money.

I felt deeply betrayed by Cynthia and shocked that she'd regurgitated everything I'd told her at a Christmas party to paint a picture of me as some sort of empty headed woman who didn't give a toss about her daughter.

It's taken a long time to come to terms with it. I am still not sure I have come to terms with it. That's one of the reasons I started to write this autobiography. Nurse Divine suggested I write it all down and get it all out. It helped but sometimes what happened still feels raw. All that betrayal. All those people I trusted.

But in those heady days of the early 1980s, I didn't have a clue. I was having fun. Did going to parties make me a bad mother? I was twenty years old for fuck's sake.

Polly

Joe came home for Christmas 1983. We had an artificial tree in the lounge decorated with tinsel and baubles and paper chains looped around the staircase in the hall. Mam loved Christmas and she'd pulled out all the stops to welcome him home.

It might have been Christmas but Joe was fixated on something else: the rumour that the Government were planning to close ninety five mines over the next three years.

"Rubbish that's what it is," Dad said dismissively as we sat around the tea table on Christmas Eve. "Don't believe everything Scargill says boy. He's full of his own sense of importance. He'd sell his own grandmother if he thought it would get him publicity."

"He's seen the letter," Joe countered as Mam set down a cheese and potato pie in front of us. "He's seen it. It's a fact Da, it's a fact. You mark my words, that government won't rest until every deep mine in this country has been closed."

Mam took her seat and dished the pie onto plates.

"They're only going to close twenty pits that aren't profitable," Da said. "Scargill's making a big drama out of it like he always does. Point is safe."

Joe picked up his knife and fork, holding them in his fists like weapons.

"And you believe that do you? That it's only going to be twenty pits? You really trust this government to do what they say? Well I for one don't trust any of them and nor do any of the boys in South Wales."

And then mam intervened.

"I don't know if you've forgotten," she said. "But it's Christmas. And you're to stop this talk right now or I'll cancel the whole thing and give the turkey to the Salvation Army."

No one argued with mam. She changed the subject to the arrangements for Christmas and how I was to cycle over to Nanny Gwynn's with her Christmas dinner in the basket and stop on the way back to fetch brandy butter from Mrs Morgan's. Joe and Da didn't mention Scargill again and after tea, Joe went out and Da settled down on the couch with the newspaper.

About five years ago, they released some government papers which showed that Scargill had been right all along. There *was* a plan in the 1980s to close hundreds of pits, not just twenty.

Maybe it's a good thing Joe wasn't around to know that.

Nellie

Extract from her unfinished biography, Street Life

On the day before Christmas Eve 1983, Chimp turned up on the doorstep with his arms full of presents.

"I thought we'd spend Christmas together," he said. "Like a proper family."

I was surprised to see him but Mrs Bennett ushered him inside and insisted he warm himself by the fire in her sitting room.

"I must say I love having them here," she said, handing him a glass of sherry. "It's a joy looking after Morwenna and Nellie is still so young. It's important she has something of a life."

"You don't leave Morwenna with her all the time do you?" Chimp said to me later. "I mean, you hardly know her."

I felt a bit bristly with him just swanning in like that and expecting me to welcome him with open arms. I hadn't heard from him for months and he never seemed to think how I managed to make ends meet. He never sent us any money and his phonecalls were few and far between.

"I worry about you and Morwenna living here," he said, pulling back the curtain and staring out into the dark. "There's a Squat round the corner and someone's sprayed *Legalise Freedom!* on the wall. Is it rough? Is there trouble?"

"No," I said. "I'm not here that much anyway."

Chimp appeared thoughtful.

"And what about this Mrs Bennett woman," he said. "How often does she look after Morwenna?"

I stood up and lit a cigarette. His questions were beginning to irritate me. He never seemed to bother most of the time and now he was picking my life apart.

"Mrs Bennett is the kindest, sweetest woman," I said, inhaling deeply. "I wouldn't be able to do my job without her and she adores Morwenna."

Chimp dropped the curtain and turned to look at me.

"Well in that case go and ask her for a suitcase," he said. "We're going to The Gower in the morning."

Nellie

Extract from her unfinished biography, Street Life

I wasn't sure I wanted to go to Wales. I had Christmas all planned and Mrs Bennett had bought a Buxted frozen turkey. Wales might have been home to Chimp but it wasn't my home. It was just a place where I'd lived for a few years.

"What if I don't want to go to Wales?" I said to him the next morning.

"Fine," he said. "You can stay here and I'll take Morwenna. Mam will be pleased to see her. You ought to make more of an effort with her Nellie. She's their only grandchild after all."

It seemed that every time he opened his mouth he was criticising me. That's what I heard. That's what I felt. And now he was saying that if I didn't go, he'd take Morwenna anyway. I wanted to point out that he hadn't bothered with her for months, that he didn't call, didn't write, didn't do anything that a father should do. And now he was waltzing into our lives wanting to play happy families.

"I'm sorry Nellie," he said, coming towards me and hooking my hair behind my ear.

"I know I haven't been in touch for a while. It's just that it's been so hectic. Boots got arrested for possession and Menace nearly left the band and my head's been all over the place. I just thought it would be nice to get away for a few days. You and me and our daughter. A few days by the sea will do us good. Remember our honeymoon? How happy we were?"

When I tell Rudi about little scenes like this, he rolls his eyes.

"He's good isn't he?" he says. "He always knew exactly what to say to pull your strings."

Rudi was right. Chimp always knew what to say to bring me round even when I wanted to stab him through the heart with a carving knife.

"And when we get back," he went on, holding my hands and pulling me to him and looking at me in that way that made my heart melt. "When we get back, we'll start looking for a house. Our very own house. This isn't the right place for you and our daughter. You deserve better than this."

My ears pricked up.

"What sort of house?" I said.

"Anything you want," he said. "A house where we can be a proper family."

"With his and hers bathrooms and a red and white kitchen?"

"If that's what you want," he said, nuzzling my neck.

"Can we afford it?" I said, trying to remain practical for a few more moments.

"If you want it we can afford it," he said.

Twenty minutes later, I rushed down the stairs and found Mrs Bennett with her hands submerged in bubbles in the kitchen sink.

"We're going to Wales," I said. "Do you have a suitcase I can borrow?"

Mrs Bennett turned and smiled at me. It was Christmas Eve and carols were playing on the transistor radio balanced on the worktop.

"That's nice dear," she said. "When are you off?"

"Well shortly I suppose," I said.

And then I read something else in her eyes.

"What about the Buxted turkey?" I said.

"Oh don't worry about that," she smiled. "I'm sure Derek and his friends will help me out. Now come with me and we'll find you a suitcase. I've got a nice brown one somewhere."

Chimp

The house where Nellie was living was this grimy old Victorian terrace just round the corner from a Rastafarian squat. And as for the landlady! Well. She was like something out of the Addams family! I was worried Nellie wasn't spending the time she should with Morwenna and was leaving Morwenna with this woman all the time. That wasn't how a mother should behave. It certainly wasn't the way my mother behaved.

When I got to the house on Christmas Eve, we had to sit downstairs in her boiling hot front room and drink this disgusting glass of sherry and as we were sitting there this huge man suddenly poked his head around the door and grinned at us.

"Oh don't mind him," this Mrs Bennett said. "That's Derek. He's always calling in. Part of the furniture aren't you dear?"

This Derek whoever he was didn't look like the sort who should always be calling in. For a start, he looked like a thug with that big woolly tea cosy on his head and his gold teeth. It just made me feel more and more uncomfortable about where my daughter was living.

Anyway you'd think Nellie would be pleased that I was back and the surprise of going to The Gower for Christmas but she wasn't. And that, I'm afraid, is Nellie all over. Ungrateful. Selfish. More interested in spending Christmas in London with that ghastly old woman and a frozen turkey than considering what might be best for her daughter.

Eventually she agreed that we should go to The Gower. I suppose I felt a bit guilty about Rhoswen and it was also my way of forgetting about what had happened with Rhoswen. It wasn't about the night I'd spent with her: it was more the way she left in the morning before it was even light outside.

"Are you going back to Greenham Common?" I asked her as she used my toothbrush to clean her teeth.

Rhoswen rolled her eyes. "I might be," she said. "What's with the questions?"

"No questions," I said. "I just wondered."

"Look Emyr," she said. "Last night was fun but that was all it was. Don't read too much into it."

That stung. Who was she to tell me not to read something into it? She was the one who had had turned up at the hotel, caused a scene, and ended up in my bed.

"Don't worry," I said. "I won't."

And she was gone.

I was pissed at her for that and a little hurt to be honest. I don't know if she meant half of what she said that night or not. It was like the things she'd said under cover of darkness evaporated in the morning light. So I wrote a song about it: ***When you Vanish with the Dawn.*** Nellie thought it was about her because when it hit the charts, that's what I told her. It only got to number 46. It was so frustrating! In the charts but nowhere near where I wanted us to be. Number one was what I was aiming for. Number one!

I couldn't possibly have known, as we set out for the Gower that Christmas, that events were about to unfold that would give me exactly what I wanted.

Be careful what you wish for. Isn't that what they say?

Polly

They called in, on Christmas Eve, completely unexpectedly. Mam put the kettle on, cut some Christmas cake and fussed over that bonny little baby.

They were going down to George's cottage on the Gower. Chimp had ants in his pants from the moment he arrived and it was clear he didn't want to hang around. He kept looking at his watch and telling Nellie they ought to get moving, that the weather was getting bad, that it would be getting dark soon. Nellie wanted to stay longer, I know she did, but if Chimp wanted to go, they had to go.

And then Joe walked in. He'd had a skinful at lunchtime down the Welfare. You could smell it on him. He stood and stared at them for a moment as Nellie bounced Morwenna on her lap.

"Can I hold her?" he said after a minute.

Chimp glared at him.

"I don't think you ought to mate," he said. "Not if you've been drinking."

Nellie glared at Chimp and let Joe take the baby. I could see that really annoyed Chimp but he couldn't make a scene could he? Not in our kitchen.

Joe was transfixed by the baby.

"She's beautiful," he said. "Hello Morwenna. Hello."

I suppose you could say Joe was a functioning alcoholic because he probably functioned better when he had a bit of the drink inside him and there was no way he would ever drop a baby. Chimp didn't like it though and after a few minutes he said

"Well thank you very much for the tea but we need to be off. We've got to call in on mam and da before we head off to The Gower."

Nellie said she needed to use the loo and went outside. Joe handed the baby back to mam – not Chimp – and left by the back door. I think he probably went back down the Welfare. He practically lived down there that Christmas.

Nellie

Extract from her unfinished biography, Street Life

I hated that outside toilet. I never understood why they didn't pull it down and get a proper one. Anyway, I didn't really need to use it, I just wanted to get out of that kitchen for a minute. Chimp always had to control things and he made me feel uncomfortable and awkward about Joe holding the baby. So I spent a few minutes in there counting to one hundred and as I came out, Joe stepped out of the shadows.

I could smell the alcohol on his breath. It came out all misty because it was December and it was cold and getting dark.

"You're looking good Nellie," he said. "Being a mother suits you."

I didn't know what to say. I hadn't expected him to be there because Polly had said he was living in South Wales.

"Thank you Joe," I said and moved to walk past him. Chimp would be getting agitated. When he wanted to go, we had to go.

Joe stopped me. He reached out his hand and he caught my arm.

"Is she mine Nellie?" he whispered. "Morwenna? I've often thought about that night…"

I shrugged his hand away. This wasn't a conversation I wanted to have.

"No Joe," I said, smiling to cover up my eagerness to end the conversation and get out of there. "She's Chimp's daughter. We got married you know."

I don't know why I did it but I held out my left hand to show him my gold wedding band like I was the most happily married woman in the world.

"Oh," he said. "Well that's good, that's good. Are you happy? Is he good to you?"

Oh I wanted to tell him! I wanted to tell him that it wasn't all I had expected it to be! I wanted to tell him about the nights wondering where he was, about the suspicions I had about other women and for a moment, I nearly did. I don't know what it was about Joe but I always felt safe with him.

The moment passed.

"I'd better go," I said, looking away.

Joe nodded and slipped away into the darkness just as a chink of light fell across the path and Chimp came out the back door with Morwenna in his arms.

"What the fuck are you doing out here?" he said. "You know we need to go."

"Sorry," I said. "I couldn't find the light switch."

He looked at me strangely.

"There isn't a light switch," he said.

"I know that now," I said, taking his arm. "I think I've been living in London too long."

Chimp

No one was ever going to believe Joe. He was just a piss head really. A typical miner who spent his days underground and his nights propping up the bar. I'm sorry if I sound harsh but half of the problem with those miners in the 1980s was that they kept harping on about the glory days and didn't realise they were gone. So they closed the pits. So they lost their jobs. Move on is what I say. I knew it wasn't the life for me very early on. Joe could have got out too. All of them could have got out.

Anyway he came up with some cock and bull story later on, during the Court case, about how Morwenna might be his. The Judge dismissed it when we got statements to show how unreliable Joe was; how he'd been part of some pretty violent behaviour with the flying pickets during the Miners' Strike; how he used to drink up to ten pints of beer a night. I mean who's going to believe someone like that? Not the Court anyway. And I don't care if his mother came to all the hearings and cried. It was nothing to do with her. I didn't need a paternity test whatever she was angling for. And the Judge was on my side about that.

"Mr Davis," he said "You strike me as an upright man of the law. Granted you spent some time in a rock band but I am aware of the good works you have done since. I dismiss Mr Evans's application as frivolous. I will treat it as a further example of the attempts being made by a small community to discredit and undermine you as a man and as a father."

I'm sorry for what happened to Joe later, really I am. But if he'd just got himself sorted out, if he'd stopped clinging to the past, if he'd found another path he could have turned it around.

Anyway, it was good to get back to Wales on Christmas Eve 1983. Mam and Da fussed around Morwenna and I was always surprised at how affectionate Da was to her: he had certainly never shown any fatherly qualities towards me! I suppose being a grandparent is different and she was, after all, their only grandchild.

We didn't stay long. Mam once told me she found Nellie *difficult* but she put up with her if it meant having time with Morwenna. Nellie wasn't the star of ***Let's Talk!*** in that house! I doubt they'd even watched it let alone heard of it. And as for her book about tips on glamourous motherhood, Mam would have laughed up her sleeve if she'd known about it. Glamourous motherhood didn't really count for much where I came from. It was baby sick down the back of your jumper and never mind the mini skirts and the lipstick.

Nellie

Extract from her unfinished biography, Street Life

Hope Cottage didn't feel the same as it did in the summer. We arrived in pitch darkness and the house was freezing cold because the generator had stopped working. All we had was a guitar and an over sized teddy bear and I had to wrap Morwenna up in all the blankets I'd brought to keep her warm. I felt like I'd been plucked out of civilisation and dumped in Tumbleweed.

"For fuck's sake stop moaning." Chimp said, as he lay half in and half out of the cellar trying to coax the generator back to life. "It's Christmas Eve."

It didn't feel like Christmas. We had no telly, no hot water, no Christmas tree and Chimp stayed in the cellar until about two o'clock in the morning fiddling with that generator. I took Morwenna to bed with me to keep her warm and all I could think about was our warm room in London and the Buxted turkey. I cursed myself for once again giving in to Chimp.

Chimp

When we got to George's cottage, it was in a bit of a state to be honest. No one had been there since we'd stayed in September. It was pretty dilapidated, because George was having difficulty finding a builder to work on it and the woman in the village who looked after it had had a fall. I worked all night to fix the generator but all Nellie did was moan.

Things got better on Christmas Day. I persuaded her that we should go out for a walk and see if we could get Christmas lunch at the pub down the road. We walked quite a long way only to find that the pub had closed down.

Nellie moaned that her feet hurt and so we got in the car and drove to Swansea. It was Christmas Day and we had to wait an hour for a table. And when we got one, Nellie complained that the sprouts were hard and there weren't enough potatoes. Morwenna cried most of the way through it which annoyed the other diners and on the way back to the cottage, Nellie got a strop on and tried to get out of the car. It took ages to persuade her to get back in and by the time we were on the road again, it was getting dark.

I often wonder, if we hadn't gone to Wales that Christmas, how different our lives might have been. Rhoswen says it's no use thinking that way. That I can't change it now. And anyway, she says, it had a happy ending didn't it?

Did it?

Nellie

Extract from her unfinished biography, Street Life

All my adult life I'd wanted a romantic Christmas with a man I loved. And there I was with my husband and baby on Christmas Day and I wasn't happy at all. Chimp did things on the spur of the moment even when it came to where we were going to eat Christmas dinner. I preferred to be more organised but he said I should stop trying to control everything. Me!

We couldn't get it right. Chimp wanted to go for a walk on the beach when we woke up but I didn't have the right shoes and that pissed him off. The local pub where he thought we'd have lunch was closed and we ended up driving to Swansea, niggling at each other all the way. When we got there everywhere was full and we had to settle for this pub where the only free table was crammed in a corner with hardly enough room to move. Morwenna picked up on the tense atmosphere and wailed her way through dinner. It was the most disgusting dinner I've ever eaten and we rushed through it because the other diners kept giving us filthy looks because we'd dared to bring a crying baby into their domain.

On the way home, Chimp pointed out all these things to Morwenna that she couldn't possibly understand because she was so young. After a while, it got on my nerves.

"Why do you keep doing that?" I said. "She's only seven months old. She doesn't understand what you're going on about."

Chimp gave me a sideways glance.

"It's important to speak to babies," he said. "Don't you speak to her when you're in London?"

Chimp had suddenly become an expert on parenthood and I felt a flare of hot anger inside me and started to undo my seatbelt.

"Stop the car," I said.

Chimp slowed down and I opened the door and got out.

"What do you think you're doing?" he said.

"You've done nothing but niggle at me all day," I said, close to tears. "I want to go home."

Chimp sighed and rolled his eyes at the car roof.

"Don't be silly Nellie. Get back in the car and close the door. It's freezing out there."

I hadn't thought it through, not really. I mean how could I get back to London with a tiny baby from there?

"You can't go back to London Nellie," he said. "Stop acting like a child and get back in the car."

I had no choice, did I? I had to get back in. I've had some Christmases since that weren't exactly perfect, especially the one during the custody battle but that one, well, it's right up there as one of the worst I've ever had.

We drove on in silence but just before we got to the lane where we turned off to Hope Cottage, a police officer waved us over. I thought we must have done something wrong but I couldn't think what.

"Road's closed," he said, crouching down by the side of the car as Chimp wound down the window. "We've got a bit of an incident going on I'm afraid."

Chimp stuck his head out of the driver's window and looked down the road but the fog was coming down and dusk was falling. "We're only going to Hope Cottage," he said.

"Sorry, sir," the police officer said. "No cars are allowed past this point until the incident is over."

Chimp turned off the engine and we sat there and looked straight ahead without speaking. Morwenna was fast asleep in her carrycot on the back seat. At least she was oblivious.

Chimp

We got pulled over by the police on the way back to Hope Cottage. It was getting dark and we'd been driving in fog for the last half hour. Now we were sitting in it, in silence. Luckily Morwenna had worn herself out crying and was fast asleep in the back of the car.

"We can't sit here all night," Nellie said, unclipping her seat belt. "This could take hours and I'm dying for a wee."

As I watched Nellie cross the road to get to the bushes on the other side, I unbuckled my seatbelt and got out of the car. I nearly jumped out of my skin when a man standing at the side of the road spoke to me. The fog was so thick I hadn't seen him. Up ahead there were more people standing around on the verge under the trees.

"What's going on?" I asked him.

"Some bloke's lost it apparently," he said in a South Wales accent. "He's holed himself up in that house at the turning with his daughter and a shotgun, threatening to blow both of them to kingdom come."

I stared ahead but I couldn't see anything. Moments later, a voice floated through the fog.

"Anyone here speak Welsh?"

"Anyone here speak Welsh?"

Nellie appeared from the other side of the road and glared at me over the roof of the car.

"Don't you dare," she said. "Don't you dare."

"Here," I said, ignoring her and holding my hand up in the air. "Here."

The crowd parted to let the police officer through.

"Speak Welsh do you?" he said.

When I nodded he beckoned me forward.

"Make way for the gentleman please. Make way."

Nellie shook her head and rolled her eyes.

I felt an immense sense of importance as I followed the officer through the parting crowd. Up ahead, there was a cluster of police cars parked at angles in front of the house at the corner of Primrose Lane with their blue lights flashing in the fog. The police officer pulled me over to the side of the road, out of earshot of the other people, and spoke to me in a low voice.

"We've got a man in there with his twelve year old daughter and a gun," he said. "He doesn't speak English and the trained negotiator we're expecting has been held up in an accident on the motorway."

I listened carefully to what he was saying. Part of me wanted to run, part of me wanted to stay.

"Ok," I said. "What do you want me to do?"

"The negotiator's made contact on the radio. Come over to the car so she can speak to you. I'm hoping she can tell you what to say and you can translate."

I stared at him.

"You want me to speak to him?"

"That's right son. You sound like a North Wales boy to me. You all speak Welsh up there don't you?"

I looked behind me. Nellie had followed me forward, holding Morwenna in her arms. I felt irritated at seeing her. We were yards away from a man with a shot gun who, by all accounts, sounded completely unhinged and she was bringing our baby forward?

"Could you tell my wife to go back to the car please?"

The officer followed my gaze.

"Oh," he said. "Yes, righto. Go back please madam. Yes, right back. That's it, that's it."

Nellie and Morwenna disappeared into the fog and for a moment I hesitated as the police officer waited by the open door of the police car. What was I supposed to do? Walk away or try to help? The man in the cottage had a 12 year old girl with him and although the police officer was calm and in control, that's how they are trained to be. I doubt the Mid Glamorgan constabulary had ever had to deal with something so fragile before.

Moments after I got into the police car, the gun went off.

Nellie

Extract from her unfinished biography, Street Life

I dropped to my knees as a crack of gun fire broke the eerie silence. I remember staring at my Christmas shoes – red, high and deadly - and squeezing Morwenna so tightly that she whimpered. There was this flash of bright light through the fog and a moment's silence before people started screaming and panicking.

"Everyone stay where you are!" a police officer shouted through a megaphone. "PLEASE! Stay where you are."

A woman wrapped in a big oversized cardigan emerged from the fog and I looked up at her from my crouching position beside the car.

"I live over the road," she said. "Come and have a cup of tea."

"My husband…" I said.

"I saw a man get in the police car," she said. "Wearing a parka."

"Oh thank goodness," I said.

The woman took Morwenna, helped me to my feet and draped her cardigan around my shoulders.

Her house was cosy and warm with a fire roaring in the grate and a silver Christmas tree glowing with fairy lights in the corner. I had to tiptoe across toys and wrapping paper strewn across the carpet and drifting down from the ceiling above me, were the thumps and bumps of children playing upstairs.

"You're the girl off the telly aren't you?" she said, squinting as we came into the light. "I thought I recognised you. Nellie isn't it? LOVE your shoes by the way."

I nodded but I was feeling so strange and light headed I wasn't sure who I was. I remember a big man wearing an orange paper hat putting a tray of tea on the table and I remember the woman taking Morwenna from me and making me sit on the couch with my head between my knees. I felt sick and cold even though it was very warm in there. I remember it all like it was an upside down world decorated with tinsel and baubles.

I'd completely forgotten it was Christmas Day.

Chimp

Suddenly I was sitting alone in the car. When the gun went off, the officer pushed my head forward so that I was looking at my lap and then he leapt out of the car and ran with his colleagues towards the house. I don't know how they do what they do. I know they're trained and all that but how do you know how you'll react when disaster strikes? All these voices were coming through the radio and I sat there staring at the house as the police rammed the front door open and ran inside.

I found myself focusing on this strange sign propped up on the porch. It was strange to see something so normal amidst the chaos erupting all around me. It was a piece of brown corrugated cardboard on which someone had written, in thick black pen NO MILK TODAY. It struck me as odd. Why would anyone put out a sign for the milkman on Christmas Day when the milkman doesn't come on Christmas Day? Had they got mixed up? Did they know it was Christmas? And if the man didn't speak English how could he have written it?

The brain is an amazing organ. It focuses and finds the mundane to focus on when something it can't comprehend or translate comes out of the blue. Maybe it's a protective mechanism, maybe it stops you from going mad or putting yourself in more danger by running or reacting in a way that could put your life at risk. So I sat there thinking about the connotations of this sign while the police dealt with a life and death situation concerning a man and a 12 year old girl shut inside a house on a Christmas Day that had turned out to be anything but full of peace and good will to all men.

It seemed like I sat there for ages before another police officer knocked on the passenger window and indicated I should wind it down.

"Are you the boy who speaks Welsh?" he said.

I nodded and he got in the driver's side and sat there staring straight ahead at the house. There were no lights on inside but from time to time I caught the flash of a torch in an upstairs window.

"I'm afraid we have a casualty situation," he said. "The man, who we believe to be the little girl's father – has shot himself. The little girl won't leave his side and doesn't appear to speak English. I've been doing this job twenty years but I've never seen anything like this."

We sat in silence for a moment.

“You want me to speak to her?” I said.

“Yes please,” he said. “Her name is Grace Chappell. That’s all we know at the moment.”

Polly

What did we know about Grace? Not much at the time. Except of course that her father shot himself in front of her on Christmas Day.

We saw it on the local News that evening.

"Bloody hell that girl gets everywhere," Da said as Nellie's face appeared on the screen and mam and I shushed him.

"Twenty five year old Emyr Davis from Flintshire, who is married to the host of Let's Talk, Nellie Morgan, was on holiday in The Gower when it happened and helped the police persuade the 12 year old girl to leave the house."

"I just did what anyone else would do," Chimp said, as the camera closed in on him. "It's not the sort of thing you expect to see on Christmas Day."

"Well well," mam said, knitting furiously. "He might at least have put a comb through his hair."

I shot a look at mam and Vincent, sitting next to me, squeezed my hand.

"Want to go for a walk?" he whispered.

It was hot in there, stifling. Da got up to put more coal on the fire but it was already warm enough to sit in the lounge in your underwear.

"Whatever makes someone do something like that?" I said to him when we were out in the crisp cold air and the stars were bright in the sky above us. "I mean what sort of effect is that going to have on a twelve year old girl?"

Vincent shook his head as we stared up at the stars.

We'd find out in the months and years to come.

Nellie

Extract from her unfinished biography, Street Life

Grace was small and thin with long raggedy brown hair and bare feet. As Chimp carried her out of the house, she clung to him like he was her last hope and refused to let go.

"I don't suppose you'd come with us to the police station," the officer said when she refused to be handed over. "I don't want to cause her more trauma by forcing her to come with us and she seems to trust you."

Chimp caught my eye over her head. I was rocking Morwenna and I wanted to go. It was so cold and Morwenna was grizzling and needed a feed.

"My wife and daughter…" he said. "They need to get to Hope Cottage."

"Well," the officer said, as Grace stuck her thumb in her mouth and stared at me over his shoulder. "We could drop them off. It's only down the road isn't it?"

Chimp nodded.

"Nellie?"

What was I supposed to say? If I protested he'd call me heartless. If I agreed, it was home alone in that dark creepy cottage.

I shrugged, saying neither yes or no but Chimp seemed to think it was settled.

"Come on then Grace," he said walking towards the police car. "Let's get you into the warm eh?"

As they walked away, she gave me this sort of triumphant smile over his shoulder. For a girl who had just been through what she'd been through it surprised me.

I think Grace made up her mind about me that night. I certainly made up my mind about her. The rest of the world was so indulgent with her afterwards but I could see right through her. I know it sounds harsh but she sent a shiver down my spine. Rudi says that I just imagine my instincts sometimes and how could a twelve year old girl do that? I don't know. All I know is that I never trusted her to be what she presented herself to be, twelve years old or not and I certainly don't trust her now.

Chimp

We waited hours at the police station for Social Services to come. Well, it was Christmas Day after all.

When the woman arrived, Grace refused to look up at her and every time she tried to take her hand she pulled it away and shook her head.

"Come on love," she said. "We're taking you to Swansea to see your auntie Megan. You'll be safe there. Safe."

Grace shuffled closer to me and stared at the floor. I couldn't imagine how she was feeling having seen her dad shoot himself. I felt so protective of her, even then. I mean, imagine… So yes, from then on, she became a part of my life. Some people say I should have left it at that and walked away and that if I hadn't got involved, if I had walked away, what happened to Rudi later on wouldn't have happened.

I re-visit that night time and time again. What if I hadn't offered to get her out of that house? What if I'd kept my mouth shut about speaking Welsh? What if we had just done a U turn in the road and gone back to the cottage the long way round? Things would have turned out so differently wouldn't they?

She's changed all our lives, Grace. Mine. Morwenna's. Nellie's. Especially Nellie's and I'm really sorry about that. Not just sorry. Heartbroken. No one deserved that. No one.

I went to see Nellie at The Suns of Life in 1989. I don't think she knew I was there. The nurses said that some days she knew where she was, other days she was completely lost. I can never think of Nellie as lost. It's not how I think of her at all.

When Morwenna asked me and Polly to write about our lives, I didn't think it would be this difficult. Sometimes I find myself just sitting and staring out of the window and I realise that hours have gone by. And I'm back there, in those strange and sometimes dark days of the 1980s and Rhoswen comes in and I look at my notebook and realise I haven't written a word for hours.

Anyway, back to Christmas Day 1983. It's a time I'll never forget for many reasons. And that shooting and Grace coming into our lives are the biggest ones.

Nellie

Extract from her unfinished biography, Street Life

Hope Cottage creaked and groaned when you were alone in it at night. I put the radio on and took Morwenna and a bottle of vodka up to bed.

All night I listened out for Chimp but he didn't come. I had a dream that I'd got lost in the fog and kept turning down all these lanes that ended at big wooden doors. If I'd been back in London I'd have left Morwenna with Mrs Bennett and gone out to find some company. But I couldn't do that in the middle of nowhere. I couldn't do anything except wait for Chimp to come home.

I was still in bed when I heard the back door open. It was about ten o'clock in the morning and daylight was peeping through the curtains. I thought he'd be annoyed that I was still in bed at that time of day – he didn't approve of lie ins.

Anyway, he wasn't annoyed. He wasn't anything but tired. He lifted Morwenna out of the bed, put her in her carrycot and got in beside me, wrapping his arms around my waist and nuzzling the back of my neck.

"Let's get back to where we were," he whispered. "Let's stop all this bickering and arguing shall we? Life is so short."

That was the thing with me and Chimp. One minute we were fighting. The next we were loving. It was that sort of relationship. People who stood outside it couldn't see into those moments, those moments when, like on that morning, we were as close as any couple could be. How we whispered in the morning light, how he stroked my hair, how he told me that he was the luckiest man in the world to have such a beautiful wife and daughter. And how he thought we should extend our stay, remain in Wales for New Year. Give us some time to chill out. Relax.

I agreed on the condition we got some decent food and a lot of alcohol and later on that day, I rang Mrs Bennett from a phone box. I felt gloriously happy and content. She said she'd see me in a few days time and that I was to enjoy myself and make hay while the sun shone, whatever that meant.

1984

Chimp

We stayed in the Gower for New Year. It was one of the most peaceful times of my life. We lived on fish and chips and pizza although Nellie did attempt to make macaroni cheese one night. Mucked Up Cheese I called it. Even Nellie laughed.

Nellie was a night owl and I was a lark so I'd leave her and Morwenna sleeping and go walking on the beach early in the morning. It was so peaceful, so beautiful with miles and miles of white sand and the sea birds calling and the winter sun on the waves. Nellie wasn't into walking at all. I don't think she owned a pair of shoes without a four inch heel! We had an argument about that when we first arrived on The Gower but after the shooting, things like that didn't seem to matter any more.

I couldn't get Grace and what had happened that night, out of my mind. How could her father have shot himself in front of her? How desperate had life become to make him do that? And then I thought about how he must have planned it all even down to putting that note out to cancel the milk. I couldn't get over that. I mean it's so bizarre isn't it, to put a note out for the milkman knowing that in a few hours' time, you're going to shoot yourself.

One morning as I was walking on the beach, the song came into my head out of nowhere, burning and insistent in my mind, clamouring to be born. I ran back to the house and wrote it down on the first thing I could find which happened to be the back of an empty pizza box.

Those scribbled words became *No Milk Today,* our greatest hit. It spent ten weeks at number one, sold over 600,000 copies and got us a gold disc. At the time, I had no idea it was the song I'd dreamed of writing for years, the song that would lift us out of the mediocre and establish us as one of the foremost bands of the 1980s.

Later that night, I picked up my guitar and sang it through to Nellie as she rocked Morwenna by the log fire.

"It's a bit dark isn't it?" she said.

"It's meant to be," I said. "It's about the loss of hope, the way life takes you to where you'd never thought you'd go. There's a lot of people struggling at the moment; there's a lot of lost hope."

"Oh," she said. "Is there?"

Nellie

Extract from her unfinished biography, Street Life

One morning, after the shooting, Chimp came running up from the beach like something was on fire or someone had drowned and shouted at me, as he came into the house, to find him a pen and something to write on. All I could find was a pen from a betting shop and an empty pizza box and so he took that and ran off up the stairs. Being married to a rock star is not all glitz and glamour!

Anyway, later that evening, Chimp came downstairs, picked up his guitar and played this song as I sat by the fire dozing with Morwenna in my lap. I thought it was a bit dark at the time.

I'm not coming out of the house today
I don't want any milk and I don't want to stay
In this world, not in this world
Give the milk back to the cow
It's getting dark and I don't know how
I'll make it, I'll make it
No milk today, I have a master plan
No more ploughing the field or working the master's land
There's no milk deliveries
In the place I want to stay
I said No milk no milk no milk
Today

It was clearly inspired by what had happened on Christmas Night. At the time I thought it was just another song out of the Chimp stable, like ***Looking at the Stars*** or ***Radical Love*** or ***When You Vanish With the Dawn.*** There were loads of songs and I knew most of them by heart. My favourite was ***Let's Not Fight Anymore.*** That was definitely about us. Definitely.

Anyway ***No Milk*** became the Sons' biggest hit. Everyone remembers that chorus. People used to say it to cashiers in supermarkets or as a joke or to each other. ***No milk no milk no milk today.*** It's a statement, it's an attitude, it's a man controlling the one thing he has left to control: his milk delivery. That's what Chimp said, anyway.

Chimp

I felt so nervous when Boots played the opening riff at Reading University at the end of January 1984. I held my breath, waiting to see how the crowd would react because it was the first time we had played *No Milk* and it could either sink like a stone or explode like a supernova. In the end, it was supernova.

The crowd went wild for it, jumping up and down and by the end of it they were punching the air and repeating the chorus back to us.

"*I said no milk, no milk, no milk today!*"

At the end of the song, I dropped the mike and stood there listening to the roar and whistle of the crowd. I felt elated, as high as a kite. We had a hit song. Finally, we had a hit song. I raised my fist in the air and shouted to the sky "*Cymru am byth! Cymru am byth!*" After that, I made that gesture and shouted those words at the end of every gig we played.

The single was released in March 1984 and it went straight to number one. We were signed by Dolphin Records and started putting an album together which we recorded at the Mono Studios in Monmouth, where Queen recorded Bohemian Rhapsody. Life changed for us overnight when *No Milk* hit the charts. Suddenly we were the hottest property around and everywhere we went, people shouted that chorus back at us. We were in all the magazines and newspapers but one thing really pissed me off and that was when some of the interviewers insisted on comparing it to *I Don't Like Mondays* by the Boomtown Rats.

I can see why because both songs were about shootings but it still annoyed me. Did they think I'd deliberating gone out looking for a shooting so that I could write a song about it? Did they really think the Sons were so unoriginal that we had to copy someone else?

Nellie interviewed me on ***Let's Talk!***

I told her not to mention *Mondays* and to be fair to her, she didn't.

Richard was swamped with fan mail, which George thought the coolest thing ever and they used to tease me about the amount of cards and letters Grace sent me. It seemed that nearly every day she sent a postcard or a letter from Swansea. I got more letters from her than from the rest of the world put together and they were always covered in love hearts.

Chimp

At the time when *No Milk* hit the charts, Grace was living with her auntie and uncle in Swansea. I went down there when I could. I felt his sort of guilty obligation to see Grace and when I walked in, she'd rush out to the hall and throw her arms around me and start chattering away in Welsh.

Little by little I learned about the life Grace had lived with her father holed up in that house near Hope Cottage on The Gower. I won't go on about it here but what I will say is that whilst it never excuses what she did later on, it goes some way to explaining it.

I mean, if your mother dies when you are a child and you never go to school or meet other children, you're going to be a little different aren't you?

"My brother was a strange one," Megan said sadly. "Yes, he was a strange one."

Part of me felt a bit guilty for making a fortune out of such misfortune, from the sad life of a man called Frank I didn't even know. Grace seemed to have a different slant on it. She used to write me letters in her spidery black writing saying how much she loved me for making us both famous. I didn't see it like that but if that was helping her get over the tragedies in her life then I accepted it. Who knows how grief and loss affect people? Who am I to judge?

Polly

It may have been all gold taps and champagne for Chimp in early 1984 but on 6th March, our world turned upside down. We were sitting at the tea table waiting for the BBC News to come on and when it did, John Humphreys tipped the world upside down.

"The National Coal Board has today announced that the agreements reached during the 1974 miners strike are invalid. Twenty pits will close with immediate effect with the loss of 20,000 jobs. In the long term, up to seventy pits will be closed across England Wales. "

Da dropped his knife and fork.

"What the bloody hell..." he said, wiping his mouth with his napkin. "They told us they were safe! They promised!"

Within minutes, the phone in the hall started to ring and Mam went to answer it.

"It's Joe," she said. "Be quick Gordon. He's in a phone box."

Mam put his dinner in the oven as Da went out to the hall. I wanted to listen but all I could hear was Da raising his voice and minutes later he came back into the room looking a little red in the face.

"I don't know where I went wrong with that boy," he said, shaking his head and sitting down at the table. "I don't know where I went wrong."

Mam took his dinner out of the oven but although Da picked up his knife and fork, he didn't eat anything and just stared at the television.

"Well?" Mam said. "What did he say?"

Da glared at her.

"A load of bloody rubbish about striking that's what," he said. "A load of bloody rubbish."

Just then the back door opened and Vincent came in, pale faced and pinched with cold.

"Have you heard?" he said. "About the pits?"

Da nodded.

"Sit down boy sit down," he said. "This is a day I don't think any of us are going to forget in a hurry."

Vincent pulled a chair up to the table and we sat in silence listening to John Humphreys as if he was God.

Mam and I didn't speak. We didn't dare.

The next day, 187,000 miners went out on strike in protest at the closure of the pits. The first pit to go out was Cortonwood in Barnsley, Yorkshire followed by Scotland, Kent and South Wales. They held a ballot at Point. Out of the 600 men who worked there, 84 voted to go on strike but the rest, including Da and Vincent, continued to work. Most of the men at Point held on to the NUM's reassurances that Point was safe.

Two days later, the National Coal Board announced five more pits would close in the next five weeks under a scheme they called "accelerated closure". We waited to see what the miners in Nottingham would do. If they went out on strike, the country would be starved of coal, the government would capitulate and everyone could go back to work.

"Nottingham won't go out," Da said. "They get too much money."

"This country's gone mad," Mam said, pummelling one of Da's shirts to death on the ironing board. "Utterly and completely mad."

Letter to Polly from Mary Williams, 1984

Dear Polly

I hope all is well with you in North Wales. Life has changed drastically in Yorkshire since the strike started at Cortonwood. Paul said he couldn't stand back and let the government take away his livelihood. Men are angry, men are desperate. All they want to do is work and they've been forced to strike to save their jobs.

Some of the wives have started up a group to support them. We run it from my kitchen and we take sandwiches up to the picket line and cook hot food for the children.

I hear the South Wales miners are out but I haven't heard anything about the two pits in North Wales. Are Joe and your dad on strike?

I can't believe how quickly life has changed. There's no money coming in and people are stealing potatoes from the fields and milk from the doorsteps. My neighbour has burned her wooden spoons and the baby's play pen just to keep them warm.

I am amazed at the generosity from other countries. We have been sent boxes and boxes of tinned food from Chile and France and Russia. Half the time we don't know what's in the tins because we can't read the writing on them. Donna Black nearly fried chips in floor cleaner last week!

We intend to stand by our men all the way through this. If Nottingham goes out. we'll be that much stronger and hopefully that will be an end to this dreadful business. They say it should all be over in eight weeks and I think we can manage until then.

Anyway I hope things are better for you in Wales and I hope you will write soon.

Yours affectionately

Mary

Polly

It's strange when I read that letter back now. Eight weeks. That's how long we thought the strike would be. Eight weeks.

In the end it was a year. One whole long year.

Nellie

Extract from her unfinished biography, Street Life

Polly and the miners! When we spoke on the phone, that was all she went on about and it was just so *boring*. I thought they were holding on to a past that had no future. It did not affect me.

I saw a dirty gaggle of them once, shaking collection tins at King's Cross Station and I walked straight past them. What did it have to do with me? Chimp and I were living in a world where the Thatcher reforms could only benefit us. She did a lot of good if you ask me. Smashed the Unions. Made people millionaires. Told us the sky was the limit, introduced individual responsibility rather than people relying on State handouts.

My main focus at that time was the house Chimp bought in St. John's Wood, North London. Mrs Bennett cried when we moved out but she was happy for us really, I know she was.

I wanted gold taps, big mirrors, a his and her bathroom and a red and white Habitat kitchen with a microwave oven. Everyone had red and white kitchens in the 1980s. I wanted our home to be modern and exotic and glamorous, like the houses I saw in the glossy magazines. And we could do it: we had money and lots of it. Chimp's star had exploded and I wasn't doing too badly either.

We were the new golden couple and I loved it. We were the darlings of the new world of the young and up coming professionals. I used to float around our new house wearing a pink silk dressing gown with a glass of wine in my hand listening to *Sade's Diamond Life*. I was living the dream.

Chimp's star may have exploded but mine was also twinkling quite nicely thank you very much. I loved working on ***Let's Talk!*** and I even interviewed Chimp! The show was becoming known for being a little avant garde! Some of the things we made the rock stars do were quite outrageous! We even persuaded Radion Helsmidt, a rock star from a big Swedish group at the time, to sit in an empty bath in his underpants whilst two girls rubbed the new avocado body moisturiser from The Body Shop into his chest as he tried to recite the alphabet backwards. It was hilarious!

Our ratings were good and increasing. I loved those days, I loved that show. I used to spend hours getting my clothes just right for it. One day I might present it in high heels with stripy red socks and a short leather mini skirt. The next I'd be in dungarees with a scarf tied around my hair. My clothes, my look, were picked up by the teen mags and there were features telling the young kids how to copy my look, how to do their hair like Nellie, how to dress like Nellie. I became known as "Nellie on the Telly". And after the show, every Friday night, there was always a big, glamorous party for all the guests and people who worked on the show. There were bottles of Bollinger and piles of cocaine in the his and her toilets. That's how we rolled in the 1980s.

I used to think of Chimp and me as a golden couple in a golden age that was emerging from the dark days of the 1970s. It was a great time to be young, a great time to be alive and we had it all. We had money, cars, a fabulous house. Apart from owning a yacht like Simon le Bon, we had it all. And so as far as I was concerned, the miners should just shut up and go back to work.

Chimp

I couldn't believe how much my life changed after ***No Milk Today*** hit the number one spot in the Charts; how fortunes can turn around overnight. It was something I'd always dreamed about but there had also been times when I seriously doubted whether it would ever happen.

And suddenly there I was, living in a big posh house in North London with Nellie and Morwenna and people were talking to me about security and burglar alarms and things I'd never had to think about before.

I didn't have time to get up to Wales to see Grace. Life was a roller coaster. Richard used to call me every morning at 10am so that we could discuss this or that, would I endorse a brand of crisps, appear on a children's TV programme, open a new supermarket. We were no longer playing the University circuits or backing other bands. We had bands backing us. We were headlining! We played at all the big venues – Wembley, Edinburgh, the Milton Keynes Bowl with Simple Minds and Big Country. Richard said we couldn't sit back on our laurels and be complacent. We had to keep touring, we had to maintain our profile and keep up the momentum and that's what we did.

Grace used to write me letters saying she'd seen me on TV. She used to say lots of things about Nellie in those letters: how she didn't the way I'd held her hand on a TV show or how she hated the dress she'd worn on ***Let's Talk!***. I didn't think anything of it at the time.

Rhoswen wrote to me saying she didn't approve of the rock star life I was living. She said I'd sold out to the capitalists! She was still setting fires in Wales and getting arrested at Greenham Common. Some days she was a distant memory, at other times she haunted me.

Polly

One night, in late March or April 1984, Mam sent me down the Welfare to fetch Da because the iron wasn't working. What Da was supposed to do about the iron at seven o'clock at night I don't know. I think it was probably an attempt to get him home. Ever since the strike had started, Da had been spending a lot of time at the Welfare.

Sidney trotted along behind me and I pushed open the door of the Welfare. It was smoky and loud with the sound of men's voices. Tom Horse was standing at the far end of the bar with a group of men and Da was standing at the other end with Frank Talbot and a larger group of men. I walked towards Tom Horse to say hello like I always did but Frank Talbot shouted over at me.

"Don't you be speaking to that lot Polly. Come over here with us."

I looked at Tom Horse and I hesitated. I could feel something different in there and the atmosphere was taut and tense.

"Well at least I'm not a scab," Tom Horse shouted back at Frank Talbot. "At least I can sleep with my conscience at night instead of getting into bed with Margaret Thatcher."

There was a burst of movement and Da and Tall Chalky grabbed Frank Talbot's arms and held him back. He looked like a dog straining to get off the leash. His face! It was dark and angry and he looked like he wanted to kill Tom Horse.

"Ay not such a big man now are ye?" Tom Horse said, raising his glass at him. "Not such a big man after all," and he turned his back and continued speaking to the men gathered around him.

"What is it Polly love?" Da said, as I stared at the men trying to work out what was going on.

I swallowed. The Welfare had never felt like this before. It was tight, tense, smoky, rumbling.

"Mam said you're to come home because the iron's broken."

A couple of men chuckled and slapped Da on the back but Da looked at me like it was the most important thing he'd ever heard.

"I'll just finish my pint and I'll be along," he said, ignoring the looks of amusement the men were exchanging. "Off you go Polly, off you go."

As I walked home with the ever loyal Sidney trotting at my heels, I replayed the scene at the Welfare in my mind, trying to pinpoint what was different. I didn't realise at the time that the men were fragmenting.

"What's a Scab?" I asked Joe when he rang a few days later.

The line went silent for a while and he sighed before replying.

"You leave that word where you found it Poll. Leave that word where you found it."

Nellie

Extract from her unfinished biography, Street Life

In the late spring of 1984, Chimp decided that Grace should come and stay in London for a few weeks.

"Megan is worried about all the publicity she's getting," he said. "Apparently reporters come to the house all the time and Grace just lets them in. Megan thinks it would do her good to get away for a while."

I did not want a thirteen year old girl coming to stay with me. I wished we'd never got involved in all that business. It was not our responsibility, it was not our life but Chimp acted like it was, like he was this great saviour of a poor little orphaned girl from South Wales.

"I thought you were going off on tour?" I said.

"I am," he said. "But she could spend some time with you and Morwenna."

I put down my Habitat coffee mug and I glared at him.

"What am I supposed to do with her?" I said. "I've got to work."

"Mrs Bennett could look after her couldn't she? When she has Morwenna? Or you could take her to work with you. I'm sure she'd love to see a TV studio. Maybe you could interview her. She's been in quite a few of the papers because of the record. It might make a good story."

I pointed out that the sort of "story" I ran did not involve bleeding hearts. It was focused on the rock star and celebrity world, not teenagers in crisis.

"Oh come on Nellie don't be so selfish. You've got this great big house all to yourself and what has she got? It would only be for a couple of weeks. Think about what she's been through."

"I thought she didn't speak English," I said as a last ditch attempt to head Grace off.

"Oh she speaks English alright," Chimp said. "It just depends on who she's talking to."

Grace arrived at Paddington station with a suitcase twice the size of her. I was an hour late picking her up and she was sulky and quiet in the taxi. I dropped her off at the house where Mrs Bennett was looking after Morwenna and continued on to the studio. *Let's Talk* was my priority, not

Grace.

The next night, Mrs Bennet babysat Morwenna while I took Grace out for a pizza in Henry J Beans. When it came she just stared at it and said nothing.

"What's wrong?" I said. "Don't you like pizza?"

"I don't like you," she said, scowling at me. "And I don't like London. I want to go home."

That's how good it was!

Another time, we were in the kitchen at home when ***Refugee*** came on the radio.

"Chimp wrote that song for me," she said as she shoved crisps into her mouth.

Honestly the way she spoke about him sometimes, it was like she was the one in the relationship with him and I was the one who had come to stay.

So when ***When You Vanish With the Dawn*** came on another time I said

"Hear that Grace? He wrote this one for me."

I didn't expect her to react the way she did. She picked up her glass of lemonade from the table and threw it across the kitchen where it smashed against the wall.

"What did you do that for?" I said, genuinely shocked. It was a good job Morwenna was upstairs at the time.

"You always spoil EVERYTHING!" she shouted and then she ran upstairs and slammed her bedroom door behind her.

These were minor incidents compared to the day I walked into Morwenna's bedroom and found her locked in the wardrobe with her mouth completely bound by sellotape.

"What the hell…"

Grace grinned at me, swaying on her feet, her hands locked behind her back.

"She gets on my nerves," she said. "So I locked her away."

Frantically I pulled at the sellotape as Morwenna stared at me with frightened eyes.

I grabbed Grace by the arms and shook her.

"Don't you ever do that again!" I said. "Go downstairs now!"

Grace stayed where she was, swaying from side to side.

"You can't make me do anything," she said. "I'm protected by Social Services."

I told Chimp about it later on when we spoke on the phone.

"She was probably just playing," he said.

"Playing? You call gagging Morwenna with sellotape *playing?*"

After that I kept Morwenna away from Grace as much as I could and gave Mrs Bennett strict instructions not to leave them alone together.

I tried with her, really I did. I took her shopping on Kensington High Street but she wasn't the type of girl who liked shopping. When I was her age I would have killed to go shopping in London.

"But I'm not you am I?" she said when I said this to her. "I'm me and I don't care about stupid old clothes."

She didn't care about makeup or hair either. She was a proper little backwoods child.

"Would you like to go to Madame Tussauds?" I tried. "Or the Tower of London? They've got dungeons there. Or how about we take a boat up the river to see the Cutty Sark?"

She didn't want to do any of it. She just wanted to stay at home and watch TV and eat crisps. I took her into the studio a few times, introduced her to people and showed her how things worked and what we did in there. I even offered to introduce her to some of the rock stars we had lined up. She wasn't interested in any of it. I don't know what she was interested in apart from Chimp! I found her sitting in front of the telly one evening holding on to one of his best shirts. She'd just helped herself out of his wardrobe and was holding the collar to her cheek like it was a comfort blanket or something. She even took it to bed with her. It was weird. She was such a weird child.

So I left her at the house watching videos and eating crisps and at the end of those two weeks I couldn't wait to get rid of her. Even Mrs

Bennett said she was the strangest child she had ever met and for Mrs Bennett to say that, well, it says it all really. There is a song that reminds me of that strange time. It's Billy Idol's *Eyes Without a Face.* They were playing it all the time at the studio back then.

Grace lives with Chimp and Rhoswen now and she's quite close to Rhoswen. Birds of a feather, I say.

But I tell you what, she'll be notorious one day, Grace. You mark my words, one day her name will be known for all the wrong reasons.

Polly

They showed it on the BBC News, the funeral. They showed his mother collapsing and people holding her up. Three thousand people attended that funeral in South Kirby. How do you bury your son?

His name was David Gareth Jones and he was a miner from Ackton Hall Colliery near Featherstone in North Yorkshire. He was just another miner who picketed mines all over the country. Flying pickets they called them. On 15th March 1984, three days after the strike officially began, he was in Ollerton to picket the Colliery in Nottingham.

David Gareth Jones was 24 years old. He had young daughters, parents, brothers and sisters. He wasn't even on the picket line. He was in a pub giving first aid to another miner who'd been injured, when someone ran in saying kids were outside damaging cars. David Gareth Jones and some others ran out of the pub and chased the kids down the road. One of them turned round and threw a brick at him. And that was it. That is how quickly life can end.

There is another more sinister part of that story that isn't always heard. The post mortem ruled out the brick as a cause of death. It was believed he died from injuries caused when he'd been crushed up against railings by the police earlier that day.

We'll never know the truth but David Jones and Ollerton have never been forgotten.

Chimp

Nellie wasn't particularly good with Grace. During those two weeks she stayed at the house in London, Nellie was on the phone to me all the time complaining that she'd done this or that.

I didn't have time for it. We were touring the States and had just released our second single ***Refugee*** which went straight to number one in the UK. ***No Milk Today*** had only got to number 45 in the States and I was hoping for greater things with ***Refugee.*** Richard said the American market was notoriously hard to crack. Not even the Beatles had made it to number one.

The important thing, he said, was to tour. So we toured. Florida, Atlanta, New Orleans. It might sound glamorous but the inside of a stadium in one town looks pretty much like the inside of a stadium in the next. There was no time for sight seeing! It was all we could do to keep Boots standing upright and George and Menace away from the girls. Girls girls girls. There were hundreds of them everywhere we went, falling at our feet, sleeping on the stairs of the hotels we stayed in. I didn't sleep with any of them despite what the papers said. I was too busy working, too busy writing new songs. I was deep sea diving in a vast blue ocean and I didn't have time to come up for air.

Polly

On 26th March 1984, one hundred flying pickets descended on Point.

"Arthur Scargill should call a national ballot," Vincent said. "That way, we'd all know where we stand."

Vincent and Da and most of the men at Point carried on working. I knew that in England and South Wales the miners were mostly out on strike but it seemed very random. For instead of the NUM saying all the miners should strike or all the miners shouldn't strike, the decision was left to the regional areas to decide.

Mam stood at the window and watched as bus load after bus load of police passed by.

"It's like we're under siege," she said. "I've never seen anything like it."

Da was not impressed.

"I don't need the boys in blue fighting my battles," he said. "And I'm not going to be told what to do by a bunch of Trotskyites either."

So Da and the men of North Wales threw their heads back and barged through the lines of pickets who spat and shouted and heckled them for going to work.

A local ballot was held and 72% of the miners in North Wales voted against strike action. It didn't matter to the flying pickets. They kept on coming, believing that if they kept up the pressure, the men at Point would give in. The pickets caused mayhem in the village, pulling up plants in front gardens and vandalising the phone box. Vincent's mam had a couple of her windows smashed and someone left a disgusting present on the doorstep of the toyshop.

On 28th March, 300 pickets from South Wales were waiting for the men at Point as they started their six o'clock shift. As the men arrived to start their shift, the pickets surged forward trying to stop the men from entering the mine. One of the pickets was Joe.

Da was so shocked that he turned around and came straight home again.

"I mean what the bloody hell is he doing? A son of mine? Standing at the pit where he worked, standing against men he worked with, men he's grown up with and drank with, telling us we can't go to work?"

Da paced around the kitchen. I'd never seen him so agitated, so upset.

"Calm down Gordon," Mam said. "You'll give yourself a stroke."

"Well if I have a stroke it will be his bloody fault. I can't believe it. I can't bloody believe it."

Vincent had followed Da back from Point and tried to calm things down. Me and Mam were no good. We seemed to make it worse.

"He's only doing what he thinks is right Da," I said. "Just like you think what you're doing is right."

I was venturing into dangerous territory and I knew it because Da swung round and glared at me.

"Been filling your head with his rubbish too has he?"

And then he walked out, slamming the back door behind him.

Vincent walked forward and put his arm around my shoulders.

"I'll put the kettle on," Mam said. "What we need is a nice cup of tea."

I wanted it all to end: the strike, the anger and the division. I couldn't see how it had infiltrated our home. But it had. It had crept in the back door when no one was looking and mam thought it could all be solved by putting the kettle on.

Polly

Despite Da and Vincent continuing to work at Point, their wages were much less as shift allowances and overtime stopped. For those who were on strike, the Government had changed the law so they couldn't claim State benefits and as they weren't working, they had no money coming in. Later, the government froze the NUM's funds which Joe always said drove starving miners back to work.

Da used to repair TVs in his spare time to make some cash and when the coal got low, we put on jumpers and stared at the empty fireplace.

Mam became an expert at making things out of corned beef. Cheesy peas was another thing she conjured up out of our new found frugality.

One Friday evening Da came back from the Welfare with his face dark and shadowy.

"Sending us bloody food parcels they are now," he said. "Like we're some sort of third world country."

My ears pricked up and I thought about Mary Williams and the women in Barnsley.

"What are they doing with it?" I asked him, trying to sound casual. "The food?"

"I don't bloody know," he said. "Great big piles of tin cans and packages dumped in the hall. No one knows what to do with it."

The next morning Mam and I went down to the Welfare and stared at the parcels and boxes stacked up in the hall.

"Right then," she said, rolling up her sleeves. "Let's get on with it."

Every Friday from then on, a lorry arrived at the Welfare bringing parcels of food and clothes and toys donated by people who worked in factories and offices in Liverpool. We sorted the donations into boxes and Mam sent Eifion the milkman around the village delivering them to the poorest families.

"I'm only supposed to carry milk, eggs and orange juice," Eifion complained as we loaded up his milk float.

One look from Mam was enough to make him bend the rules.

Morwenna

I loved Uncle Joe and I loved the stories he told me about my mum. Listening to them was like catching a fragrance on the breeze. I was hungry for his stories because Granpy and Nanna and dad didn't talk about her when I was around.

I don't know why Granpy and Nanna let me spend so much time with Uncle Joe seeing as he wasn't part of the family. I think Auntie Polly had something to do with it. Auntie Polly is a force of nature! She's the only one I've ever seen who can put my dad in his place. She doesn't care that he's a sold a million records or that he's raised all this money for charity. She remembers him when he was a skinny, dishevelled, scruffy kid, who went around in a dirty old parka coat. That's what she says anyway.

I loved Uncle Joe. People used to think I was his daughter; we looked so alike. He'd sing this song "***I'd like to be… under the sea, in an octopus's garden…***" and he took me to see magical things like the rusty old ship docked at Llannerch -Y- Mor.

Once, we got lost in the Hidden Valley, in the Clwydian Hills. It was getting dark and the mist was coming down but I wasn't scared. I was never scared when he was around. He kept telling me it was an adventure and that we were explorers of an ancient land that was thousands of years old. In the end we found a red phone box in the middle of nowhere and rang Auntie Polly.

Another time, we drove me over to Llandudno to see the feral goats on Great Orm and ran out of petrol on the way home. Auntie Polly was always coming to our rescue.

I was very young when the Miners' Strike broke out in 1984. Uncle Joe used to say that no one could possibly understand it all unless they'd lived through it.

"Your mum didn't have time for any of it," he'd say. "She couldn't stand Wales at the best of times."

To me she is like a princess in my memory, someone who floated in and out of my life in beautiful clothes leaving a trail of perfume behind her. Dad gets irritated when I describe her like that and Rhoswen rolls her eyes and shakes her head. What do they expect me to say? She was my mother and I loved her and I used to blame myself for what happened.

I'm 36 years old now but I still feel that way sometimes and so I understand when Auntie Polly says scars run deep.

Polly

More and more women started helping us sort out the Friday food parcels and we formed a little group. We cooked hot food on Sundays in the Welfare kitchen and turned the bar into a makeshift dining hall. We didn't officially call our group Women Against Pit Closures like the women in Yorkshire did; it never got that official. What bound us together and drove us on was the worry about Point closing. Every family in Ffynnongroyw depended on that mine and some nights I couldn't sleep for worrying about the future. It wasn't me I was worried about: it was about men like Da and Tom Horse and what would become of them. The mine was all they had ever known and it held our village together by invisible gossamer threads.

Da was always too busy to speak to Joe when he rang on Sunday evenings but I always spoke to him at length.

"Why don't you come down here?" Joe said. "You could join the women's group in Merthyr. They're doing a good job despite the chaos. You wouldn't believe what's going on down here."

"It's not exactly a picnic up here," I said.

"No but it's different down here. You've got two pits up there and most of the men are still working aren't they? Well down here they're not. Down here they are all on strike. Just this morning I watched a group of kids going through the bins. They didn't have any shoes on. Everyone's struggling."

That night I tossed and turned in my bed. We were managing in Ffynnongroyw. Ok so times were the hardest we'd ever known but no kids ran down our streets without shoes on their feet or went through the dustbins after dark.

"If you want to go, go," Vincent as we sat on the bench outside the chapel one night wishing we could afford a bag of chips.

"But what about Da?" I said. "Wouldn't he see it as taking Joe's side?"

Vincent took my hand and looked across at the distant mountains.

"There aren't any sides in this," he said. "We're all fighting for the same thing in the end: to keep the mines open. Joe and your Da are just doing it in different ways."

"And what about Nanny Gwynn?" I said. "She's so used to me

coming over on Saturday afternoons."

"I'll keep an eye on her," he said. "I can talk about spitfires for hours."

By the time Joe rang the following Sunday evening, I had made up my mind.

Polly

Merthyr Vale was very different from Ffynnongroyw. It looked like it had been dropped into a valley between the hills and you could taste the coal dust in your mouth and smell it in the air. Compared to the open skies of Ffynnongroyw, Merthyr felt claustrophobic, as if everyone was trapped in the valleys and there was no escape.

Joe came and collected me on an overcast day in May 1984. Mam cried on the doorstep and Da stayed away but Vincent was there, keeping me strong, moving me on.

"I'll look after her," Joe said, leaning out of the driver's window.

Joe had borrowed Badger Jones's car, an old orange Volvo and off we went down the A470.

"Do you remember when you used to borrow Bryn Thomas's old car?" I said, trying to keep it light. I was upset Da hadn't come home from the Welfare to see me off and leaving Mam and Vincent hadn't been easy. "Bit of a heap wasn't it?"

Joe scowled at the road.

"Aye 'n he's a Scab now and all," Joe said. "Sorry Poll. I shouldn't use that word in front of you."

"It's alright," I said, looking out the window as the landscape flashed by. "It's part of our language now."

We took Sidney with us in mam's old wicker shopping basket. He sat on the back seat popping his head up every so often to look out of the window. I liked the fact he was coming with me. He was something familiar, something from home.

Joe had moved out of Uncle Frank's house to make way for me and was living in digs just around the corner. My three cousins still lived with their parents and so it was a bit of a squash at times with three grown men in the house but they'd opened up an attic room for me and me and Sidney were quite happy up there.

Uncle Frank and his sons used to get up at three o'clock in the morning to picket Cwm, the mine where they worked with Joe. They walked up Mynydd Methyr and over the ridge to avoid the police roadblocks on the main roads. And later, as things got worse, I often went with them.

Letter from Mary Williams
1984

Dear Polly

So you've moved to South Wales! What a brave thing to do! I am sure it is nice having Sidney with you. There is something about cats that makes you feel like you are never alone. I hope you aren't missing your mam and da and Vincent too much but it must be good to be with your brother again.

It is still pretty grim up here.

Men knock on my door all the time asking for food. People are starving and broke. Families are losing their homes and men are turned against men. Just last week one of the men went back to work and in the middle of the night, they set fire to his shed and smashed his windows.

Did any of us anticipate this when it all started? That men would turn against each other like this? Sometimes I don't understand this hatred, this anger, this rage. Paul can't understand why Arthur Scargill doesn't hold a national ballot instead of leaving regional areas to decide whether to strike or not. He says this way, it can only end in disaster.

I used to think happiness was going down to London to see a show. What would make me happy now? The world as it used to be. A hot bath, a fire in the grate and food in the cupboard.

Write soon and tell me how it is in your part of the world.

With love

Mary

Polly

Alison had started a Women Against Pit Closures group at the local Welfare and on my first day in Merthyr, we walked down the hill to the hall. It was only eight o'clock in the morning but already women and children were queuing round the block. Outside the door cardboard boxes were stacked up overflowing with tins of food and clothes.

Alison unlocked the door and I joined the women sorting through the donations whilst Alison went off to the kitchen. I was a little shy at first but when they found out I had come down from North Wales to help my brother, they went out of their way to make me feel at home. I was probably the youngest there! Boxes arrived all the time full of clothes and toys and tins of food and when Alison opened the doors a tidal wave of women rushed in to grab things for their families.

At lunchtime people came to eat soup and tinned spaghetti at the tables set up in the skittle alley and in the afternoon, we walked up to the picket line at Cwm with flasks of soup and cigarettes. I was given a placard to hold that said **CLOSE A PIT, KILL A COMMUNITY!** and when we got to the picket line, the police stared at us, made us wait five minutes and then waved us through.

The miners stood outside the gates in their black donkey jackets, stamping their feet and rubbing their hands to keep warm, shouting at lorries to turn back and hurling abuse at the drivers if they didn't.

I saw Joe amongst them and went over to see him.

"Why are there so many police?" I asked him, handing him a flask of soup and a packet of Benson & Hedges.

"You tell me," he said. "You tell me. Some people say some of them are army boys sent in by Thatcher."

Joe unscrewed the flask and poured steaming soup into the plastic cup.

"Tomato soup," he said, sipping it carefully. "Food of the gods."

We used to spend hours up there waving our banners and chanting slogans. *Coal not dole! Scargill giz us a ballot!* We stayed out there in all weathers, supporting the men and shouting at the working miners trying to get through the picket lines. I didn't like doing it at first because I wouldn't want anyone to do that to Da and Vincent at Point but I had to show support for the women and I couldn't do anything else now I was part of the WAPC. The men who tried to get through the picket line were punched and kicked and spat at, called all the names under the sun and pelted with sanitary towels, apple cores, rubbish and rotten fruit. And there we were, a bunch of women in plastic rain hats, waving our banners in the rain right in the thick of it, doing all we could to stop the government from destroying our communities, trying to support the men who were fighting to preserve our way of life.

At times, it felt like a civil war.

Nellie

Extract from her unfinished biography, Street Life

Summer 1984. The time of *Frankie Says Relax* t-shirts, *Club Tropicana* and Cyndi Lauper singing about girls wanting to have fun.

We introduced a new feature called *Socks Appeal* on ***Let's Talk!*** I'd interview a rock star or an actor sitting on the famous purple couch and the camera would focus on the socks he was wearing. Viewers had to ring or write in and guess who he was and the winner got a signed photo of the person wearing the socks and a tub of chocolate body paint.

I saw an angle for writing another book. I'd call it *Sex in Socks* and it would be full of photographs of naked men in their socks with a cuddly toy covering up their private parts. Tom Wainwright was as supportive as always and so every guest we had on was asked, after they took part in the sock competition, if they would mind posing for a photograph.

Chimp refused to take any part in the competition or be photographed for the book.

"What are you trying to do to me?" he said. "Sell me like a cheap suit?"

Morwenna

When I was five or six years old, Uncle Joe found me locked in the coal shed with Grace sitting with her back against the door.

Uncle Joe never lost his temper. He was always gentle and kind to me but that day he was angry. He lifted Grace out of the way and came inside to rescue me.

"If you were my daughter," he told her, breathing heavily. "I'd put you across my knee and give you a good hiding."

Grace stuck her tongue out at him and seemed unrepentant.

"But I'm not am I," she said defiantly. "And if you do anything to me I'll tell Chimp and he won't let you see Morticia anymore."

Uncle Joe struggled to contain his anger.

"Who are you calling Morticia?" he said.

"Your little pet," she said, tossing her hair and going off into Welsh which she did when she wanted to annoy people. What she didn't appreciate was that Uncle Joe understood every word of it.

Uncle Joe took me into town afterwards to see the ducks on the pond and buy me an icecream.

"Has she done this to you before?" he said as we threw bread at the water.

I didn't want to tell him the truth because I was scared he would say something to my dad and Grace would take it out on me. I dreaded her coming to Nanny and Granpy's because she seemed to delight in making me unhappy.

I have never understood why Dad and Rhoswen are so defensive of Grace. I know exactly what she is but they have never been able to see it, not even after what happened to Rudi and my mum. All I know is that I was told to be kind to Grace because she'd had a very sad childhood. So in our world, it was always Grace who had the power and she knew it. But I tell you something I used to cry with relief when she went home.

Polly

Joe was one of the flying pickets who went all over the country to put pressure on working miners and those unloading and loading coal at coking plants, railways and power stations.

"If Scargill called a national ballot," he said. "Nottingham would come out and there'd be no need for any of it. If they came out, the power stations would grind to a halt, industry would come to a standstill and the government would have to give in."

But the Nottingham pits weren't having any of it. The miners kept working, supplying the power stations with coal to keep the country running.

On 17th June 1984, Arthur Scargill addressed a massive crowd at Wakefield urging the miners to mass picket the coking plant at Orgreave, South Yorkshire and stop the coal entering the plant. The following day, five thousand pickets descended on Orgreave. One of them was Joe.

Six thousand riot police were deployed; the first time riot police had ever been deployed in an industrial dispute. It was unheard of.

"It was the police who charged first," Joe told me afterwards. "It was a boiling hot day and some of us had our shirts off and a lot of the boys were lying around sunbathing. And suddenly, out of nowhere, the police charged. We were chased up a hill and through a village and into a field where we were kettled, like a herd of cattle. There was no way backwards and no way forwards. Grown men were dragged down the hillside and beaten by the police. It's not true what they say in the papers about the pickets starting it. How could we start it? Ok some of us were throwing stones and bottles but only after they charged at us on horseback, swiping down, left and right, with their batons. John Jones got knocked unconscious and I went to help him and got whacked over the head. I could hardly see there was so much blood pouring into my eyes. I've never been a great fan of the boys in blue but that day, well, they lost control."

The footage they showed on the News didn't show the true picture. The cameras didn't show any police brutality, of course they didn't. They just showed pickets with their shirts off, being led away by the police. It was filming by suggestion. It showed the miners in the worst possible light so that the public didn't have any sympathy for them. One of them was pictured holding what the Press said was a large stone. It turned out to be a pork pie.

Ninety five men were arrested that day, including Joe. Seventy five of them were charged with riot which, in those days, was punishable by life imprisonment. Twenty four men, including Joe, were charged with violent disorder and taken to the local police station. It wasn't far from where Mary lived and she and the women of the local WAPC marched down there and refused to leave until they got answers.

"They didn't know what to do when we turned up," she told me later in one of her letters. "A great gaggle of angry women blowing whistles and waving banners invading a sleepy little police station. The desk sergeant tried to ignore us at first but more and more women kept turning up and we sat on the floor and sang and refused to budge. All we wanted to know was what was happening to the ninety five men they'd arrested. Ninety five men couldn't just disappear like that and we weren't moving until they gave us some answers."

The men were kept incommunicado for 24 hours and denied food and water. Some of them were beaten.

The following day they were taken to Court where every single charge was dismissed because the evidence the police provided wasn't worth the paper it was written on.

When Joe and the other men returned to Merthyr, they were given a hero's welcome. Cwm's brass band marched through the streets with the colliery banner held high and defiantly above their heads.

"I don't feel like a hero," he said later that afternoon as we sat in Alison and Frank's kitchen drinking a cup of tea. He had stitches in his head and he looked unusually pale.

"How do you feel then?" I asked him.

Sidney jumped up on his lap and butted his face into his chest.

"Baffled," he said. "Well and truly baffled."

Four years ago, in 2015, the IPCC found that the South Yorkshire police used exceptional force at Orgreave and had come dangerously close to being an instrument of the State. Evidence was provided that the police had written false statements and committed perjury and tried to cover it all up in the trials that followed.

The following year, the Home Secretary Amber Rudd, said that despite this, there would be no public enquiry or independent review.

You might say oh let it go, it's such a long time ago. Norman Tebbit says that people should forget about Orgreave and move on with their lives. The same Norman Tebbit who told everyone to get on their bikes in the 1980s and find work. There weren't many bikes in Wales at that time.

The miners who were there have been looking for justice for thirty years and no one listens.

Who cares about the Miners' Strike now? Who cares?

Chimp

In the late summer of 1984, Richard arranged for Rhoswen to spend a week at Hope Cottage.

"She needs a break," he told George. "And a week in your cottage is just what the doctor ordered."

I hung around eavesdropping on the conversation. I hadn't seen Rhoswen for so long and the last time we'd met hadn't exactly been on good terms.

"Is she ok?" I asked Richard, trying to sound casual about it.

"Would you be ok if you'd just spent six weeks in Holloway prison?" he said.

I questioned George about it later and in my mind a plan began to form. Oh I know I had Nellie and Morwenna. I know I had it all but there was something about Rhoswen that still called to me. I wanted to see her. It was as simple as that.

We were on a short break from touring and I casually told Nellie that I was going to spend a few days in Wales, see Grace, call in on my mum and dad.

"I don't suppose you could get some time off and come with me?" I said, knowing full well she would refuse point blank.

"You think I can just drop everything and go to Wales?" she said. "You never seem to realise, Chimp, that I have a career to think about. Are you staying at the haunted house?"

"I don't know yet," I lied. "I don't know yet."

Chimp

I drove down to Swansea on the same day Richard drove Rhoswen down to The Gower.

Megan and Paul knew I was coming but they kept it a secret from Grace so it would be a surprise.

When she heard my voice in the hall, she came bowling down the stairs and nearly knocked me over, clamping her long skinny arms around my waist and refusing to let go.

"Maybe Chimp would like a cup of tea, after his long drive," Paul suggested. "And afterwards, perhaps you could show him your Special Collection."

The Special Collection was Grace's treasure trove of paraphernalia relating to *The Sons*. She had everything. T-shirts, mugs, stickers, photographs, all set out on a table in her bedroom like a shrine. My photo was in the middle in a heart shaped frame.

"I kiss it every night before I go to sleep," she said.

I stayed for about an hour. We had lunch and I declined their invitation to spend the afternoon with them at the zoo.

"Do you think the miners will go back to work soon?" Paul asked while Grace went off to her bedroom to fetch her collection of fluffy haired trolls which I think she hoped would persuade me to stay.

"Don't know much about it really mate," I said. "I've been living in a different world."

Megan came into the room.

"We see you all the time on TV," she said. "Grace is quite obsessed with the band. She's doing well," she said. "Really well."

Paul leaned forward and put his cup of tea down on the table.

"She has her moments Megan, be fair."

I saw a glance pass between the two of them but it wasn't mine to interpret.

Just then there was a knock on the back door and Megan got up to answer it. Paul and I sat there in awkward silence. He was such a deep thinker Paul. I never knew what to say to him.

"Collection for the miners," Megan said, coming back into the room. "They come to the door all the time. A little boy in my class brought his teddy bear in last week. He wanted to sell it to get his mam and dad money to buy food. All the kids come to school wearing those yellow *Coal not Dole* stickers on their school jumpers. The Head has turned a blind eye for now but where will this end? Where will this end? Me and some of the other teachers buy breakfast for the children some mornings. They look so cold, so thin, so hungry."

I didn't know what to say. I wasn't interested in the miners. It wasn't my concern.

Grace returned with her trolls.

"This one's called Chimp," she said, holding out the one with bright orange hair. "And this one is Nellie."

The one called Nellie had no hair and gouges all over its brown plastic body.

Megan jumped forward and took it away from her looking at it in dismay.

"What did you do that for?" she asked Grace.

Grace sat back on her heels and smiled.

"I don't like that one," she said. "It lives all on its own in the cupboard."

I didn't give it much thought at the time. I wanted to be off. I wanted to see Rhoswen.

I wasn't sure how she might react when I turned up unannounced at the cottage but I decided if she was hostile and didn't want me there, I'd just turn the car around and head up to Ffynnongroyw. I didn't particularly want to go home but mam would be pleased to see me.

When she opened the door, I was prepared for a black eye or a mouthful of invective but instead, she was calm and together.

"I had a feeling you'd come," she said.

"So you're not going to scratch my eyes out or hit me over the head with a frying pan?"

Her eyes glinted with amusement.

"That depends," she said. "If you're staying or going."

I stayed. Of course I stayed. The cottage felt different with Rhoswen in it. Nellie was like a fish out of water in that place but it suited Rhoswen and she loved it, despite all its quirks and failings.

Where Nellie used to complain that the seagulls woke her up in the morning, Rhoswen loved to hear them because they told her she was by the sea. Where Nellie used to complain about the cold, Rhoswen relished it by snuggling up in thick jumpers and blankets by the fire. Where Nellie complained the hot water didn't work, Rhoswen took a cold bath. And Rhoswen wanted to see Dylan Thomas's boathouse and Laugharne Castle which Nellie wasn't interested in at all. So they were very different, yes, very different.

One morning I was woken by a strange noise. Rhoswen's side of the bed was empty, the sheet crumpled where she'd slept. I got out of bed and pulled back the curtain and there she was, outside in the yard chopping wood in her dressing gown and wellies.

That image has stayed with me through the years. I think that's when I realised I was in far deeper than I ever intended to be.

Chimp

Snatching those few days with Rhoswen down on The Gower was just what I needed. We hadn't stopped, as a band, for months, not since ***No Milk Today*** came out of nowhere and took the charts by storm.

I showed Rhoswen the house that had inspired it. The windows were boarded up and there was a *For Sale* sign staked in the overgrown front garden.

"Spooky," she said shivering a little. "Who ever would want to live there after what happened?"

At night, we kept the curtains open so we could see the stars. She knew the stars just like I did.

"So can I meet this Grace?" she said one night as we lay in bed.

I wasn't sure. I mean what if it got back to Nellie?

"You can introduce me as your friend Emyr," she said, reading my mind. "You're allowed to have friends aren't you?"

That day, we drove into Swansea and had lunch in a pub and on the way out, a photographer leapt out of the bushes and snapped a photo as I was getting in the car.

"Occupational hazard," I said to Rhoswen as we drove off. "It happens all the time these days."

In Swansea, Megan and Paul gave Rhoswen a warm welcome.

Grace did her usual thing of flying down the stairs, her feet unable to propel her fast enough when she heard my voice in the hall and then she stopped and looked at Rhoswen and I thought uh oh here we go. Rhoswen crouched down, took off her necklace and hung it around Grace's neck.

"You like it?" she said in Welsh "It's yours now."

Grace looked down at the shell hanging on a silver chain and her face split into the widest smile I'd ever seen.

"Have you got any crisps?" she said.

"Yes," Rhoswen said. "Bags and bags of them. In the car. You want some?"

And that was it: an alliance formed out of a seashell necklace and salt and vinegar crisps. Grace was shallow enough to be bribed by trinkets and material things. Or was it more than that? Was it the kindness Rhoswen showed her? The understanding? The indulgence? Nellie hadn't had that approach but perhaps if she had, things wouldn't have turned out the way they did.

Nellie

Extract from her unfinished biography, Street Life

Mrs Bennett showed me the photograph in the paper.

A black and white photograph of Chimp getting out of a car.

ROCK STAR TAKES TIME OUT!

"*Emyr Davis, lead singer with The Sons of Glendower leaving his secret holiday destination on The Gower with a mystery woman.*"

I could see someone standing by the passenger door of the car and although her shape was blurred, I knew exactly who it was.

"It's probably nothing," Mrs Bennett said. "You know what these newspapers are like."

That night when Chimp rang to speak to Morwenna, I came straight out with it. It had been on my mind all day.

"What's with this photograph in the papers of you and Rhoswen in The Gower?"

Chimp sighed down the phone.

"I told you," he said. "I went down there to see Grace."

"With Rhoswen?" I asked.

He sighed again, a sure sign he was having to think fast on his feet.

"She's a friend Nellie that's all. She was down there, I was down there. We met up."

"Bit of a coincidence isn't it? I thought she was hanging out with the lesbians at Greenham Common growing her armpit hair."

"There's no need to be like that."

"Well what am I supposed to be like when my husband's face is splashed all over the paper with a mystery woman?"

"Put Morwenna on the phone," he said.

"She's asleep." I lied and then I put the phone down.

I stared at it for a while willing him to ring me back but he didn't. Chimp never did things like that.

Polly

It was a foggy, gloomy day in November when David Wilkie died. We were in the kitchen at the Welfare chopping vegetables when Julie Jones came in.

"There's been an accident up at Heads of Valley," she said. "I've been stuck in traffic for half an hour. They're saying someone dropped a concrete block over the bridge at Rhymney and killed a taxi driver."

I was wrestling with a cabbage that me and Julie Jones had stolen from a farmer's field the night before. There was silence in the kitchen for a moment, silence except for the sound of women chopping and boiling and stirring and thinking and then Julie said

"They're saying it's pickets what done it."

Immediately I thought of Joe and my heart sank. Surely Joe wouldn't get involved in something like that.

"That's what they always say," Jackie Evans said. "The pickets get the blame for everything."

That night, everyone crowded round the telly propped on the bar at the Welfare. Joe wasn't there and I was becoming increasingly worried that he had something to do with the accident at Rhymney. It was the leading story on the News that night. It was 30th November 1984.

"*A taxi driver from Treforest in South Wales was killed today when a concrete pillar was dropped over a bridge on the Heads of Valley Road near Merthyr Tydfil.*

David Wilkie, 35, a taxi driver from Treforest, was driving a strike breaker to work at the Merthyr Vale Colliery when the accident happened.

Police are looking for two men seen running across the bridge shortly after the accident happened just after five o'clock this morning. The passenger in the taxi, miner David Williams, escaped with minor injuries.

Twenty eight police officers have been injured in the last eight days in picket line clashes outside the Merthyr Vale Colliery. Earlier today, Neil Kinnock addressed a rally at Stoke on Trent where he denounced the leader of the NUM, Arthur Scargill for failing to hold a national ballot on strike action.

The Miners Strike, which started in March, is now in its eighth month."

The men in the Welfare started muttering and jeering at the screen and then they started to sing.

"***Arthur Scargill, Arthur Scargill***
We'll support you ever more (ever more)
We'll support you ever more!"

I needed to get out of there. I couldn't breathe. I made a bolt for the door and once outside, I threw up in the bushes. I was sitting on the bench breathing in great big gulps of air when Joe's voice came through the darkness.

"Everything all right Poll?"

Relief flooded through me as the big dark shape of Joe appeared in front of me and handed me his handkerchief.

"What the blazing armpits are you doing out here in the cold?" he said. "You look very pale Poll. Are you sick?"

"No," I said. "No… Joe you didn't have anything to do with those men did you? The taxi driver? The men on the bridge?"

Joe sat down next to me and hunkered forward, staring at the dark shapes of the bushes in front of us.

"Not me, no," he said. "But I know the boys who did it. Want me to walk you back?"

"I was so worried… I thought…"

"Never mind what you thought. Come on. I'll walk you back. I could do with some fresh air. I can't have my little sister vomiting in the rose bushes. Against Union rules it is."

He smiled and stood up and held out his hand like I was five years old.

Joe the big brother. Always the big brother.

Polly

By Christmas 1984 I had been in South Wales with Joe for seven months. And during that time, Da refused to speak to either of us. Our mam was a bit different. Frosty on the phone she was but at least she spoke.

"So when are you coming home for Christmas?" she said when I rang her in early December.

"I'm not sure mam," I said.

To be honest, I didn't fancy sitting around the table in paper hats while Da and Joe shot daggers at each other

"What do you mean you're not sure? You're coming home for Christmas aren't you? You and Joe?"

I hesitated. I wanted to spend Christmas with the people I'd come to think of as my second family and as for Joe, well, he'd be happy with a pint wherever he was.

"We'll see mam ok? I'm not sure what's going on down here yet."

There was a hurt silence at the other end.

"Oh I see like that is it? Well if you want to spend Christmas with strangers that's your look out Polly but your Da won't be pleased. He won't be pleased at all."

I doubted he would care one way or the other. I couldn't imagine sitting at the table pulling crackers and reading out trivial jokes like we used to. Not now. Not when so much had happened. And besides, I'd organised all the Christmas parties for the WAPC that year: for the little children and the older children and I couldn't just disappear back home for a few days.

Also, some of the women had got talking about arranging a benefit concert. That Christmas the song *Feed the World* was number one and it inspired everyone with its funding raising focus on the starving children of Ethiopia.

"Perhaps we could put on a concert for the miners," Julie Jones suggested one Tuesday night at the weekly meeting of the WAPC. "You know Emyr Davis don't you Polly? Perhaps we could get his band to come."

All eyes turned to me and my cheeks burned.

"I don't really know him that well," I said. "But I could ask I suppose. Yes I could ask."

The women started chattering excitedly about it as plans and foundations started to form.

"We could use my uncle's farm," Julie said, warming to the subject. "We could put a big stage up in the farmyard. He's waiting to sell it," she added when the women looked curious. "All the animals have gone."

The women nodded. Empty farms were another sign of the times.

"I think Polly should be in charge of organising it," Mary Wright said. "I mean look what a good job she's done with organising the Christmas parties."

"And she knows *The Sons*," Julie chipped in. "Well Polly?"

What could I say? I wanted to help and to be seen to help and so before I knew it I was nodding my head. I didn't have a clue how to organise a benefit concert but I was about to find out.

Nellie

Extract from her unfinished biography, Street Life

I got quite a few phonecalls from Polly around Christmas time. I was busy with the show and ***Sex in Socks*** and we were also recording a special Christmas edition of ***Let's Talk!*** where our fabulous guests would sit in a bath eating Christmas pudding fed to them by half naked elves and reciting passages from the Bible. Honestly how we got away with it I don't know! There were hundreds of complaints after that show aired and Mary Whitehouse was outraged. Tom didn't care. He thought it was great publicity and she didn't even notice when the following week, I appeared surrounded by a dozen phallic shaped cactuses! That was Tom's joke on her.

Anyway to get Polly off the phone, I said that yes I would speak to Chimp about the band playing a benefit gig for the miners in South Wales. And when he called and told me that he might not be back for Christmas I said

"I bet you'd make the effort for a benefit concert though wouldn't you?"

It was meant to be sarcastic, a jab at him, a reference to the fact that he couldn't make time for me and Morwenna but would probably move heaven and earth for the band.

"What concert?" he said.

"Oh I don't know," I said because I was pissed off about Christmas. "Something Polly's organising for next February. She wants to know if *The Sons* would play that's all."

"Give her Richard's phone number," he said. "I've got to go."

Polly

Nellie gave me Richard's phone number and when I rang him to see if the band were free on 16th February 1985, he checked the diary and said that they were.

"Does that mean they will?" I said.

"These benefit concerts are hot potatoes," he said. "There's loads going on in London for the miners. I'm sure they will, seeing it's for the men of Wales."

"Is that a yes?" I pushed.

Sometimes I surprised myself with how different I'd become. Mam used to say when I was little that I wouldn't say boo to a goose and now look at me!

"I think you could say it's 90% certain."

I ran out of that phone box and down the road to the Welfare because I couldn't wait to tell someone, anyone, what had just happened and there was always someone from the WAPC in our little room upstairs. I ran up those stairs but unusually, there was no one there so I came back downstairs where Joe was huddled at the bar with a group of men who were speaking in low voices.

"Bloody scabs," I heard one of them say. "They need to be taught a lesson."

When Joe saw me he straightened up and looked a little guilty, like he'd been caught with his hand in the sweet jar. I had this sinking feeling they were up to something.

"Joe?" I said. "What's going on?"

Joe sighed and shook his head.

"Some of the men are talking about going back to work," he said. "Nothing for you to worry about Polly. Nothing at all. This is men's stuff this is."

I looked behind him to where there was a picture of Mrs Thatcher ripped out of the newspaper and pinned up on the dartboard. There were pin marks all over her face.

I searched his face for a clue about what he was up to.

"You're not going to do anything daft are you?"

"Just go home Polly," he said. "Just go home and lock the doors."

Polly

When I got home to Frank and Alison's, I felt uneasy. As I turned the key in the lock, I looked around me. The streets were silent, dark and deserted. What had Joe meant, go home and lock the doors?

I kept Sidney in at night. There were often fights late at night and men out drinking and it was no place for a half blind cat. I was so caught up in my thoughts as I opened the door that I forgot to check he wasn't waiting behind it and in a flash he darted out on to the street.

I wanted nothing more than to go to my bed. It had been a long day and my feet hurt but I couldn't leave Sidney out there so I ran after him, down alley ways and lanes that ran behind the terraced houses. No sooner did I get close to him than he ran off again.

It was as I ran down Pleasant Row that I first heard the shouting and I slowed down. Sidney jumped up on to a fence and I grabbed him and stepped back into the shadows. The back door of the house was open and I watched as a man was dragged outside despite his wife's screams and the man's protests. Once outside, four or five men dressed in dark donkey jackets holding pieces of wood up in the air hit him again and again and again. I closed my eyes. I felt sick. I wanted to run but the only way was past the house and that way, the men would see us. The noise, the screams, were dreadful. I had never heard a man scream before.

I was so cold by the time the men dispersed and it was safe for us to go back home. As I stepped back into the street lights, a car came crawling down the road towards us with its headlights off. I knew it was Julie's brother, Badger, out delivering illicit coal after dark.

"What are you doing out here so late?" he said, winding down the passenger window and leaning across from the driver's seat.

"Oh," I said brightly. "Sidney escaped. I had to go after him."

"See anything did you?" he said, testing me.

"No," I said, shaking my head. "I didn't see anything."

It was the right thing to say. No one dared speak about the beatings delivered after dark to miners suspected of being about to go back to work. I walked past that house the next day and all the windows were smashed. I don't know what happened to the man.

I'd learned there were many things you might see in Merthyr that you didn't mention. Instead, I concentrated on helping to make Christmas 1984 the best we could, given the circumstances. We had to make do with little or nothing but it's surprising what you can do with little or nothing.

We had a cartoon pinned up on the WAPC kitchen wall. It showed a policeman holding up his truncheon and stopping Father Christmas and his reindeer.

"*Alright,*" the caption said, "*I'll let you go. As long as you promise none of the presents are for the MINERS' CHILDREN!*"

We had carols in the church and a party for the children down the Welfare. Frank dressed up as Santa and the children ran around bursting balloons and playing games.

Afterwards, after the children had gone home and most of the adults had drifted off to the bar, I sat with Joe in the empty hall. Home made paper chains hung from the ceiling and the lights on the Christmas tree flashed on off on off.

"I hope 1985 is a better year," I said. "It's got to be better hasn't it?"

"I'm not so sure," he said, staring into his pint glass. "The future doesn't look that bright to me Poll, not if the mines go. Because there will be empty spaces if the mines go. Empty spaces in men's hearts and men's minds and I don't know how you fill those spaces."

We sat there as Frankie Goes to Hollywood's song, *The Power of Love* soared up to the ceiling. We were on the verge of an uncertain future but that song gave me hope. Hope that no matter how dark it got, there was always love in the world, shining out somewhere from the darkness. It didn't always feel like that in 1984, not in a world where men could get arrested for calling a working miner a Scab.

Nellie

Extract from her unfinished biography, Street Life

What was Christmas 1984 like?

We spent Christmas Day in Ffynnongroyw and were back in London by midnight. Then we had a stupid argument about who'd left the fridge door open and Chimp went off to bed leaving me with the Christmas tree and a bottle of vodka.

The next day I had a roaring hangover which I didn't need because out of the blue, my mum turned up on the doorstep.

If Chimp hadn't come into the hall to see who it was I think I would have shut the door on her but he came up behind me and he said

"Let her in Nell. It's Christmas. Let's hear what she's got to say for herself."

I was suspicious of her because not once had she tried to contact me since I left Wales, not even after Morwenna was born.

"This is nice," she said, looking around her as she shrugged off her coat in the hall.

Nice? It had costs thousands in interior design and furniture and she described it as nice?

She said yes to a cup of tea and then Morwenna came tottering along in her sparkly party tights and Christmas dress that I'd bought on Oxford Street. She looked like a little princess caught up in the magic of Christmas. She held her doll out to my mother as if she was giving her a Christmas present.

"Morwenna," I said. "Your granddaughter."

I saw her eyes fill with tears as she looked up at me.

"She's just like you were at that age."

I put a mug of tea down on the table in front of her.

"I'm surprised you remember."

"Don't be like that," she said, looking past me and catching sight of her reflection in the mirror behind me. She touched her hair. Still mum. Still vain.

She stayed for about an hour. She had bought Morwenna a Paddington Bear which she loved and a woolly hat which she didn't.

Chimp had vanished. He was in his den with his guitar and a can of beer. I didn't blame him really. It was awkward enough for me. I mean, what do you say to a woman who brought you up and calls herself your mother when you don't really know her? I'd never really known her. I was just an aside to her life as she was pulled by any wind that blew.

"Owen's not well," she said, sipping her tea. "Two bouts of pneumonia and he needs a hip operation. We sold the Castle Bay last year and we moved to Pinner. Owen runs a dog food business from home. It's a bit of a poky little house but I suppose I should be grateful."

She didn't sound grateful and I was suspicious of her. The mum I remembered didn't just call in to see people, not even if they were related to her.

"What do you want mum?"

She put her tea down on the table and adopted a hurt look.

"Want?" she said. "I don't want anything. I was just passing."

"On Boxing Day?" I said. "From Pinner?"

She pulled at an imaginary thread on her skirt, Her nails were immaculate and painted pink.

"I didn't want to ask you… it's just… well… we've been struggling a bit what with Owen being unwell. I don't suppose you could see your way to lending us a few quid could you? I mean you're not exactly short of a bob or two are you?"

So that was it. Here it was.

"How much do you want?" I said.

She looked up at me then and her eyes were the clearest grey.

"A thousand pounds should do it."

I stared at her. A thousand pounds? Had she really just asked me for a thousand pounds?

"Ok," I said, leaning forward as Morwenna piled her toys into her lap. "I tell you what. You tell me who my dad was and I'll think about it."

She sat bolt upright then, like she'd been struck by lightning and those clear grey eyes clouded. That did it. That brought the old Gillian back.

"It's always got to come back to you hasn't it?" she said, standing up and letting all the toys Morwenna had brought her fall to the ground. "I shouldn't have come. Owen told me not to come. He said you wouldn't help us and he was right wasn't he?"

"Why won't you tell me who he is?" I pushed.

She stood up and stared at me.

"Why can't you just let it go?"

I stood up as well. I was taller than her these days, even in my bare feet.

"Maybe it's got something to do with the fact that he was my dad," I said. "Maybe I'd like to know who my father was."

She rolled her eyes and I scooped up Morwenna who was sitting at her feet surrounded by toys and held her close to me.

She walked out into the hall and lifted her coat off the banister.

"I'm sorry I wasn't as welcome as I hoped I'd be," she said in that hurt sort of voice I remembered so well.

I stood holding Morwenna as she left, heading off down the street in a cherry red coat. She didn't look back. Not once. Flashes of memory. Of watching her leave from the windows of the houses we had lived in. ***Don't go mummy, don't go***.

But she did. Just like she'd always done. Vanished in a red coat into thin air.

And all these years later, I still don't know who my dad was.

1985

Polly

By early 1985, the miners were drifting back to work. There was a rumour that every returning miner would be paid £1,400.

"Over my dead body," Joe said; a sentiment shared by most of the miners in South Wales. It was hard and it was tough to stay out on strike but it was even harder to go back. Those who tried had their windows smashed, or graffiti sprayed on the walls or got "spoken to" down an alley after dark. I knew this: I'd seen it for myself.

Vincent and I could not agree on the strike. We still have completely different views even all these years later. The sticking point is always Arthur Scargill and whether he should have called a national ballot to unite the men into taking compulsory and unified strike action. I say he shouldn't, Vincent says he should. Men still debate it in the local pub.

The women of the Women Against Pit Closures Movement never received the recognition they deserved for what they did during the Strike. In every part of the country, they supported the strikers, fed the hungry and ministered to the sick. I knew many women who went without food just so their children could eat. I have never forgotten those women. They taught me to be strong and to think for myself and with them, I grew up.

Some years after the Strike, the WAPC applied for affiliate membership of the NUM. The NUM refused.

Chimp

The benefit concert was arranged for 16th February 1985. The band weren't that keen on going back to Wales, especially South Wales with all that was going on down there. We'd played some of the biggest stadiums in the world and *The Sons* were an international band. Why would we want to play there? Richard however was convinced that a benefit concert would show us in a good light and boost record sales and despite the grumblings, the band wouldn't go against what their manager said.

Privately I thought the miners were just old dinosaurs who couldn't let go, who couldn't step into the 20th century without coal dust on their boots. I didn't say this of course but I felt it every time I went home to Wales. Yes I had passions, particularly for keeping Wales Welsh but this was different. The strike was crucifying the country that I loved and none of them could see it.

The Miners' Strike was something I couldn't discuss with Rhoswen. She was a passionate supporter of it and was impressed that we were taking part in the concert and raising funds for the miners. At that time, she was always accusing me of drifting away from my roots, having my head turned by fame and fortune and I was determined to prove her wrong. There are very few people I've ever wanted to impress but Rhoswen has always been one of them.

Nellie

Extract from her unfinished biography, Street Life

Polly was surprised when I said I was coming down for the benefit concert.

"I didn't think it would be your thing," she said. "I thought you'd be busy with the show."

I was always busy with the show but if Chimp was going, if *The Sons* were playing, I was going. And besides, I was still their unofficial photographer wasn't I?

"We can't put you up," she said. "Alison and Frank's is crowded enough as it is. Where will you stay?"

Eventually Chimp decided we would stay at Hope Cottage with the band because it was only an hour's drive from Merthyr Vale. Great, I thought. Great. Stinking socks everywhere and pubes in the bath.

It was bloody freezing that winter of 1985 and about a week before the concert, South Wales was completely whited out by snow.

"I'm not going to let a bit of snow put us off," Polly said during one of our phone calls. "The roads should be clear by then."

"Chimp says the tour bus can get through anywhere," I said, filing my nails. "He's not worried about it either."

The Sons' tour bus was completely state of the art. Chimp had wanted one that was sleek and gold and he got one that was sleek and gold. It was my first time travelling in the tour bus and it was very different from George's dad's old van. It even had a bar and a toilet with a padded seat.

Despite Chimp's optimism, the journey wasn't good. Our driver was ex army and he navigated while the band lounged around at the back, jamming on their guitars, playing cards and drinking from the bar. There were delays everywhere and when we got off the M4 and crossed the Severn Bridge the countryside and the fields looked like someone had topped them with meringue. Morwenna stared out of the window, mesmerised by the transformation of the world. She had Mr Boo, her toy rabbit with her and she held him up against the window and talked to him in a low voice, telling him stories about the snow.

We hadn't gone far when we were waved over by a police roadblock.

Chimp went down the front to see what was going on and three policemen met him at the door.

"Sorry mate," one of them said. "We've got orders to check every bus that comes through in case there's pickets on it."

"Pickets?" Chimp said. "Can't you see this is a tour bus? Don't you know who we are?"

The police officer turned bright red.

"Ah," he said. "Yes I do now. I'm very sorry Mr Davis. Would you mind signing your autograph for my granddaughter?"

After they waved us on, we headed off into the back of beyond through winding and narrow lanes. We had to stop every so often so that our driver Dave could get out and shovel the snow away. Someone had taken down the local road signs so we got lost a few times.

"More attempts to confuse the pickets," George muttered morosely as he looked out of the window. "High tech stuff."

By the time we reached Merthyr, I'd drunk half a bottle of vodka. If you've travelled on those roads, particularly if you've travelled on those roads in the snow, you will understand that you can't do it sober.

We found Polly in the local Welfare wrapping up food parcels with a gaggle of women who wore the most old fashioned clothes I'd ever seen! The band stayed on the bus and she grinned at me as I walked in with Morwenna.

"You made it then," she said as we hugged. It was so good to see her. It had been so long.

The band agreed to follow us to the farm and Polly and Morwenna and I got into this old custard coloured mini that smelt of damp and cabbages. Polly drove off without putting her seatbelt on.

"No one's that bothered around here," she said. "The police are more interested in pickets."

She had changed. I couldn't put my finger on exactly how because she looked the same old Polly but the old Polly would never have gone anywhere without wearing a seatbelt. She hadn't done much with her hair but she had grown it long and tied it back and she was wearing these old dungarees and what I swore was a man's shirt. She kept up a constant stream of chatter as we drove, about the bands that were coming, about how she hoped the snow wouldn't cause a problem and how they had sold 100 tickets. Morwenna sat happily in the back, pointing out of the window and chattering away to Mr Boo.

The concert was being held on an abandoned dairy farm. The owners, Polly said, were selling it as farming just wasn't viable anymore. It was happening all over the place. Old industries, old things giving way to the new. I was cushioned by vodka and drifted in and out of what she was saying.

When I saw the stage in the farmyard, I knew Chimp and the band wouldn't be impressed.

"Badger Jones and his mates stayed up all night finishing it off," Polly said proudly as we walked around it. "What do you think?"

Luckily Chimp and the band arrived so I didn't have to answer, spilling out of the tour bus in jeans and cowboy boots. Boots was off his face and fell into a bank of snow and stomped off with a moody look on his face when we laughed at him. Menace kept singing *Old MacDonald had a farm* until George got pissed off with his duck noises and told him to shut up.

The concert was scheduled for the next day. Polly gave us all a flyer with *The Sons'* name at the top and underneath, the names of the other bands who would be playing. Some names I recognised, others I didn't.

"Who's *Powder Room*?" Chimp said, reading the flyer out loud.

"You'll have to ask Richard," Polly said. "He booked all the bands. An American rock group I think. Or maybe they're from Canada."

"Never heard of them," he said.

"They sound like hot chicks to me," Menace said. "I bet they're hot chicks."

Chimp circled the stage with George while Boots and Menace sat on a low stone wall smoking.

"We'll come early tomorrow to do the lighting and sound checks and get set up," Chimp said. I was surprised that he didn't criticise it. Maybe Chimp was mellowing.

We said goodbye to Polly and got back on the tour bus. I had more vodka as we headed down to Hope Cottage.

"That stage is a pile of shit," Chimp said. "People don't have a clue do they?"

I stared at him. Not so mellow after all.

Polly

Nellie caused quite a stir turning up at the Welfare dressed in that gold mini dress and fringed white boots.

"You're Nellie on the Telly aren't you?" Julie Jones said. "You're the one who interviews all those half naked men."

The women crowded round and cooed over Morwenna and asked for Nellie's autograph which annoyed me a bit because we had so much to do what with getting the food parcels ready and the concert.

The band followed us up to the farm in their tour bus. It was a big gold beast of a thing. I've never seen anything like it. We had old cars and pushbikes and that was it.

I don't know what *The Sons* thought about the stage. Badger Jones and his mates had stayed up all night building it and Chimp just looked at it and said they'd come early the next day to set up. Chimp hadn't changed. He still had his scruffy hair and parka and as for the other three band members, well. I am sure one of them was wearing his dad's pyjamas!

So off they went in that not so subtle gold bus to stay in George's cottage on the Gower and I just hoped Nellie had brought a coat with her because she was hardly dressed for winter in Wales!

Nellie

Extract from her unfinished biography, Street Life

I didn't know it when I woke up that morning, but Saturday 16th February 1985 was a day that would change my life forever. It didn't start off well.

Chimp had arranged for Tom Horse to drive down from Ffynnongroyw, collect Morwenna and take her back to stay with them for the weekend. I never liked being away from her but also I was looking forward to a good party.

We weren't sure what the A470 down from Ffynnongroyw would be like but Tom Horse made it through and arrived on time.

"Nellie," he said, nodding at me when I opened the front door.

Tom was keen to get back on the road because more snow was forecast and he wasn't a man who hung around making small talk. Morwenna was grizzling because we couldn't find Mr Boo and she didn't go anywhere without Mr Boo.

I ran upstairs to have another look for him in our bedroom. Morwenna had slept with us the night before, much to Chimp's irritation.

In the end, he got up and slept downstairs on the couch and in the morning, I tiptoed around quietly so I didn't irritate him further.

Up in the bedroom, I pulled back the sheets and I turned over the pillows. No Mr Boo. I crouched down and patted around under the bed with the flat of my palm. I kept my eyes shut because I was sure there were dreadful things under that bed – dust balls and sandwiches from the 1950s, maybe a skeleton or two – and I found Mr Boo and brought him out from his hiding place and dusted him down. And that's when the ear ring fell on the floor. It must have got attached to his fur. I picked it up and I looked at it. It was a single silver rose and it wasn't mine.

As I sat there staring at it, Chimp shouted up the stairs.

"Come on Nellie! Dad wants to go! If you can't find it she'll have to go without!"

I slipped the ear ring into the pocket of my Levis 501s and I came down the stairs with a bright smile on my face waggling Mr Boo's arms at Morwenna.

"Look who I found hiding under the bed!"

Her face lit up with this beautiful smile and she held out her arms and welcomed him home. I crouched down and fastened the buttons on her little wool coat and reminded her to be good for Granpy and Nanna. She nodded solemnly and I kissed her and inhaled that wonderful scent of daughter and my heart ached at the thought of being separated from her for a few days.

And then they were gone, Morwenna and Mr Boo, her little gloved hand held in Tom's big working hand as they walked to the car and she waved out of the window as the car pulled out on the road and I watched until I couldn't see them any more.

And then I went back inside. George was walking up the stairs in his socks and underpants carrying a plate of peanut butter on toast. Menace and Boots were still sleeping.

I went into the kitchen. Chimp was sitting at the table with a big mug of tea in front of him reading the paper. I took the ear ring out of my jeans pocket and I threw it on the table.

"What's this?" I said.

Chimp stared at it and when he looked up, guilt was written all over his face.

"Are you sleeping with her?" I said, my heart pounding in my chest. "Are you?"

Chimp sighed.

"It's not what you think Nellie," he said. "It's not what you think."

I slammed the kitchen door and I went back upstairs. I sat on the bed and I thought about that photograph I'd seen in the paper and the ear ring I'd found under the bed. Suddenly it all started to make sense.

I wish I'd packed my things earlier that morning and taken Morwenna back to London. If I'd done that they would never have been able to take her away from me later on.

On the other hand, I would never have met Rudi.

Morwenna

I love that bit where she describes coming down the stairs with Mr Boo. Where she says she inhaled the scent of daughter. It made me cry when I first read it. I can see her, my mother, young and hopeful standing at the top of the stairs probably wearing some completely unsuitable outfit. I don't have many memories of her – I was too young – but her words create them.

Sometimes I touch her photographs, trace the outline of her face, try to piece her together, try to see what was behind the face she presented to the camera. It is as if by touching her, I can somehow magically make her appear like the genie in the lamp.

I remember being in the car with Uncle Joe once when the oil light came on – that red oil can graphic – and when I asked him what it was, he said

"It means you get three wishes."

I used every single one of them wishing my mother would magically appear from the mountains.

Reading her unfinished autobiography has helped in some ways but made her loss more raw in others, especially when she gives details like that. When I first read it, I went through a whole host of emotions from feeling like I was intruding to feeling furious with my dad. Some days I couldn't speak to him it was so strong.

Chimp

What could I say? All I know is that we had a gig to prepare for and I could do without Nellie throwing a strop like that. So she'd found an ear ring under the bed. It wasn't the end of the world although being Nellie, she acted like it was, throwing it at me and flouncing out of the kitchen.

I was a bit concerned about my dad and distracted by it – I'd smelt the booze on him when he collected Morwenna that morning but when I asked him if he was ok, he just brushed me off and said they'd better get going because there was more snow on the way.

I didn't mention my concerns about him to Nellie. Relations between us for the rest of the day were what you would call decidedly cool and I was glad to get away, to throw myself into what I did best. The music.

Nellie

Extract from her unfinished biography, Street Life

I suppose I was drinking quite a bit by then. Not as much as they made out in Court later but Count Smirnoff was definitely a very close friend!

Who says you can't start drinking before midday? I frequently did except when I was looking after Morwenna although later on, Chimp's barrister tried to suggest otherwise. That man tried to throw everything at me he possibly could to paint me as an unreliable, drink sodden mother. It wasn't true. I would never put Morwenna at risk.

I have identified the triggers for my drinking now. *The Suns of Life* made me address those and I had to learn some hard lessons. But back then, every time I felt unsettled or anxious – and Chimp was a master at making me feel that way – I reached for the vodka bottle.

I decided that I would go to the gig in the most outrageous outfit I could find. I wasn't going to let Chimp pull me down. I was Nellie on the Telly, loved by the public and copied by teenage girls everywhere. Nellie, the face of Friday night was, despite everything else, pretty good on the telly but my personal life was a different story. I drank to blot out the truth that my marriage was not the perfect shiny thing I wanted it to be. I drank to blot out the reality that my husband was often non committal and cold. I drank to blot out the fact that I had recently found an earring belonging to another woman under the bed and the suspicions gnawing at the edge of my world: that he was having an affair with Rhoswen Jones and that perhaps she wasn't a lesbian after all.

I always think that getting ready is the best part of going out. After the band left, I topped up my vodka and turned on the music. I had a tape of my favourite songs with me: *Private Dancer by Tina Turner, Native New Yorker* by Odyssey, *Young Hearts Run Free* by Candi Staton and oh yes *Street Life* by *Randy Crawford.*

I also had a ballgown I'd picked up in Soho. It was pink with darker pink rosebuds around the hem. I teamed it with black Doc Marten boots without laces and a jean jacket. That was my look. The princess and the street walker. Well, I was a bit of both wasn't I?

Dressing up for me was like putting on a suit of armour. It made me feel quirky, rebellious, strong. I wasn't going to put on sack cloth and ashes after finding that earring. I was going to be Nellie in all her true colours.

And so when I met Rhoswen and Grace later that day, it made me feel defiant and strong. It made me feel Nellie. I **was** Nellie on the Telly and no one was going to get under my skin.

Polly

I am sure Nellie was a bit pissed when she turned up at the farm on the back of Joe's motorbike. She denied it of course and said she was just feeling nervous for Chimp. She didn't tell me about the earring until later. She didn't tell me about the photograph of them in Swansea either. It was if by denying these things, not saying them out loud, they weren't true. But I saw Chimp with Rhoswen that night and a seed of suspicion sprouted in my mind before Nellie said anything at all. Joe saw it too although he had no time for Chimp and would have accused him of anything.

"Why are they even playing down here?" he said. "It's not as if he's interested in the miners."

The snow hadn't finished with us yet. Some bands got through, others got stranded or cancelled as soon as they looked out the window. Billy Bragg got stuck on the M1 and had to turn back. He was probably the most famous person we had coming apart from *The Sons*. I had hoped for Paul Weller because he really seemed to get what was going on with Thatcher and the miners but Richard told me Chimp didn't want any big names to eclipse his and had only agreed to Billy Bragg because Rhoswen liked him.

The bands were a mix of all sorts of music, from African rhythms to rock. *The Sons* were the headliners, playing as the sky darkened and the lights from the stage illuminated the snow falling all around them. It was quite atmospheric, seeing their Welsh flags blowing out behind them and hearing Chimp shout out to the elements at the end "*Cymru am Byth!*"

I think it was a success. We raised over a thousand pounds for the miners which was the main thing but in other ways, that night changed the course of all of our futures. We just didn't know it at the time.

Nellie

Extract from her unfinished biography, Street Life

When Polly said Joe would come and collect me I wasn't expecting him to arrive on a motorbike.

I ran down the stairs and met him outside. It felt exciting standing in the snow in a ballgown. Magical.

"What the blazing armpits is this?" he said, looking up at the cottage. "The House of Horrors?"

Despite the day I'd had so far I couldn't help but laugh. Joe had a way of saying things you were thinking but didn't dare say out loud.

"It belongs to George," I said. "And Chimp loves it so don't let him hear you say that."

"How is Simon le Bon?" he said. "Still strutting about on stage is he?"

"You can ask him yourself later," I said.

"I thought you were coming in a car," I said. "How am I going to ride on a motorbike in this?"

Joe laughed.

"Well you'll just have to ride side saddle won't you," he said. "So how are you Nellie? And how is Morwenna?"

"Oh fine," I said. "Everything's really good Joe. I've got a new book on the go and the show is going really well. And Morwenna well she's a proper little girl now. She's beautiful Joe, really she is."

Joe dropped his eyes so that I couldn't read what was in them and when he looked up again the shadows had gone.

"Right then," he said. "Let's get you on mounted on this trusty steed shall we?"

I had forgotten how it felt to laugh. I mean, really laugh. Joe had that gift. If it was Chimp picking me up on a motorbike he would have made me go back into the house and change and we would have argued until he got his way and I would have remained silent and sulky on the back of that bike all the way to the farm. Joe was different. He relished a challenge even if it involved getting a woman in a ballgown to sit on the back of a motorbike and not tip it over. He found it all quite funny I think.

"Remember to lean when we go round the corners," he said. "Otherwise you'll end up arse over tit by the side of the road with me on top of you. And we'll put that bottle of vodka and the camera in the pannier shall we?"

I nodded and let him take over. The bike wobbled and we almost tipped over a few times and he made all these whoa noises and somehow turned it into something crazy and fun. I hadn't had so much fun in ages. I mean I had it all, I could have bought fun in great big bite sized chunks in whatever form I wanted but you couldn't buy fun with money could you? And I tell you what I laughed like I hadn't done in years. I mean really laughed, helpless laughed, tears running down your face laughed.

Joe pulled over a few times to make sure I was ok and we got quite a few strange looks as we drove along.

"Don't worry about them!" Joe shouted back over his shoulder above the roar of the motorbike. "They're just the village idiots."

Joe picked me up that day, not just physically, but mentally too. The snow sparkled in the winter sun and I had *Native New Yorker* playing in my mind. I felt like I was in a James Bond film and I was almost sorry when we got to the farm and the adventure was over.

He held the bike steady while I climbed off and then he got off too and removed his helmet and took my bottle of vodka and the camera out of the pannier.

"There you are Cinderella," he said. "And lo and behold, you've still got your shoes on."

We were standing there laughing when I suddenly heard Chimp's voice behind us.

"What the bloody hell do you think you're doing roaring in here like that? We're trying to do a soundcheck!"

Joe kept his cool.

"No offence mate," he said. "I was just giving Nellie a lift that's all."

Chimp glared at me and then he turned on his heel and stomped off back to the stage.

"Artistic temperament," Joe said, watching him go. "Or complete wanker."

"Joe!" I giggled.

Joe was still watching him.

"Well," he said. "He wants to remember where he came from, that one."

And then he turned back to me and there was this curious light in his eyes.

"Is he good to you Nellie?" he said. "Does he treat you proper?"

I looked straight ahead because I had this ridiculous feeling I might cry.

"Of course he does," I said. "He just gets a bit stressed before a gig that's all."

I looked over at the entrance to the farmyard and saw a woman and a girl standing there. My heart sank as I registered Rhoswen and Grace and the laughter and the magic of my sleigh ride through the snow faded.

I wanted to blurt it out then. I wanted to tell him that I'd found this ear ring, seen this photo… but Polly came over and she looked me up and down and she said

"You didn't come on the bike in that did you?"

"Yes Polly I did," I said, and wandered off to find the bar.

Morwenna

That's another of my favourite stories from her autobiography. The one where she rides on the motorbike with Uncle Joe in the snow. I asked him about it once and he said it had been magical and crazy and that you wouldn't get away with it now, not with all the police about. Sometimes Uncle Joe seemed so sad but when he talked about Nellie it brought light back to his eyes.

"Ah," he said. "She was a wild one your mother. And you know what? She managed to keep her shoes on even though we went down all these windy, twisty lanes. No laces, you see. No laces."

I think he was in love with her. It wasn't something I could ask him but I had this feeling. I mean you just know, don't you? Because whenever we talked about her, a light came into his eyes. He kept her alive for me, Uncle Joe, he painted pictures. Sometimes we forget that our mothers are women as well as mothers but he always brought her home to me, woman, mother, Nellie on the Telly, a beautiful enigma, fragranced with the perfume of the wind.

Polly

Powder Room were not, as Menace had suggested, a bunch of hot chicks. Instead they were this wild rock n roll band from the States. I'd never seen anything like them. They installed themselves in one of the old stables and the next day, Agnes Carter told me she'd found 37 empty bottles of Jack Daniels when they were cleaning up.

The farm had been transformed. Fairy lights were strung across the stage and the farmyard and the stables had become dressing rooms, a bar, a room with food laid out on a table and a toilet. Around the stage were hay bales for people to sit on and people with guitars and spiky hair styles wandered around mingling with the roadies who humped speakers and lights and cables.

Powder Room arrived early and Richard said they were big in America and about to take the UK by storm. I was there when they did their sound checks and I remember thinking they were so loud they'd hear them all the way to Abertillery!

Anyway I was waiting for Vincent to arrive as I wandered around checking everything was in order. Rock concerts weren't his thing but he said he'd be down. They weren't my thing either – my ears were ringing by the end of the night and I had a splitting headache – but we weren't doing it for us.

I saw Nellie flitting around the place in that ridiculous ballgown taking photographs but we didn't really have time to speak because I was busy making sure that things went smoothly, that the bands had all they needed, that the food we'd laid on was going to be enough. I was impressed by how many people turned out despite the weather but I kept a worried eye on the skies that evening. Vincent was late and I was concerned that if the weather got too bad we might have to abandon ship in the middle of the concert. You can cope with almost any eventuality when you're planning something but the weather is always beyond your control.

I think there was some tension between Nellie and Chimp that night but it didn't surprise me because there was always something firing up between them and I had my mind on other things, like where Vincent was and what the weather was going to do.

Nellie

Extract from her unfinished biography, Street Life

Can a man be beautiful?

I don't know but what I do know is that the image of Rudi standing at the front of the stage while the snow fell softly all around him has never left me. It promoted him to god like status but I couldn't work out why the snow didn't do that to any of the other bands who performed that night. Maybe it was his leather trousers! All I know is I was mesmerised. There was something raw about Rudi Delawayo, something primitive, something I felt crackle through the air like electricity. You can see it in the photos I took.

I had never heard of *Powder Room* but circumstances conspired to give me a front row seat or maybe, as Rudi says, it was fate. I mean how else would I ever have met him if I hadn't gone to that concert? If I hadn't been so harshly evicted from Chimp's dressing room?

He was a welcome distraction, something wild and exotic to look at, taking my mind off what had happened with Chimp an hour or so earlier. I remember my thoughts racing, thinking how I must interview him for ***Let's Talk!***, how he had to be in ***Sex in Socks!***

I'd found Chimp and the band in one of the old stables which they'd set up as their dressing room. That old farm was a rag tag of hidden places, wooden ladders leading to lofts, quirky little out houses, barns and stalls.

So I wandered in there and immediately felt like I'd intruded. Grace and Rhoswen were standing laughing with Chimp in a little huddle and when I walked in, they stopped laughing and Rhoswen looked me up and down like I was something the dog brought in.

"Nellie," she said, nodding at me.

"Rhoswen," I said, staring at her rose ear rings.

She was wearing jeans and a black shirt. No dressing up for her!

"Why are you wearing a ballgown?" Grace said, sticking her thumb in her mouth. I wanted to tell her that she was too old to be sucking her thumb. I mean she was, what, fourteen, by then.

"Well Grace," I said. "It's like this. I wear a ballgown and you suck your thumb. Funny how people are so different isn't it?"

"Nellie..." Chimp said as Menace and George and Boots slipped out of the door.

I didn't care. What did I care? I had drunk quite a lot of vodka by then and I felt quite justified in saying words that had been stuck in my head all day.

"Did you lose an earring Rhoswen?" I said. "Because I found one under our bed at Hope Cottage this morning."

"Nellie..." Chimp said again, trying to warn me off.

Rhoswen didn't flinch. She just stood there and stared right back at me. She didn't have any words though. I mean what could she say? Oh yes I left it there when I was shagging your husband?

"Rhoswen gave me this," Grace piped up, holding out a shell on a string she was wearing round her neck. "It's nicer than anything you've given me."

You could have cut the atmosphere with a knife. And I caused it, I know I did but what was I supposed to do, walk in there and pretend everything was hunky dory? I tell you my heart was hammering nineteen to the dozen. I was angry, I was hurt, I was out of my league in that hostile place.

"I think you'd better go and sober up," Chimp said, moving forward. That made me even more mad because I felt like he was taking sides. That I, his wife, the mother of his child, was the thorn in their side, that I, his wife, the mother of his child, was causing a problem and that I should just disappear.

"Is she drunk?" Grace said, turning her face up to look at Rhoswen. Rhoswen kept her eyes fixed on me.

"Don't ruin it Nellie," she said. "This isn't about you today."

Chimp caught my wrist before I could slap her. She deserved a slap the moody self satisfied cow standing there like some sort of lesbian warrior.

"Nellie," he hissed at me through clenched teeth. "Go and sober up. Don't make a scene."

He pushed me out of the door and I would have gone flying into the snow if Joe hadn't caught me.

"Nellie?" he said, catching my camera before it fell into the snow. "Is everything alright?"

I found my feet, wobbled a little and was just about to let a stream of invective fly about Chimp when I saw a girl standing next to Joe.

"This is Lisa," he said proudly, taking her hand. "My new girlfriend."

Chimp

It was unfortunate that Nellie and Rhoswen met like that. I knew it might happen, that it probably would happen, and it had made me feel a bit edgy all day. I remember feeling pissed about that, the fact that I might have to deal with some cat fight when I was headlining with the band and had to perform. I could have done without it.

We could have sorted it out like adults but oh no. Nellie had to come in half pissed and shout her mouth off at Rhoswen. And in front of Grace too! At least the band had sense, they snuck off as soon as Nellie walked in. They knew that where she walked, trouble often followed.

Anyway I suggested she go and sober up. I didn't want anything to distract me from what I had to do. I almost wished none of them were there. My music and my personal life were different things and if I had to choose, my music would always come first.

After Nellie left, Rhoswen turned to me and there were questions in her dark eyes.

"She found an earring under the bed this morning," I shrugged. "It's probably been there for years but for some reason, she thinks it's yours."

I said it more for Grace's sake really. The conversation was for a later time and place when Rhoswen and I were on our own.

"Is it?" Grace asked. "Is it your ear ring Rhoswen?"

Rhoswen gave a short false laugh.

"Of course it isn't sweetheart," she said, her eyes glued to mine above her head.

"Why would my earring be under your daddy's bed?"

Grace put her thumb in her mouth, shrugged and took it out again.

"If you had sex with him it might be yours," she said.

Out of the mouths of babes. They know far more than we credit them for don't they?

Grace was fourteen by then although at times she still acted like a child: the thumbsucking for example. Megan and Paul were worried about it but the child psychologist from Barnardo's had reassured them she'd grow out of it in time and advised them not to make an issue of it. Grace, they suggested, felt more comfortable as a child at times and needed to be allowed to return to that safe place if she was to move forward into adulthood.

Anyway, Rhoswen suggested she take Grace off to get some food and I was grateful that I was finally on my own. I took some deep breaths and I ran through the order of songs in my mind. I didn't give any more thought to what had just happened. I had to perform.

Polly

Vincent had a difficult drive down from Ffynnongroyw that night. I was so pleased to see him striding across the farmyard and he picked me up and whirled me around.

"I've missed you," he said. "I've missed you."

We didn't have more than a few moments together because everyone needed me to do something. Barney was battling to keep the old generator running and the bar had run out of orange squash.

Vincent was, as always, quite laid back about it all and I think he wandered off to the bar or to find Joe or something. But later, as the snow fell, and the bands were up and running, I relaxed a little and that was when Vincent took me by the hand and led me away to a quieter place.

"I had a long drive down," he said, as *Powder Room* belted out the loudest music I've ever heard. "And lots of time to think about what's important. So this might not be the most romantic way of doing it but you are the most important thing in my life Polly Evans."

And then, right there in the snow, in the middle of a farmyard, he got down on one knee.

"Polly Evans," he said. "Will you marry me?"

The snow was tumbling down around us in great swirls of white and I stood there staring at him for a moment, not quite believing what I'd just heard.

"Yes!" I said. "Yes of course I will you silly fool!"

He picked me up and swirled me round and looked up at me as he held me up in the air.

"You've just made me the happiest man in the world," he said.

"Put me down Vincent Peters," I said. "Let's go and find Nellie. I can't wait to tell her!"

We found Nellie sitting on a haybale watching *Powder Room* with a bottle of vodka and her camera by her side.

"Vincent's just proposed!" I shouted over the music. "We're getting married!"

Nellie looked up and her blue eyes were out of focus.

"Good for you Poll," she said, unscrewing the vodka and taking a swig. "Good for you."

There was something in her eyes that looked sad. I wanted to know more but I had just got engaged and I wanted to savour that moment with my future husband and so there wasn't time to ask, there wasn't time to take it any further and I put it down to Nellie having had quite a bit to drink which, to be honest, could sometimes make her quite melancholy.

Nellie

Extract from her unfinished biography, Street Life

After Chimp pushed me out of the dressing room, I retrieved the vodka I'd stashed behind the bar and found a haybale where I could sit and watch the bands on stage. I took some photographs and I got some good shots. There were hundreds of people there that night but I have never felt more alone.

I watched Chimp and the band impassively; like I might watch a band I didn't know. He was good but he didn't have that animal magnetism I'd witnessed in the lead singer from *Powder Room* who'd played just before *The Sons* headlined.

By the time they'd finished, the farmyard was pretty much deserted as people drifted away, keen to get home because of the snow. I closed my eyes and enjoyed the emptiness in my head, the empty space that drink used to bring, when Chimp's voice suddenly cut through it.

"We need to go Nellie," he said.

When I looked up at him, he was a little out of focus, a little blurred around the edges.

"I'm not coming," I said.

He rolled his eyes and looked heavenwards.

"Oh don't start this again," he said. "We need to get going. The roads are bad."

"I thought you'd be going home with Rhoswen and Grace," I said.

"We're dropping them off on the way," he said. "They're staying in a guest house. What's with you? Time of the month?"

I hated him for saying that; like my hormones were responsible for my behaviour instead of the way he'd spoken to me and the way he'd pushed me out of their makeshift dressing room.

"NOT. GOING," I repeated.

Chimp sighed.

"You know you don't do yourself any favours getting drunk like this," he said. "You're a mess Nellie. A mess."

He stomped away, striding out towards that big gold monster of a tour bus. When he was nearly there, he turned and barked my name but I shook my head and stayed where I was.

The snow fell softly on my shoulders and the fairy lights strung up across the farmyard glowed pink and green and blue. All around me was evidence that the party was over but I would rather be there than shut inside Hope Cottage with Chimp and its darkness.

The bus drove off but I didn't mind. It was peaceful. There is something about falling snow that's quite bewitching.

I wandered over to the stable that was converted to a bar. I stashed my camera behind it and helped myself to a half empty bottle of vodka.

I would find somewhere to lie down, somewhere to watch the snow fall as I fell asleep.

Chimp

Nellie refused to leave the farm and come with us in the bus that night. So I left her there. I had Grace to think of and Dave, our driver, was already warning about the snow on the roads.

I wasn't in the best of moods. That stage had been as rickety as hell and at one stage I thought I was going to fall through it. The crowd was fairly sparse because of the snow and had drifted away towards the end.

George was wide eyed and incredulous when I told Dave to drive off.

"You can't just leave her there," he said.

"Why not," I said. "She's a grown woman."

George let out a low whistle.

"Nellie's clearly made a decision," Rhoswen said. "She'd old enough to do that."

George and Rhoswen exchanged sharp looks.

"Polly will take care of her," I said, irritated by George sticking his nose into my business.

The atmosphere between me and George was frosty for the rest of that journey.

"I'm glad we left her behind," Grace said snuggling up to me at the back of the bus. "I don't like Nellie."

Dave did his best to get us through but the snow had blocked most of the roads and it was hopeless. I've never driven in a snow storm before or since and it's not an experience I'd recommend. I don't think it would have mattered so much if it had just been me and the boys but Grace and Rhoswen were on board and I was acutely conscious of that.

In the end Dave pulled into a layby and I walked down to the front of the bus.

"Not sure what to do mate," he said. "I've tried every possible road out but they're all blocked."

We were in a layby miles from anywhere and all around us was nothing but the silence and white out of snow. It was too late to hope that anywhere might still be open to offer us shelter even if we could find somewhere.

So we stayed where we were. On the bus. In a layby. In a way it was a bit like the old days when me and the boys used to bunk down in that old van at the side of the road but in other ways it wasn't like that at all because we had Rhoswen and Grace with us.

So me and Rhoswen and Grace hunkered down at the back – Rhoswen's theory was that if we stuck together we could share our body heat – and the boys and Dave slept in the seats nearer the front. It was freezing cold and I hardly slept at all but Grace did – fast asleep between me and Rhoswen.

Nellie

Extract from her unfinished biography, Street Life

Rudi told me later that when he heard footsteps coming up the ladder, he grabbed an empty bottle of Jack Daniels ready to defend himself against an unwanted intruder. I suppose that's the sort of thing you do when you grow up in New York. And then, when he saw my head appear in the doorway, he put the bottle down because he thought an angel had come to take him up to heaven.

In reality, it was me climbing up a ladder to a hayloft. I did it one handed because I was holding a bottle of vodka and it wasn't the easiest of manoeuvres to execute in a ballgown when I was three sheets to the wind. If I'd been sober, I probably wouldn't have tried.

"Hey Princess," he said. "Did you get lost on the way to the ball?"

Those were the first words he ever said to me.

Hey Princess. Did you get lost on the way to the ball?

He had such a gentle voice, rich, American, amused, but I couldn't see his face clearly because it was so dark. I heard a Zippo firing up and he came alive in the flame, Rudi Delawayo, the lead singer of *Powder Room.*

He caught my wrist and held on. For a moment our eyes locked and we both smiled, like we'd been waiting for each other forever.

"I got you," he said. "I got you. Here, give me that bottle."

I handed him the vodka and crawled into the loft. I could smell hay and snow and man.

"You're cold and damp," he said. "Take that dress off before you freeze to death. It's ok it's ok," he said, seeing the look on my face. "I won't look and you can put this on."

He threw a pale green t-shirt towards me which had a big red phoenix on the front. I've still got it. It's my treasure t-shirt and I used to wear it at *The Suns of Life* when he wasn't with me.

It wasn't easy getting out of that ballgown in a loft but somehow I did it.

"You'd better get in here," he said, unzipping the side of his sleeping bag. "Unless you're planning on moving on."

I heard the smile in his voice and crawled across the wooden floor and got inside the sleeping bag. Instantly I was warm. Instantly I was safe.

"You make a habit of doing this?" he said into my hair as I snuggled into his chest.

"Only on Saturdays," I said, smiling in the dark.

I know it sounds far fetched but it didn't feel strange at all. I felt this instant bond with him, like I'd known him a thousand years and I'd never felt like that before, not even with Chimp.

We talked most of the night. It was innocent, two people keeping each other warm on a snowy night. I think it was the most romantic night of my life. I expected him to try it on because there was always payback. Except this time, there wasn't.

I don't think I've ever been so hypnotised by the sound of someone's voice. It was so deep, so rich. He told me about growing up in New York, funny little stories from his childhood, how he had a one eyed dog, how he fell out of a window, how his sister used to pay him a dollar to keep an eye out for their parents when she was out back with her new boyfriend. He told me how he loved to read books. Books about anything and everything. I said I couldn't equate that with the wild rock star I'd seen on stage earlier.

"It's all part of the act," he said. "You are never who you are in real life when you're on stage."

I could identify with that. Nellie on the Telly was very different from Nellie in real life. I offered stories from my world but I didn't dwell on the dark stuff. I also told him I was married to Chimp and had a little girl. For the first time in my life I didn't make things up. With him I wanted to be honest, with him I was just Nellie Morgan who sounded Welsh but wasn't. How could I be anyone else when I was in his sleeping bag in a hayloft in the middle of a snow storm? It was like the rest of the world had melted or slipped away and we were the only ones left on the planet.

I did wonder, as I drifted off to sleep, why he hadn't tried it on with me and whether he was queer or just didn't fancy me but the thought floated away as I slept in the warmth of his arms and outside, the snow fell softly all around us.

Polly

I don't know how we got back to Alison and Frank's but we did. Vincent gave me a piggyback for some of the way because it was so hard walking in that snow. I never realised before how disorientating snow can be, how exhausting.

It was three o'clock in the morning when we got back to Frank and Alison's. Frank was still up because he'd been worried about me and Sidney of course gave us a royal welcome.

Frank made up a bed for Vincent on the couch. I went up to the attic but I couldn't sleep. I kept thinking about how he'd proposed to me, how our wedding day would be; how I'd have pink roses in my bouquet and a honeymoon in Scotland. And then there was this tap on my door and when I opened it, Vincent was standing on the landing in his socks with his finger to his lips and mischief dancing in his eyes.

"I'm scared of the dark," he said.

I felt a bit guilty about letting him in my room because it was Frank and Alison's house and I wasn't sure what they might think so in the end I went downstairs with him and we slept on the couch with Sidney on top of us.

"That cat thinks he's your bodyguard," Vincent said, stroking his head.

"Yes," I smiled. "Yes he does."

The next day dawned bright and sunny. Alison cooked bacon and eggs and the boys met Vincent and shook his hand and we sat around the Sunday morning breakfast table. They had nothing that family but they welcomed Vincent with open arms and piled his plate up high. I was on tenterhooks in case the subject of the Miners' Strike came up and they discovered Vincent was a working miner but the conversation was all about the snow and how we might get back to the farm to tidy up.

"I'll walk over to Michael East's," Frank said. "He's got a tractor. He'll take you there."

So we arrived back at the farm on the back of a tractor, just in time to see Nellie coming down the ladder from the hayloft in her ballgown.

Nellie

Extract from her unfinished biography, Street Life

By the time the sun came up, I knew I was in love. It can happen that quickly, love. It can come in the snow, in the dark or with the dawn. Magic can happen when you're least expecting it.

And then Polly and Vincent arrived on the back of a tractor.

I was climbing down the ladder in my ballgown when they came as I desperately needed a pee. The sun was so bright on the snow it hurt my eyes and then, out of the silence came Polly's voice.

"Nellie Morgan what on earth are you doing?"

And before I had time to make something up, Rudi stuck his head out of the loft.

"Good morning!" he said. "What a beautiful day!"

I froze on the ladder and Polly shielded her eyes from the sun and stared up at me.

"Have you been up there all night?"

It was obvious I had. I mean why would I be climbing down a ladder if I was just passing through?

Vincent rushed over and held his arm out to guide me down the last few rungs of the ladder and Rudi came down after me bare chested, in just his leather trousers.

"Yes we have," he said, looping his arm around my shoulders. "And I'd highly recommend this hay loft to anyone."

Polly looked from me to him and back to me.

"You do know she's married," she said. "With a two year old daughter?"

"Yes ma'am," Rudi said, nodding his head solemnly. "And she also knows that I am nothing but a gentleman."

Polly flushed red at the implications of this and Vincent suppressed a smile.

"Fancy some breakfast?" he said. "We could give you a lift back to the house if you like."

So that's what we did: we rode back to Polly's house on a tractor.

Vincent lent me his sunglasses and took a photograph of me and Rudi, sitting up on the back of the tractor looking happy and relaxed with his arm looped around my shoulders. We have it framed in the hallway and I love it because it captures the day we first met, with the sun glinting off the snow and me in shades and a ballgown! Everyone remarks on it. Some people ask if it was staged and I say no, it's real, it's one hundred per cent real.

Polly

I was shocked when I found out Nellie had spent the night in a hayloft with the lead singer of *Powder Room*. Vincent told me not to be such a prude but I knew Nellie and how good she was at getting herself into situations that ended in tears.

When we got back to Alison and Frank's, Frank said that Chimp had telephoned five times asking where Nellie was.

"He sounded a bit fed up," he said. "Apparently they spent the night in a layby."

Nellie laughed at this but Frank was concerned and he and the boys set off with shovels and chains to find them.

I lent Nellie a pair of jeans and a jumper. They were way too big for her and the sleeves dangled down past her wrists but she still looked stunning.

"You better go before Chimp gets here," I said as I watched her change in my bedroom. I was worried about what would happen if Frank and the boys brought Chimp back to the house. "Honestly Nellie you're getting too old for one night stands."

She looked at me then and her eyes twinkled.

"It wasn't," she said. "It wasn't a one night stand."

I rolled my eyes and shook my head.

"What's Chimp going to say if he finds out?" I said.

"I don't know and I don't care," she said.

We went back downstairs and into the kitchen. Alison had put on the radio and of all the songs that could be playing, it had to be *No Milk Today*.

Nellie helped herself to another cup of tea and when I saw the smile Rudi gave her, I knew she'd told the truth.

Chimp

It was not my finest hour. I had long grown out of sleeping in laybys and by the time the rescue party arrived, I was not in the best of moods. I wanted a cup of coffee and a cigarette and I was very short on sleep.

Dave insisted on staying with the bus and the rescue party got to work with shovels and chains to try to get the bus moving again. The rest of us were taken in relays on a tractor back to this guy called Frank's house where Polly was staying. Polly confirmed Nellie had been there but had left not long before we arrived. Polly seemed cagey like she didn't want to speak to me or tell me anything more.

We managed to get down to Hope Cottage later that day and all I could think about was Nellie and where she'd gone. My dad was due to bring Morwenna down that afternoon so we could all travel back to England together. I was on edge about that because now of course we had Rhoswen and Grace with us and the journey was going to be difficult to say the least. It was typical of Nellie to do her own thing without a thought for anyone else.

I used Frank's phone to ring my dad and felt even more pissed off and irritated when he told me Nellie had already telephoned and agreed Morwenna could stay in Ffynnongroyw for two more days. I didn't let on that I didn't know where Nellie was but when I came off the phone I snapped at Rhoswen. I didn't mean to take it out on her but I was furious with Nellie. All she ever thought about was herself and now she had disappeared in a snow bombed Wales! Typical.

Nellie

Extract from her unfinished biography, Street Life

Where did I go? Why with Rudi of course. Yes. Just like that. I spent a night with a man in a hayloft and two days later I was living with him.

I didn't know it would happen, I didn't know what would happen. But when we were alone in the kitchen that morning, when Alison went out to the bathroom or somewhere, he leaned across the table and took hold of my hand.

"I can't leave it like this," he said. "I know it sounds kinda strange but I can't leave it like this."

I looked at him, hardly daring to breathe.

"Come with me," he said. "Come with me."

At first I thought he meant to America and my head reeled.

"I can't go to America," I said. "My daughter…"

Rudi grinned.

"Not America," he said. "Not yet anyhow. We're in the middle of a UK tour. We rent a house in Sussex. You know Sussex?"

"It's by the sea," I said.

"Right by the sea," he said. "So, are you coming with me?"

I searched his face. It was crazy. Ridiculous. I had only just met him.

"Yes," I heard myself saying, because in my mind there had never been any doubt at all.

Rudi grinned and let go of my hand.

"Way to go baby," he said. "Way to go."

Alison let me use the phone and I rang Tom and I spoke to Morwenna and told her mummy was on a little bit of an adventure and that I would see her soon. Tom and Sarah were quite happy to keep her for a little bit longer. She was their only grandchild after all.

Rudi used the phone to ring the band who were sleeping in the bus at the farm. I was so impressed they had a phone on the bus.

"Everyone has cell phones in the States," he said.

Not long after, this big black bus pulled up in the lane outside. There were no problems with that bus getting through the lanes. More American technology I supposed.

Polly asked me if I knew what I was doing. What about Chimp. What about Morwenna. What about ***Let's Talk!***. I wasn't worried about ***Let's Talk!***. I could get to the studio from Sussex. And Morwenna could come to live with me. Rudi was fine with that. So, we had it all sussed and so yes, I knew what I was doing.

"You don't even know him Nellie," she said as she stood by the door of their tour bus. "He might be a mad axe wielding maniac."

I grinned at her.

"He isn't," I said. "Trust me."

Rudi came up behind me, slung his arm around my shoulders and grinned at Polly.

"I'll look after her," he said. "Don't worry."

The rest of *Powder Room* welcomed me from the start. They were a tight knit group and there wasn't any of the back biting they had in *The Sons*. Maybe it was because they were all cousins. Maybe it's because they had been playing together since they were kids. Whatever it was it was a very different atmosphere on that bus. They welcomed me and made me feel like I belonged. By the time we stopped for a drink at a service station on the M4, I felt like I was part of the family and I'd never felt like that before.

Polly

I was worried about Nellie going off like that with a man she hardly knew and what Chimp might do when he found out. Most of all I was worried about what would happen to Morwenna.

"Will you stop worrying about everyone else and let me have some time with you?" Vincent said. "We got engaged last night and I'll be heading off soon."

In the whirlwind of what was happening, the concert, the snow, Nellie, I had almost forgotten about him going back to North Wales.

"I don't suppose you're ready to come home yet are you?"

I shook my head. As much as I loved Vincent, I wasn't ready to leave South Wales.

"Not yet," I said. "Not yet."

"Ah well all in good time," he said. "I mean you will come home one day won't you?"

I walked over to him and looped my arms around his neck.

"Of course I will," I said. "I'm going to be Mrs Peters aren't I?"

Vincent smiled and kissed my forehead.

"I'll put our names down for a Council House," he said. "And in the meantime, we can move in with my mum. I mean this strike will be over soon. The men can't stay out much longer can they?"

"Is that what you think?" I asked him, feeling my heart sink a little. "That they'll go back?"

"It's bound to happen," Vincent said. "Bound to."

Chimp

She had a nerve, Nellie, she really did. We flew out to Berlin shortly after that benefit concert in South Wales and I was in Germany not knowing what was happening at home. I telephoned our house in London about four times a day but Nellie never answered. She might have been pissed off because of the earring and because I'd gone off in the bus without her but this was taking the piss. How dare she ignore me! I was also worried about Morwenna and what I was going to do about her being in Wales. How could Nellie just go off and abandon her like that?

Two days after we arrived in Berlin, I rang my dad to discuss what we were going to do.

"Oh it's all sorted," he said. "Joe collected Morwenna yesterday and she's back with her mother. Nothing for you to worry about son."

I was livid.

"Joe collected her?" I said. "And you agreed to it?"

Da sighed down the phone.

"Look," he said. "I don't know what's going on between the two of you and it's none of my business but Nellie rang and the arrangements were made and that's that. I mean you're in Germany. You can't exactly collect her yourself can you?"

I put the phone down and immediately rang Polly but she was as cagey as fuck and wouldn't say anything apart from that Morwenna was with Nellie.

"So where exactly is Nellie for fuck's sake?" I said.

Polly caught her breath.

"There's no need to swear," she said.

I didn't know what to do. I paced up and down my hotel room. I punched walls. I couldn't concentrate on anything and the band avoided me because all I did was snap at them. I was like a lion with a thorn in its paw. In the end I called Rhoswen. She was such a support at that time. I mean, imagine not knowing where your daughter is. Imagine being ignored by your wife and not just ignored but cut out completely with a wall of silence. I didn't eat, I drank too much and I popped too many pills. I couldn't think about anything else.

Rhoswen did some detective work and flew out to Berlin to tell me what she'd discovered. We were in a bar and when she told me, I threw a glass at the wall and we got thrown out. We walked the streets while I ranted and raved about Nellie. I was sleep deprived, high on uppers and addled by alcohol. They were not days I would ever want to live again. And now Rhoswen was telling me Nellie had shacked up with the lead singer of *Powder Room* and that Morwenna, my beautiful little daughter, was living with them.

We caught the next plane home.

Nellie

Extract from her unfinished biography, Street Life

I didn't know love could be like this. I can remember those first weeks like they were yesterday and it's been four years now. When I look back, it's all bathed in a golden, sparkly light. And that is when the darkness in my life ended.

Before I met Rudi, I thought love was drama, arguments, being left alone at night. I didn't know that the proper stuff could be so delicious, so quiet, so gentle, so life affirming. That it was more about shared interests, supporting each other, interpreting the world together and holding hands when the storms raged.

Those first few weeks in the farmhouse in Sussex were like a honeymoon. Rudi says we're still on honeymoon, the longest honeymoon any couple could ever wish for, and that it will continue for ever. I hope so because you can't get complacent can you, I keep expecting it to end, that something will take it away from me but Rudi says that's just the way my mind thinks, the residue of the years I lived through before we met. Spending time at *The Suns of Life* helped but it didn't hoover up everything. There is still stuff I have to deal with when it jumps out at me from behind the bushes but I'm getting there.

The farmhouse in Sussex was by the sea and not the lonely expanse of dark grey foreboding sea of North Wales. This was a different sea. And although it was called a farmhouse, the house where we lived was far more than that.

Rudi and I had the coach house in the grounds and the other three members of *Powder Room* lived in the old farmhouse. Between the two was a small annexe where Toto and Shirley lived. They were a sort of live in couple if you like, who did everything from cooking to cleaning to house repairs.

I loved the coach house. It was warm and cosy and had a real fire. There was one room which had white fur rugs thrown over bare floorboards and nothing else except a grand piano. On summer nights, I'd sit by the French windows, the voile curtains moving in the breeze as Rudi picked out the notes of a new song or played an old one. He always played with a frown on his face, a tumbler of whisky on top of the piano and sometimes a cigarette hanging from his lower lip.

Rudi didn't write songs like Chimp wrote songs. He didn't do it for the money. He didn't do social causes or refugees or shootings in rural areas. He wrote songs about love, about walking out and walking in; about broken hearts and passion and he put them to raw, rough music – bass guitar and sax – and they made you ***feel.*** They really did. ***Mesmerise*** is my absolute favourite. It's about how love can hijack the senses and hypnotise every part of your heart and mind.

Despite the passion and the drama of those songs, Rudi wasn't like that in real life. He was funny, steady, the life and soul. He didn't walk out or walk in to make his point. He just was.

"It's all the different blood in me," he'd say. "And it comes out in the music, a little bit Cuban, a little bit Salsa, a little bit native American."

Madonna released ***Crazy for You*** in June 1985. It seemed that whenever I turned on the radio it was playing. That's our song. It always reminds me of the summer of 1985, our first summer together. And yes, I'm still crazy about Rudi Delawayo. Head over heels crazy.

Polly

I didn't expect people to react in the way that they did. All I wanted to do was help and so when David Wilkie's cousin contacted me, I thought the least I could do was give them some of the money we'd raised from the benefit concert.

I was excited about the meeting, excited about letting the women know exactly how much we'd raised for the miners and I sat upstairs in the WAPC room as they came in and took their seats.

I'd done all the work. I'd arranged the concert, collected the ticket money, marshalled the bands on the night and I'd loved every minute. I was almost sorry it was over.

Alison opened the meeting and ran through the agenda as she always did. We remained brightly optimistic despite the cracks appearing in the solid front the men presented to the world, despite some of them drifting back to work.

"And now over to Polly whose got some good news about the concert," she said, beaming at me. The women gave me a round of applause and when it died away, I started to speak.

"We raised over £2,000," I said proudly, looking at the written figures set out in front of me. "To be donated as follows. £500 for repairs to the roof at the Welfare, £500 to the children's group, £1,500 to the miner's funds and £500 to Pauline Mason. She's the cousin of David Wilkie," I added. "You know, the taxi driver who got killed at Heads of Valley last November."

I sat back in my chair and waited for more applause but it didn't come. Instead the women remained silent and stiff and stared at me.

Alison stood up to break the awkward atmosphere and addressed the women in front of us.

"I believe there's been a mistake with that last entry," she said. "We'll be cancelling it and adding the money to the miners' hardship fund instead."

I stared at her.

"But I've already promised," I said, my heart thumping in my chest. "And Mick Marshall's signed the cheque. I sent it out in the post last night."

A gasp ran around the room and the smile slipped from Alison's face.

"You had no right to do that!" Julie Jones said, standing up and pointing her finger at me. "You had no right! Ever since you came here you've thought you're better than the rest of us!"

Alison stood up again.

"Sit down please Julie. There's no need to be like that."

"But she's right!" another woman added. "She had no right! What does it look like eh? Like we're supporting the scabs that's what!"

"David Wilkie was the taxi driver," Alison said patiently. "Not the miner. I'm sure Polly did it for all the right reasons."

"Taking a scab to work he was!" another woman said. "We don't give money to scabs! They should be supporting the miners, not helping the government get the scabs to work!"

Things were getting heated. The women were all standing now and I was glad there was a table between us. Alison waved her hands to try to get them to calm down. She was on her feet, facing a barrage of angry women whilst I sat at the table wishing the floor would open up and swallow me whole.

"I think we all need to calm down," Alison said. "Let's go home and sleep on this and we'll come back tomorrow with fresh eyes."

The women muttered and started to filter out of the door but not before they cast long, reproachful glances at me. I looked down at the table.

"I'm sorry," I said but I don't think any of them heard me. "I'm sorry."

Life in Merthyr changed from that moment on. When I worked in the kitchens, the women remained silent and didn't speak to me. Not even Julie Jones, my vegetable stealing companion, would speak to me.

Alison was the only one who showed any kindness and of course I was still living in her house but the atmosphere was uncomfortable and at night, instead of joining them for tea at the table as I usually did, I got into the habit of taking toast up to my room and eating it with Sidney.

Joe didn't think it was anything to worry about.

"Aye well maybe you shouldn't have done it Polly but you didn't mean any harm, I know you didn't. It will blow over. It will all blow over."

It didn't. People spat in the street when I walked past or crossed the road when I approached. I was bewildered.

One night, in the kitchen, Frank sat down at the table and could hardly look me in the eye.

"Maybe it's best you go home," he said. "You've been a great help to the women down here Polly but sometimes things come to an end. Sometimes it's best to move on."

He did it so gently. I could see the regret and sadness in his eyes but they'd had a few windows smashed and his pushbike had been twisted up and it wasn't because Frank and his sons were out on strike. It was because I was living there. I didn't know how to make it right.

"You can't," Vincent said when I rang him from the phone box sobbing my heart out and looking out at the rain and the mist hanging over the hills. "You can't make it right. It's too big, it's beyond you."

"But I gave them everything I had," I sniffed. "I've put my heart and soul into this for the last ten months."

"I know," he sighed. "Come home now Polly. Come home."

Chimp

We found them with the help of a private detective who traced them to a farmhouse in Sussex. I don't know how he did it but he certainly charged for the pleasure. As soon as we found out where they were, I wanted to get in the car and drive there immediately but Rhoswen pointed out it was ten o'clock at night and said we should sleep on it and think it through in the morning. Rhoswen is so sensible! She really did keep my feet on the ground during those dreadful weeks when I didn't know where Morwenna was.

The next morning, we left London early and headed off to Sussex.

Nellie

Extract from her unfinished biography, Street Life

He didn't do it because he loved me. He did it because he wanted Morwenna and couldn't bear to think I'd taken her away from him. I think he thought it was a competition but for me it was just life. I had fallen out of love with him and in love with Rudi. It was a simple as that.

I didn't tear Morwenna away from her family home as he liked to put it later on. I just took her with me. She was my daughter. What else would I do?

I was sitting out by the pool enjoying the warm Spring sunshine when Chimp turned up. Rudi had gone for a run and Morwenna was splashing about at the shallow end of the pool when there was all this banging on the front door.

I thought that either Shirley or Toto would answer it. After all, they were the ones who did everything about the place, cleaning, cooking, you name it, they did it.

Suddenly Shirley walked out through the French windows making strange faces at me and before she could say anything, Chimp crashed into paradise.

"What the hell do you think you're doing?!"

I got up from the sun lounger and I lifted Morwenna out of the pool and held her close to me. A cloud passed across the sun and Shirley hopped from one foot to another.

"Shall I get Toto?" she said.

Chimp swung round and glared at her.

"Who the fuck are you anyway?" he said.

"Don't swear in front of Morwenna," I said, feeling cold despite the warmth of the sun. "Shirley lives here."

Chimp looked around him.

"Oh," he said. "A *menage a trois*. I might have guessed."

I didn't know what that meant but before I could say anything, Rhoswen came through the curtains on to the patio.

"My daughter's coming home with me," Chimp said stepping forward and trying to grab Morwenna. Morwenna's face crumpled and she shied away from him and hid her face in my shoulder.

"What have you done to her?" he fumed. "You've poisoned her against me haven't you? You've poisoned her."

Chimp looked dreadful. He hadn't shaved and he looked like he'd been sleeping in his clothes for weeks. I mean Chimp was never turned out like a city gent but this time he was even more of a mess and he stunk like a polecat. No wonder Morwenna was scared. I swung her to my other hip and Rhoswen stepped in.

"We just want to talk Nellie," she said in that low man's voice of hers.

I glared at her. She might have wanted to talk but I wanted to punch her in the face and push her in the pool. My heart was pounding.

"I think this is between me and Chimp," I said. "Don't you? "

"Suit yourself," she shrugged, stepping back. "I'm just trying to help."

I didn't care about Chimp anymore but Rhoswen made me mad. I mean she had probably been carrying on with him behind my back for years and now she was standing on the patio in my house acting like the United Nations.

"It's a bit late for that isn't it?"

Shirley was almost biting her nails off.

"Shall I ring the police?" she said.

I handed Morwenna to her and told her to take her inside. I didn't want her getting any more upset than she already was.

"She's coming home with me," Chimp said after she'd gone, pointing his finger at me. "There's laws about this sort of stuff. You can't just take her away from me."

I don't know how I stayed so calm I really don't. And I don't know what I would have done if Rudi hadn't arrived. He always came in from a run the back way and as he ran in, he quickly sized up the situation and stopped by the pool instead of jumping into it, like he usually did.

"Rudi Delawayo," he said, holding out his hand to Chimp. "Pleased to meet you."

Polly

It was strange going back home to Ffynnongroyw and even stranger for me and Sidney to move in with Vincent and his mum.

When I got back, I went round to see Mam and Da. Their house was cold and Mam moaned at me for keeping the door open and letting the heat out.

"So how's Da?" I said as I stood awkwardly in the kitchen of the house I'd grown up in.

"How do you think he is?" she said.

There was no answer to that and I didn't stay long.

A few days later, on 4th March 1985, I was sitting at the breakfast table when we heard the letter box go and Vincent went out to fetch the paper. He came back into the kitchen with his eyes glued to the front page of the Daily Express.

"That's it then," he said. "Strike's over."

I stared at him.

"What do you mean?" I said.

"The NUM have voted for the miners to return to work," he said. "Ninety eight votes to ninety one."

I stood up and he held the paper out to me so I could read the headlines.

"Has the Government agreed to keep the pits open?" I said.

Vincent scanned the words and shook his head slowly.

"It doesn't say so here," he said.

I sank down on to a chair.

"Well they must have come to some agreement," I said. "Otherwise, what was it all about?"

Vincent sighed and threw the paper onto the draining board.

"You tell me," he said. "You tell me."

I stood up, my brain working in overdrive.

"I need to ring Joe," I said. "Have you got any ten pees?"

Vincent put his hand in his trouser pocket and drew out a handful of silver coins.

"Aren't you going to get dressed first?" he said.

"No," I said.

"I'll come with you," Vincent said, fetching his donkey jacket. "Come on."

So we walked down the road to the phone box with me in my dressing gown and I didn't care if people stared at me. People were always staring and muttering but it wasn't because I went out in my dressing gown.

Vincent waited outside the phone box as I dialled the number of Joe's digs and pushed ten pence pieces into the slot.

"Have you heard?" I said as soon as he answered.

"Aye," he said. "Aye I've heard. Some of the boys are saying it's not legal, that the agreement isn't worth the paper it's written on. They can't just tell us to go back to work. We'll stay out until we get an agreement that no more mines will close. We'll stay out for ever if that's what it takes. This isn't over. This isn't over by a long chalk."

I heard the fighting talk, I heard Joe's anger but in my heart of hearts I knew they'd lost. I knew it was all over.

That afternoon, Vincent and I walked down to Coed y Garth woods. It was too early for bluebells and the fields were empty. We stopped and I looked up at the winding wheel of Point looming high against the sky.

"How long?" I said. "How long has Point got left? How long have any of the mines got left?"

Vincent lit a cigarette and blew out the smoke before answering.

"Sometimes it's best not to look too far ahead," he said.

Polly

These mist covered mountains
Are a home for me now
But my home was the lowlands
And always will be
Someday you'll return to
Your valleys and farms
And you'll no longer burn to be
Brothers in Arms
Through these fields of destruction
Baptism of fire
I've watched all your suffering
As the battle raged high
And though they did hurt me so bad
In the fear and alarm
You did not desert me
My brothers in arms
- Dire Straits, Brothers in Arms

That was the song that played through my mind as I watched the miners returning to work on the TV. They marched proudly behind their colliery banners with their heads held high as the newsreader summarised the story of the miners' strike.

Just days after the NUM capitulated, the Government put their accelerated closure plan in place and started closing mines. The public was told it was cheaper to import coal from Columbia and Australia and America than it was to dig it up in Britain.

The miners who had worked through the strike blamed the miners who had gone on strike and the miners who had gone on strike blamed those who had worked. Every day when Vincent came off shift, he told me about the fights and arguments that had broken out at Point.

It wasn't just the miners who were divided, it was the families too. Da and Tom Horse, who'd known each other forever, still refused to drink together in the Welfare and when I went to the shops, women who had known me since I was a little girl crossed the road to avoid me and men who'd worked with Joe spat in the street.

"They'll get over it in time," Vincent said. "They'll get over it."

Most of the town had supported the men who remained working and a girl who had gone to South Wales to support the striking miners was never going to be welcome.

There were other changes too: the Toy Shop had closed down and Mrs Murgatroyd had gone to Birmingham and Nanny Gwynn had gone to a nursing home in Rhyl after she nearly set her bungalow on fire.

Ffynnongroyw might have looked the same on the surface but it wasn't the same underneath. There were so many consequences of the Miners' Strike that you never read about in the newspapers. It changed the mining communities for ever: it shattered them into pieces, threw them up in the air and as the pieces floated back down to earth, they never made the same shape again.

Nellie

Extract from her unfinished biography, Street Life

After Chimp and Rhoswen left that day, I was shaking. I was so scared Chimp would just grab Morwenna and run. He was in that sort of mood. Dark and unpredictable. It's a good job that Rudi came back when he did.

Rudi was nothing but the diplomat. He suggested we all go inside, sit down and try to work something out. Chimp wasn't having any of it.

"You haven't heard the last of this," he said, jabbing his finger at me before he left.

After he'd gone I felt so unsettled I had to have a drink. Shirley brought it out to me by the pool and told me there were some black bags dumped outside the front door. My stuff. All my stuff. Just dumped there without a word.

"What if he tries to take her away?" I asked Rudi.

Rudi reassured me that Chimp wouldn't do anything, that he was full of bullshit and what could he do anyway? I was Morwenna's mother. I had rights.

I sat with Morwenna on my lap for ages as she played with Mr Boo. I kept kissing her hair even though she wanted to run and play. I didn't want to let go. It was like I had a premonition that our time together was limited.

If only Chimp had been more reasonable we could have worked something out but it was like he'd declared war, it really was.

The next day I went to the doctor who said I needed to get more sleep. He refused to give me any tablets to help me get that sleep or calm my nerves. Toto came to the rescue. He had every pill you could think of to make the sun come out and Shirley was so kind, always fetching them for me when she sensed I was on edge.

I thought we could trust Toto and Shirley, I really did. I didn't know they would turn out to be snakes in the grass I thought was so green.

Chimp

Morwenna was two in May 1985 and I didn't get to see her on her birthday. I was all for driving to Sussex and demanding time with her but Rhoswen persuaded me to get out of the car and telephone Nellie instead. It wasn't the same speaking to Morwenna on the phone. How do you speak to a two year old on the phone? I'd bought her a singing dinosaur and I so wanted to see her face when she ripped open the wrapping paper but it wasn't to be.

The band were falling apart. Boots got arrested for possessing heroin and headbutted the police officer who arrested him. *The Sun* had fun with that one, plastering it across their front page under the heading *Sons of Satan.*

George and I seemed to wind each other up just by being in the same room and as for Menace, well he fell in love with a Russian girl and dreamed of going to live in Moscow. Moscow!

The biggest thing that caused the band to split though, was my decision not to play Live Aid in July 1985. In the autobiography George wrote years later, he described me as "self opinionated and difficult to work with". But the truth was, I wasn't in the mood to play Live Aid and I refused to play it. I didn't think it would be as big as it was or as iconic as it came to be. So I'll admit I was wrong about that one but that didn't mean I was self opinionated did it? He wrote three pages about Live Aid in that book. He was still stewing over it years later.

To be honest I had other fish to fry at that time. And in the true spirit of all rock bands, I thought we could take a break and go back a little while later and everything would be the same. What you don't realise is that your fans are fickle: they move on and the music scene changes. New bands come up all the time and fans switch allegiances.

The gigs were falling away and I hadn't written a song for months. I was stressed out over Morwenna and was in the process of selling our house in London. It was too Nellie for me and I couldn't stand being there.

"Why don't we just go back to the cottage in Wrexham?" Rhoswen suggested. "Take a break for a while. Get back to our roots. I've had enough of Greenham Common anyway."

It seemed a perfect solution and so that is what we did.

Nellie

Extract from her unfinished biography, Street Life

At Home With Nellie. That's what they called it. A double page spread in *The News of the World* Sunday supplement. I loved it! I got to wear some beautiful clothes and pose around the swimming pool. The photographer took a photograph of me and Rudi lying on our Queen sized bed surrounded by pink fluffy cushions and another one of me in rubber gloves dressed up like a 1950s housewife in a head scarf pretending to clean the toilet with a brush. That one was just for fun.

The journalist wanted my views on Chimp and what I thought about the band breaking up but I didn't want to slag him off in the papers and so I just said I wished him well and when they pushed me for reasons for our break up, I said we had fallen out of love with each other.

I don't know why it wound him up so much but when the article came out, he got on the phone and let off a whole trail of abuse at me. After I put the phone down, I had to take three Xanax to take the edge off.

It didn't take much to wind him up at that time. He wasn't in a good place with the band splitting up and he did become a bit obsessed about me and Morwenna. It was almost like he couldn't bear us to be so happy when he was so miserable and I lived on edge wondering what he might do next.

I interviewed Rudi on ***Let's Talk!*** and I put him in my book ***Sex in Socks*** which was published in September '85. It sold like hot cakes and the picture of him, well, it smouldered to be honest but that's Rudi. I sometimes wonder what a man like him ever sees in me. I mean he is one hundred per cent stunning inside and out and he's had some beautiful girlfriends. He says they are like books he read and enjoyed at the time but now they're back on the shelf. I used to feel a little insecure about that. I mean was I just another book? Another story? And he'd laugh and say I was the story to end all stories, his magnum opus, his masterpiece.

Our life was perfect. Rudi was like a father to Morwenna. He used to sit her on his knee when he was playing the piano and she'd reach out her little hands and he'd hold them and pretend it was her making the music and she'd look up into his face in wonder at what her hands were doing and he'd laugh. Music just came out of him. We could be anywhere and he'd start scribbling in a notebook or say

"What do you think about this?"

We tried to be reasonable about Chimp seeing Morwenna. Rudi used to speak to Rhoswen – I couldn't – on the phone and arrange when they could come and collect her and take her out. I resisted her staying overnight with them because I just didn't trust him to bring her back. It wasn't anything else. It wasn't me being difficult or having to have things my way like he tried to make out later on.

But Chimp never stuck to the plans. He would arrive on days we hadn't arranged or at odd hours of the day or night. He didn't understand that she was going to a party or that we had other plans or why he couldn't drive her down to Wales at three o'clock in the morning. He always made a scene and it became exhausting. Rudi was away touring for a while and he'd ring me every night and tell me not to stress over Chimp, that things would settle down. They didn't settle down. Chimp continued to make life as difficult as possible and on the days I allowed him to take Morwenna to see her grandparents in Ffynnongroyw, I took extra Xanax to calm the fear he wouldn't bring her back again.

When Rudi got home, he tried to reason with him on the phone.

"C'mon man," he'd say. "This isn't the way to go about things. We had a plan. Let's stick to it."

It didn't work. Chimp just kept on doing what he wanted to do.

Polly

In May 1985, two men received life sentences for the murder of the taxi driver, David Wilkie. When the news broke, 700 miners In South Wales walked out in protest. Four years later, their conviction for murder was reduced to manslaughter and their sentences cut to four years. When the news broke, seven hundred miners walked out of Cwm in South Wales in protest.

Most of the miners were back at work by this time. The pits in South Wales and Kent held out the longest but in the end they didn't have much choice. The government knew they were in a stronger position and refused to agree that only mines that were uneconomically viable should be closed.

At the end of the year, Joe came back from South Wales and he and Lisa rented a house near Coed y Garth. None of his old friends from Point would speak to him and he couldn't get his old job back.

"Why did you come back?" I asked him one day as we walked in the woods.

Joe made up something about wanting to come home but it didn't really ring true. He had been settled in South Wales and had seemed happy there. Years later Lisa told me it was because he'd had a fight with Cwm's colliery manager that had ended up with him in hospital. He was a local man and despite the friendships Joe had made, despite standing next to the men day in day out on that picket line, some of the men turned against him and Frank had suggested he come home.

Joe never said it but he must have felt like a drifter: not welcome here or there.

It was one more dark cloud he had to live with.

1986

Nellie

Extract from her unfinished biography, Street Life

On 4th January 1986, Phil Lynott, the lead singer with the rock band *Thin Lizzy*, died. He was 37 years old. Rudi was devastated. He'd played with *Thin Lizzy*, he said, a couple of years back at the Reading Rock Festival.

Rudi's reaction to Phil Lynott's death wasn't the same as Chimp's reaction to the death of Sid Vicious on my sixteenth birthday. He was just quietly sad.

"He was only thirty seven," he said. "All that talent. Gone."

For the next few days, the farmhouse reverberated with the sounds of ***The Boys are Back in Town, Don't Believe a Word*** and ***Whisky in the Jar.*** The *Powder Room* boys knew how to party and I went right along with them. Morwenna was staying in Wales with Chimp's parents and partying took the edge off my fears that he wouldn't bring her back. I stayed up all night, we slept most of the day and then the band gradually sobered up as the date for them to tour the States came closer.

Powder Room had been touring England since I met Rudi but England was proving a difficult nut to crack.

"Are you coming back?" I asked him the night they were due to fly out.

"Hey," he said, coming over to me and putting his arms around me. "Where did that come from?"

I shrugged.

"You think I'd do that?" he said, pulling me closer to him. "Leave the two most precious things in my life behind? I won't be away for long honey. I'll be back before you know it. And when I come back we'll get this Chimp stuff sorted ok?"

I leaned into his warmth. Rudi always made everything feel safe and strong.

Polly

Vincent and I celebrated the New Year with a bottle of Blue Nun and a pizza from the Co-op. His mum got a little maudlin as she listened to old Frank Sinatra records and Sidney vomited up a mouse on our bed so it was definitely one to remember.

"So," Vincent said. "What do you think about setting the 12th July for our wedding day? The pit will be on shut down and we might even get some good weather."

I felt so happy but poor Elizabeth started crying all over again. It wasn't easy for her. She had been a widow for so long.

Chimp

In early 1986, we drove down to see Grace in Swansea. I felt guilty we hadn't seen her for several months but my focus had been on Morwenna.

"You didn't come," Grace said when we got there. "You didn't come on Christmas Day."

I crouched down and looked into her face and felt a pang of guilt.

"I'm sorry," I said. "I was up in Ffynnongroyw at Christmas with Morwenna."

Something flickered in her eyes and a shadow crossed her face.

"Oh Morwenna Morwenna Morwenna!" she said, stamping her foot and turning away from me. "That's all you care about! You don't care about me!"

Rhoswen caught her arm to stop her running up the stairs and we exchanged a look over her head.

"It's not like that *cariad*," she said gently, crouching down to speak to her. "It's just Chimp doesn't get to see her much these days."

Grace was nearly fifteen but sometimes she acted like she was five.

"I'm sorry Grace," I said. "Things have been a bit difficult but we're living in Wrexham now and you can come and stay whenever you like. You can have your own room if you want."

Grace stared at me.

"Can I paint it black?"

"If you like," I said. "If you like."

"And can I live there all the time?"

I looked at Rhoswen.

"You live here," I said. "With Megan and Paul."

"But I'd rather live with you," she said, putting her arms around my waist and resting her head against my stomach. "I'd rather live with you."

I lifted her arms and gently disentangled her.

"We'll see shall we. We'll see."

Afterwards, when we were having a cup of tea with Megan and Paul, they told us how difficult she'd been at Christmas.

"Maybe it might do her good to get a change of scenery," Megan sighed. "Because sometimes I honestly don't know what to do with her."

Nellie

Extract from her unfinished biography, Street Life

I once asked Rudi why they had called the band *Powder Room.* His eyes twinkled as he rolled a joint and he took his time before he answered.

"*Powder Room* is where the ladies go," he said. "So the boys say."

Powder Room never really made it in the UK despite their best efforts. Rudi said the UK market was notoriously hard to crack for an American band and they were always bigger in the States and Canada and Australia than they ever were here.

Rudi is a contradiction and he fascinates me. One minute he's prowling around the stage looking like he tames wild animals for a living and the next he's sitting quietly under a lamp reading a book on philosophy. He never really lets things get under his skin. He didn't take it personally that the band couldn't break the UK. He just took it in his stride. Maybe that's why we work so well together. I liven him up and he calms me down!

It was about that time, early in 1986, that Chimp told me Grace was living with him and Rhoswen in Wrexham. It was just before Morwenna was due to go to Wales to spend time with her grandparents.

"So she'll be staying with us instead," he said, just like that.

I didn't want Morwenna near Grace. I had never forgotten the day I found her with her mouth bound with Sellotape.

"She's not staying in Wrexham if Grace is there," I said. "You can see her at your mum and dad's."

"You can't dictate to me what I can and can't do," Chimp said. "I'm her father. I've got rights."

"I've got more," I said. "I'm her mother."

There was an awkward silence for a moment.

"Why do you have to be so difficult about everything?" he said. "And why do you have to be so unkind about Grace. She's just a fifteen year old girl."

"She's more than that," I said. "Only you can't see it."

"Nellie…"

I put the phone down. That was the end of it as far as I was concerned.

He didn't let it go, of course he didn't. He started to ring at all hours of the day and night and we had some terrible arguments. Rudi tried to speak to him but Chimp refused to listen so in the end I stopped answering the phone.

So there we were. I was refusing to let Chimp take Morwenna and he was going mad on the phone. Secretly I felt pleased that finally I was the one with the power. Is it wrong to say that? I don't know. All I know is that it was the first time in our relationship that I held the strings. And he didn't like that one bit.

I drank more, I took more drugs to blot it out. I used to dread that phone ringing. He used to ring at all hours of the day and night, three o'clock in the morning sometimes. Why didn't I just let the answerphone take it? Because he'd fill up the tape with long rambling vitriolic messages I didn't want Morwenna to hear.

I thought that leaving Chimp and being with Rudi would be a much easier life. It was in many ways apart from what was going on with Chimp. He wasn't going to let go that easily. Not when he wanted Morwenna.

Polly

We got married at Brethnaer village church on Saturday 12th July 1986. Vincent chose July so it didn't clash with the World Cup!

I asked Nellie to be a matron of honour but she refused. I don't think she liked the idea of being a matron! But to be fair, she had all this stuff going on with Chimp and when she came to the wedding, she'd lost a lot of weight, not that there was much of her to start with.

I always had so much time for Rudi. He had this way of listening to you, of being so quietly courteous. It still breaks my heart when I think of what happened to him. He was a lovely man, very special. I could see why Nellie loved him so much.

He was also very good with Morwenna who looked so pretty in a little blue dress with a matching ribbon in her hair. She had this gorgeous long dark brown hair and blue eyes. She was such a pretty little girl and now she's a beautiful woman.

Best of all, Da came to the wedding to give me away. Walking down the aisle holding his arm meant the world to me. Since I'd returned to Ffynnongroyw he had been distant and difficult with me but he had always thought a lot of Vincent and they still worked together at Point.

"Make sure you look after her," he told Vincent afterwards. "She doesn't always do what she's told but she's a good girl at heart."

Joe came in a suit he hired from Moss Bros and spent most of the time watching Nellie and Morwenna and if Lisa noticed, she was too polite to say anything. When you look at the photographs, you wouldn't believe there were so many ripples going on under the surface that day. Every one looks happy, like they are supposed to do at a wedding.

We couldn't afford a honeymoon so Nellie invited us to the farm in Sussex.

"We're right by the sea and we've got a pool," she said. "And a lovely guest bedroom that looks out over the water."

We went to stay during the last week in August 1986. What a wash out it was! They say 1986 was the wettest summer of the 20th century and I remember Bank Holiday Monday was atrocious. We stayed inside as the rain ran down the windows and I kept looking at my wedding ring and pinching myself because I couldn't believe I was Mrs Vincent Peters.

I didn't see anything odd at the house. Unless you count Shirley and that strange boy Toto. Well he wasn't a boy he was a sort of a man, maybe something in between. The Judge asked me questions about it later, whether I'd noticed anything but I honestly couldn't say I had. It wasn't like they made out. They weren't living a drug crazed bohemian lifestyle at the farmhouse like they said in the papers. It wasn't like that at all.

Chimp

We didn't get invited to Polly's wedding. She said it would cause too much trouble because Nellie and Rudi were going.

Oh Nellie and Rudi, Rudi and Nellie! Weren't their stars burning bright? He was no threat to me. I mean who were *Powder Room* anyway? They hadn't had three number one singles in the UK. They couldn't even get into the top forty! I watched her interview him on that stupid ***Let's Talk!*** Programme. And then I opened the Sunday paper one day and there they were beaming out at me from their farmhouse in Sussex. They were everywhere and the more I saw them the angrier I got that they had got away with stealing my daughter and playing happy families. That's how I saw it anyway.

"Social climbers," Rhoswen said when she saw the double page spread in the Sunday papers. "They're the sort of people who only put value in material possessions. They're shallow, that's what they are. Shallow."

It was certainly a world away from how we lived. We lived in a cottage without running water and now we had a teenage girl living with us. We lived a quiet life which is just what we wanted but when we went into Wrexham, there were men begging on the streets and sleeping in doorways. There were empty shops and long queues outside the dole office and Margaret Thatcher would appear on the telly at night saying how Britain was working again. I have always admired her but sometimes I wasn't sure what planet she was on.

"Do you know there's over 3 million unemployed people in the UK?" Rhoswen said to me one morning as we sat at the breakfast table. "For the fifth year in a row."

Meibion Glyndwr was still operating but they'd stopped fire setting when a more moderate leadership took over. Rhoswen had disagreed with their approach and no longer attended their meetings but her social conscience was as raw as ever and needed somewhere to land.

"What do you think about setting up a charity?" she said. "To help the unemployed in Wales? We could run drop in centres, help people find work and offer the families a hot meal while we're at it. How they survive on the dole I don't know."

I stared at her. I wasn't feeling particularly charitable. The situation with Nellie and Morwenna was eating me up.

"Do you good to focus on something else," she said. "The Coal Board's selling off a lot of land and I've got my inheritance."

"I don't know," I sighed. "I don't know."

"Well I do," she said. "And I'm going to do it, with or without your support."

Our first Hope Centre opened in Liverpool in 1987 and over the next five years, we opened twenty Hope Centres in the North West of England and Yorkshire. I have always believed Rhoswen could run the world if she put her mind to it and I still believe that now.

Nellie

Extract from her unfinished biography, Street Life

It is true that at times, we smoked heroin but I swear to God that we didn't ever keep it in the house. It was something we did occasionally when the band had an impromptu party so the stuff they found in our kitchen drawer must have belonged to Toto and Shirley. It wasn't ours and it didn't belong to any of the band.

The Judge dismissed my theory as ***fanciful***, saying that sadly, he saw this behaviour all too often in those who lived our sort of lifestyle, in people who thought the laws about possessing drugs didn't apply to them.

He was a pompous old fart that Judge and the police who arrested us were even worse.

Polly

The first we knew of Rudi and Nellie being arrested for possessing heroin was when we saw them on the BBC News leaving a London police station with the Press charging after them with cameras and microphones. Nellie was wearing dark sunglasses. She looked so thin and pale.

Vincent stared at the telly with his mouth open.

"I don't bloody believe it," he said. "Possession of heroin? They're no more heroin users than I am."

Vincent, went into the kitchen and got himself a beer and that's saying something because it was a Wednesday night and Vincent never drinks beer on a Wednesday night.

I tried to ring Nellie but there was no answer and it was three days before we managed to speak. When we did, Nellie was a complete mess.

"They've taken Morwenna," she sobbed. "They've taken Morwenna Polly and I don't know what to do."

I spoke to Rudi who made more sense. He sounded quietly shocked, that's the only way I can describe it, but at least I got more information out of him. He said the police had raided in the middle of the night and found heroin in the kitchen drawer.

"It wasn't ours," he said. "It definitely wasn't ours and I don't know how it got there."

"Where's Morwenna?" I asked closing my eyes and dreading the answer.

"Social Services took her to her grandparents in Wales," he said. "I keep trying to ring them but they're not answering."

I asked him if he wanted us to come. We didn't have a car, we were miles away but I would have got there somehow.

"Let's see how things are in the morning," he said. "It's late and the doctor has given Nellie an injection to help her sleep. I'll look after her. Don't worry. I'll look after her."

When Rudi said that you knew it was true. He was so good to Nellie. He accepted her for all she was and I don't think any man has done that before. When she burned, he put out her fire. He was such a gentle person for all his wild antics on stage. I still get this pang deep in my heart when I think about what happened to him. The night they got arrested put a whole chain of events into motion we couldn't imagine would end the way they did.

I came off the phone and I burst into tears. I just felt so much for Nellie and Morwenna. What had happened? Why had they taken her away like that?

"That's what they do," Vincent said, folding me into his arms. "That's what they do."

It was the sort of night that made you want to do something comforting like eat rice pudding and watch Des O'Connor on the telly.

So that's what we did.

Chimp

Nellie had some fanciful idea that I planted the heroin in the kitchen drawer and tipped off the police. All I'll say to that is if you dabble in drugs, you have to take the consequences. At that time she blamed me for everything and even if it rained, I suspect it was my fault.

It's not right is it? Taking drugs when there's a young child in the house? Mothers should be role models, standing at the stove and baking cakes not getting off their heads on chemical substances every night.

We had a flurry of phonecalls from the police and Social Services when Nellie and Rudi got arrested. I wanted Morwenna to come and stay with us but Grace threw a tantrum and locked herself in the bathroom so I suggested my parents' address instead. When I rang mum and dad, they were shocked to hear Nellie had been arrested and were only too happy to give sanctuary to Morwenna. I don't think my mum knew what drugs were. She didn't even take aspirin.

Morwenna arrived at my parents' house in a police car in the middle of the night and I was there to meet her. It was so good to have her home. I picked her up and I breathed her in and she pushed my nose and said ***daddy.*** She took it all in her stride. She didn't even question why she had been driven all the way to Wales in the middle of the night. As long as she had Mr Boo the world was alright with her.

The next morning I went to see a solicitor and I started proceedings to get custody of my daughter. It's what any father would do isn't it?

Nellie

Extract from her unfinished biography, Street Life

Our lives changed from that moment on. I'll never forget the way armed police broke into our house in the middle of the night, leaving mud on the carpets, shouting at us and telling us to stay where we were as if we had guns, as if we were hardened criminals on the run. We were in bed, we'd been asleep, we were hardly likely to do anything. I didn't know they could just come into your house like that but there was a lot I didn't know at the time.

Rudi kept trying to find out what was going on but they told him to shut up and stay where he was. They opened cupboards and drawers and threw everything on the floor and there wasn't anything we could do about it. I was worried about Morwenna but they wouldn't let me go to her and she remained asleep in her bedroom at the back of the house.

They found the heroin in the kitchen drawer and as soon as they found it the police got angry. They read our rights to us and pushed us out of the house into two separate police cars. Rudi whispered to me before we separated not to say anything and to make sure I got a lawyer. I didn't want to be separated from him but they tore me away and pushed me into the back of the second car.

I was kept in a cell for hours with only my thoughts for company. I wanted to know where my daughter was but they wouldn't tell me anything. They just kept me shut up in this cell with its ghastly yellow painted walls and a thin navy blue mattress.

I was dying for the loo but I didn't want to use the one in the cell in case they were watching me on the camera.

A duty solicitor came and told me not to say anything. I don't know if that was a mistake or not because I wanted to say something, I wanted to tell the police that the heroin wasn't ours and that I had no idea it was in the kitchen drawer. He said that wouldn't do me any good and it was best to say no comment to all their questions.

The police don't like it when you say no comment. They take it personally. They make out that you're on your last chance and that serious things will happen if you don't speak to them. I didn't know that at the time. I had never been arrested before, I was in an alien world and I think the police enjoyed having Nellie on the Telly and the lead singer from

Powder Room locked up in their provincial police station like our celebrity status bestowed something important on them.

They kept us there all night and it was the longest night of my life. There's something about being anxious and alone at three o'clock in the morning that is horrific at the worst of times let alone when you're in a police cell. It was bloody freezing and they hadn't even let me take a coat from the house. I'd grabbed the nearest thing I could find when they barked their orders to get out of bed and get dressed and I was wearing a thin t-shirt and a pair of jeans. I needed a shower. I needed Rudi. I needed to know where Morwenna was. It's amazing how quickly you can go from being a glamorous woman on the telly to being a dirty urchin in the police station. Life can turn on the head of a pin.

I pressed the cell bell all through the night and I kept asking the same thing.

"Where's my daughter? Please tell me where my daughter is."

And they kept giving me the same answer:

"Stop ringing the bell."

In the morning I was taken to the sergeant's desk, told to sign some papers and released on bail. I was standing outside shivering when Rudi called my name and came up behind me and I felt the sudden warmth of his leather jacket around my shoulders.

The Press must have been camping outside the police station all night because they suddenly appeared from behind the bushes and trees and Rudi grabbed my hand and we ran. I felt such a mess as well, so dirty, and they kept snapping away, taking our photographs like we were some sort of public property, some sort of animals released from a cage at the zoo.

We ran into a phone box where Rudi rang Ricky Rich and asked him to come and get us. Even then the Press didn't let up, banging on the glass and trying to open the door. Rudi kept one hand against it and his other arm around me. I honestly thought that if they got in they would kill us. They were like a pack of wolves.

It seemed like only minutes later that Ricky Rich came screeching around the corner in his Opel Manta like something out of *Starsky and Hutch*. When he saw us in the phone box, he leapt out of the driver's door, pushing people out of his way so that he could get to us. He yanked open the door, shielding us from the men pushing up behind him and we made a run for the car. They got in our faces, they flashed light bulbs, they shoved microphones under our chins and Ricky Rich pushed them all away and if, in the scuffle, his fist happened to make contact with some of their faces that was their problem wasn't it? He got done for that later on, believe it or not. Done for assault.

"Fuck that," was his verdict. "They were lucky I wasn't loaded."

Somehow we bundled into the car, somehow Ricky managed to get us away and I collapsed into Rudi's arms in the back seat. They carried on running after the car for a while but Ricky Rich was driving so fast they didn't have a chance.

When we got back to the house we stood in the doorway and stared at the mess the police had made.

"Fuck man," Ricky Rich said, shaking his head. "The Feds did this?"

I ran upstairs to Morwenna's room but her bed was empty. I screamed and Rudi ran up after me and told me it was alright, he was going to sort it all out, he would make some phonecalls, it was alright.

It took quite a few phonecalls to find out where she was. I sat on the sofa in numb disbelief. I couldn't believe people could take my daughter away and had no obligation to tell me where she was.

Toto and Shirley were nowhere to be seen so Ricky Rich rolled me a joint and told me to inhale deep and slow. It took the edge off and I needed to take the edge off. It was all too horrible, too stark, too nightmarish to comprehend sober.

"Why the fuck didn't you put the heroin in some other place?" he said.

"It wasn't ours," I said. "Honestly Ricky it wasn't ours."

Polly

What people do to each other. People who've gone to sleep side by side, people who have shared life's ups and downs, had a child together, exchanged marriage vows. Perhaps that's the worst thing about it. That someone you thought you knew could turn into your worst enemy. It's probably worse than what strangers do to each other. As if knowing someone gives you permission to act as badly as possible.

That's what I thought about Chimp and Nellie. Neither of them was perfect but I couldn't get over what had happened. I didn't for a moment believe Nellie and Rudi were out and out heroin addicts. What they said in the papers about that was ridiculous. Nellie was many things but she was not a heroin addict.

Joe and Lisa drove over to see us when they heard what happened. They were living in a little Council house near Mostyn at the time and Joe had got work at Bersham. He looked much brighter and happier now he was back down the mines and despite the situation with Nellie, it made me feel a little better.

Joe didn't believe the story about the heroin either.

"I'll bet my shirt on it that wanker Chimp Davis is behind this," he said as he sat on the couch cracking open a can of beer. "And if I ever get hold of him, I'll rip his head off."

Lisa put her hand on his arm. She was good for him, Lisa and I liked the calming influence she had.

"It's too early to judge what's happened," Vincent said. "We don't know the facts yet, we don't know the facts."

I rang Nellie every day. I asked her if she wanted to come to Wales or if she wanted me to go and stay with her. Sometimes she was so spaced out she couldn't string her words together. Other times she just cried down the phone. The Court had made an interim Order granting custody to Chimp's parents and now there was going to be a Court case to decide who Morwenna would live with. It was unbelievable. Every day brought a new twist or turn.

"Surely they wouldn't stop a child living with her mother just because of a few drugs," I said to Vincent one night. "I mean it's not like she was beating her black and blue is it?"

I still had faith in the Court system at that time and I remained optimistic that justice would prevail.

Vincent kept quiet. I think he knew it didn't work like that but while I had hope, he wasn't going to destroy it.

Nellie

Extract from her unfinished biography, Street Life

Every time I stepped outside the house, the reporters and the cameramen were camped outside so in the end, I stopped going out. It was like we were prisoners in our own home. One morning I pulled back the curtains on the patio window and this man flashed a camera through the glass. I kept the curtains closed after that.

The only time we went out was when we had to go to Court. I used to start worrying about that days ahead and the more I worried the more Valium and Xanax I took.

We were sure the heroin belonged to Shirley and Toto and that it had all been a terrible mistake. Rudi said all we had to do was find them and they could go to Court and explain.

The problem was that Shirley and Toto had disappeared and judging by the state of the annexe, they had left in a hurry. I couldn't think why Toto would store his drugs in our kitchen drawer but Rudi said it made sense because if the police raided the annexe, he wouldn't be caught. Even so, why would he do that? It wasn't as if we were constantly at risk from a police raid or living in a crack den.

Sometimes I got so confused about it all.

"Are you sure it wasn't yours Rudi. Did the band put it there and you just forgot?"

Rudi paced up and down and ran his hands through his hair.

"No way," he said. "I'd remember something like that."

Toto and Shirley left the annexe in a terrible mess. I was shocked by the piles of dirty plates, the overflowing ashtrays, the half empty glasses of alcohol. Shirley had kept the houses on the farm spick and span but clearly, in her own domain, things were different.

We didn't care about the mess, we just wanted to find them so we could call them to Court as our witnesses and get Morwenna back.

The trouble was they had vanished into thin air and we didn't have a clue how to find them.

Chimp

I don't know why Da did it and when I tried to speak to him about it, he became quite defensive.

"She's living with us for the time being," he said. "And while she's living with us, I'll decide who she can see and who she can't see."

I was pissed off but I couldn't do anything about it. I could have taken Morwenna to our house but I couldn't breach the rules of the interim Court Order. I just didn't understand why Da was letting Joe see Morwenna.

I saw Joe as part of the enemy camp and now he was creeping around spending time with my daughter.

I met him one day coming out of the house and he just stared at me and said

"I've got your number boy. Don't think I don't know what you're up to. I've got your number Emyr Davis."

I mean??

I wondered if Nellie had put him up to it, if he was a spy in the camp.

"Don't be so paranoid," Rhoswen said. "There's probably a perfectly good reason for it."

"Like what?" I said.

"Well…" she hesitated. "I don't know. Maybe Joe just asked and he said yes."

"But why?" I pushed. "Why would Joe want to see Morwenna?"

Rhoswen sighed.

"Look," she said, turning away from the sink where she was potting Spring plants. "I don't know but what I do know is that we've got enough going on with Grace and the charities and this Court case without throwing paranoia into the mix."

I didn't want anything going wrong with my plans. I was quite convinced the Court would find in our favour and award custody to us. I mean why wouldn't they? They would never let Morwenna go back to a house with an unstable drug taking mother would they? Even so I didn't like it. I didn't like Joe hanging around.

The other problem we had was Grace. Whenever we brought Morwenna over from Ffynnongroyw, she played up. I caught her once, plaiting Morwenna's hair so tightly that Morwenna cried and another time I found Mr Boo strung up by a shoe lace from the light fitting in her bedroom and Morwenna standing underneath, sobbing her heart out.

I tried to talk to Grace about it but she went completely off on one.

"You always take her side!" she said, her eyes blazing. "You don't love me as much as you love Morwenna."

We tried to reassure her. We tried to tell her we had to look after Morwenna because she might not be able to live with her mum anymore. We didn't dare say we were hoping she would come to live with us permanently.

We put her behaviour down to all the damage Grace had suffered as a child: the insecurities, witnessing her father beating her mother and locking Grace under the stairs and of course, his eventual suicide. Eventually we consulted our GP and he referred her back to Barnado's for more counselling. It was all we could do really. I mean we thought we were doing the right thing. Neither of us had had to deal with a teenager before and we weren't sure whether this type of behaviour was normal or not.

"Stay with it," the counsellor said when I told her about the recent behaviour with Morwenna.

"The important thing is not to make an issue of it. Grace needs to know that whatever she does you will still love her. It's a sort of testing process if you like. It will pass with time, when she feels more secure."

Polly

I didn't know Tom Horse had such a problem with the drink until Joe told me. And when he told me about that night on the railway bridge it made me cry.

The rise in alcohol consumption and the increase in suicide rates in the mining communities was not something the Government publicised. They were more keen on privatising industries and making the Great British Public share holders.

"It cost £6.7 million to float British Telecom on the stock market," Vincent said one evening, shaking his head as he read the paper. "£6.7 million! I can't imagine that sort of money."

So, the rich might have been getting richer but the poor were struggling to survive. It wasn't so bad for us in Ffynnongroyw because Point was still up and running. It's sister pit, Bersham, closed just weeks after Joe started working there and he was unemployed again. It was just one of hundreds of pits closing across South Wales and England as the government stepped up their accelerated closure plan with little regard for the people it affected. In the end, over 100,000 miners lost their jobs.

Many of the miners found themselves out of work for the first time in their lives. Men who found themselves cast loose and adrift after years of going down the pits. They lost their jobs, they lost their sense of purpose and most of all they lost the sense of camaraderie they'd had down the mines. Instead there was poverty, drug abuse, divorce, and a complete loss of hope in many of the communities where mining had thrived for centuries. It was all so bleak.

Tom Horse had always struck me as a big strong man but even big strong men aren't invincible. They may have strong bodies but you can't see inside their minds. You can't see how broken they've become and the thought of him sitting on that railway bridge contemplating suicide is shocking.

Joe spent two hours persuading him not to jump, persuading him that life was worth living, that it wasn't as bleak as he thought it was. He didn't tell me much more than that, just that they'd talked this way and they'd talked that way and the rain came down and soaked them to the skin and eventually Tom let Joe lead him away from the bridge and take him home. That night created a bond between them when one man had lost all hope and the other gave it back to him and so when Joe asked if he could spend time with Morwenna, Tom Horse readily agreed.

"All I can do is keep an eye on her," Joe said. "Make sure she's safe. You make sure you tell Nellie she's safe, Poll, tell her I'm keeping an eye out and no harm will come to her. Not on my watch."

I used to worry Chimp would make a fuss and accuse him of interfering, meddling, and get funny about it

"So what's he going to do?" Joe said "Write a song about it? "

Despite my concerns, despite the sadness I felt for Tom Horse, that made me laugh because me and Joe had this private joke that Chimp would write a song about any misfortune he came across that might make him some money. Really, it wasn't funny at all. It wasn't funny that Morwenna had been taken away from Nellie and it wasn't funny that a grown man like Tom Horse had got so broken that he'd almost jumped from a railway bridge in the middle of the night.

Nellie

Extract from her unfinished biography, Street Life

Our solicitor told us to plead guilty. It was the best way, he said, because that way we'd probably get a rap on the knuckles and a fine and it would all be done and dusted by lunchtime.

I didn't want to plead guilty because we hadn't done anything wrong. The heroin wasn't ours so why should we plead guilty to it? I wanted to go to Court and explain this to the Judge and jury. They'd believe us when they'd heard what we had to say.

"They won't," the solicitor said. "It was found in the kitchen drawer of your house and you have nothing to back up your story that someone else put it there. If you go to trial you will be found guilty."

So that was how the law worked. I'd had no experience of it before. Like other citizens I put my faith in the system only to realise it wasn't about faith. It was about something completely different.

"What about Morwenna" I said.

I'd popped three Valium before we went to his office and the room was hazy with cigarette smoke.

"If we're found guilty of possessing heroin they'll never let her come home."

The solicitor sighed. I got the feeling that he had other things to do and that his patience with us, with me, was rapidly running out.

"That's a different issue," he said. "A matter for the Family Court. All I can do is advise you on the criminal law. I'm not a family lawyer. And my advice is that if you go to trial, you'll be found guilty anyway. With a guilty plea, you will get a lesser sentence."

It was October and outside the window, it was getting dark. The leaves were falling and autumn was coming. I had this feeling of being removed from it all, that it wasn't really happening. That it was too unreal to be real.

Rudi stood up.

"We'll think about it," he said, holding out his hand to me to signify we were leaving.

"Don't think about it for too long," the solicitor said." If you're going to plead guilty you need to do it at the hearing next week."

For once, the Press weren't waiting outside for us but Ricky Rich was and he got us home in record time. Rudi used to tease him about his driving. He used to say he'd missed his vocation in life, that he should have been a getaway driver. I let them chat away in the front while I floated away in the back. Life just didn't seem real. None of it seemed real.

Polly

There was hardly room in the public gallery that day. Honestly you'd think they were up for murder. Most of the people there were Press, jostling and pushing in the foyer to get the best photograph they possibly could of two people down on their luck. It made me so angry. Didn't they have anything better to do with their time like following that story about the missing estate agent - Suzy Lamplugh – for example? She'd gone missing in July and that wasn't getting half as much publicity as Nellie and Rudi were getting for pleading guilty to possessing heroin.

Me and Vincent felt like the country cousins that day. We were completely out of our depth in that Court. We were just a simple couple who lived a simple life on a day out from Wales. That day out was a real eye opener.

We couldn't get near Nellie and Rudi. They were jostled by the Press in the Court and chased down the road afterwards. I saw it later, on the News. Nellie had her head down and she was wearing these huge black sunglasses. She could hardly walk along the pavement for the photographers shoving their cameras in her face. Rudi pushed them out of the way and a car pulled up, a white Opel Manta, and they dived into the back seat and it tore away at speed. We didn't have time to speak to them. It was all so frantic.

The next day there were damning headlines in *The Sun* and the *News of the World.*

Nell's Hell!

Not On Your Nellie!

Underneath the headlines they published just about the worst photographs they could find: Nellie falling out of a car, Nellie staring blankly at a camera with mascara lines down her face. It was all so unfair.

After the hearing, we drove back to Wales in thick fog. The heater in the Ford Cortina Vincent had borrowed packed up and it was freezing cold. All I could think about was that Nellie and Rudi had pleaded guilty and what effect that was going to have on Nellie getting Morwenna back.

It was a long journey home.

1987

Nellie

Extract from her unfinished biography, Street Life

Christmas 1986 was miserable without Morwenna, what I remember of it anyway. I remember ringing up Tom and Sarah on Christmas Day to speak to her but I didn't realise I'd rung them thirteen times. I thought they were unreasonable when they asked me to stop ringing. I mean it was Christmas Day wasn't it? It was Christmas Day and I wanted to speak to my daughter. I missed my daughter and there were all these presents under the tree waiting for her and she wasn't there.

I was still allowed to see her. No one had stopped that. I mean they couldn't could they? But let's just say Chimp's family didn't make it easy for me. She was in North Wales. I was in Sussex. It wasn't an easy journey and it wasn't as if we could just pop in whenever we felt like it. I hated going to Wales at the best of times: that journey was so long and it broke my heart when we had to leave without her. I used to cry all the way home. I don't know what I would have done without Rudi, if I'd had to deal with it all on my own.

When I look back, I remember those days as dark, very dark, like perpetual winter. It seemed we were always leaving our house or the house in Wales, in the dark and that it was always raining. It can't have been like that every time but that is how I remember it and I try not to remember it too much because it can make me feel so hollow and sad. I had to explore it all at *The Suns of Life* and it was hard.

We didn't manage to get to Wales to deliver the Christmas presents and that was something else Chimp brought up later on, during the custody proceedings. He said that it showed I wasn't as heartbroken as I made out because if I had been, I would have made the effort to get there. The truth was I could hardly get out of bed some days. Some days I just lay on the bathroom floor and not even the thought of seeing Morwenna could get me up. It wasn't the sort of thing you told people. I wasn't ashamed, I didn't have enough strength to be ashamed. I was just very sad, very lost and the world was a very dark place for me.

So it wasn't me being unreliable. It was me being lost in the depths of a deep dark depression but I wasn't going to expose that to the world. I was Nellie on the Telly, bright and young and go ahead. Except I wasn't. Not behind closed doors. It was all an act and I couldn't act anymore. I couldn't even get to the studios and so after I missed a few shows, Tom Wainwright rang up and said that perhaps we should suspend ***Let's Talk!*** for a while. It never came back. That was the end of it. If it had happened when the world was normal, I would have been heartbroken but at that time all I wanted was my daughter and nothing else mattered.

The New Year snowed us in. I was glad about that. It kept the Press away, it cut us off from the world and it gave us time to breathe. The custody proceedings were due to start in February. I hadn't thought it would go that far. I thought that Morwenna would stay with her grandparents for a few weeks and then come home once the drug thing blew over. It didn't turn out like that. It grew into a monster. Chimp was determined to get his daughter back and at that time, he was so much stronger than I was.

And then just a few weeks before we were due to go to Court, Shirley and Toto sold their story to the papers.

Chimp

For me, 1987 dawned full of promise. Morwenna was living in North Wales and soon, I was convinced, that would be a permanent arrangement. Our Hope Charity was up and running and through it, we'd managed to buy land in Yorkshire and Nottingham from the National Coal Board and sell it on to developers at a handsome profit.

"Are we doing the right thing?" Rhoswen questioned one night. "I thought we were going to build places on the land for the unemployed, not sell it on to a third party."

I didn't see it that way at all. What I saw was an opportunity to make money that was too good to miss.

"We're still doing that," I countered. "They'll build supermarkets and factories and shops on the land and create new jobs. It's just we're doing it in a different way that's all."

Margaret Thatcher was certainly sorting out the UK. Out of the ashes of strikes and industrial unrest, she was creating a much more settled future. She made you feel that you could do anything if you put your mind to it. You could buy shares in big companies. You could be anything you wanted to be. Rhoswen was not a great fan of Mrs Thatcher but I was. I felt like there was a tide in the affairs of men which, if taken at full flood, would help us ride into the golden future she promised could be ours.

The only fly in the ointment was Nellie. I don't know why she couldn't act like an adult and face the fact that due to her own actions, she had lost her daughter. We had the Court case set for February and instead of acting like a mature, composed woman, she used to ring me up at all times of the day and night and scream abuse at me down the phone. Everything was my fault. It was even my fault when that weird couple that used to work for them sold their story to the papers. Let me tell you that was nothing to do with me. It was to do with them riding their own tides. If Nellie hadn't lived that lifestyle they wouldn't have anything to expose would they? That was the thing: she could never take responsibility, never see that it was her actions that got her to the places where she didn't want to be.

Mam and Da were pretty fed up with her ringing up all the time to speak to Morwenna and in the end I suggested they change their phone number. I mean what sort of person rings up over twenty times on Christmas Day? Sad though it is, Nellie had problems and it was up to her to fix them and move on.

Not everything was my fault.

Polly

It wasn't what Nellie needed. I couldn't believe it when I opened *The News of the World* and saw the double page spread. Shirley and Toto went to town on them they really did and why? From what I could see they'd been treated really well.

"Money," Vincent said. "They'll get a pretty penny for that."

I read that article and I felt sick because the timing couldn't have been worse. They painted Nellie and Rudi like a couple of drug taking bohemians. Worse than that, they said they'd leave Morwenna on her own to go out partying, that they'd once found cocaine on a spoon in her bedroom and that Nellie used to put whisky in Morwenna's milk to make her sleep at night so that they could party downstairs undisturbed. They described the rest of *Powder Room* as a bunch of unkempt, Bourbon swilling Americans who used to regularly throw drug parties and God knows what else. How could they get away with writing stuff like that?

"To sell papers," Vincent said. "That's what it's all about these days. Making money and not caring who you shoot down in the process."

Was it really like that? Sadly I think it was. Margaret Thatcher promoted the idea of every man for himself and sod everyone else. She had no time for socialism, for community spirit. She just encouraged everyone to run for the money and never mind who you knocked over in the process.

It should have been a happy time for us. We'd moved into this lovely little council house in Ffynnongroyw that had roses in the flowerbed and a shed in the back garden. Elizabeth cried when we moved out but we assured her we were only down the road. Sidney used to sleep out on the shed roof in rain, snow or sun. Honestly for a cat with no tail and failing eyesight, he was quite a nifty little creature. I used to worry about Point closing but Vincent assured me that one, it wouldn't and two, if it did, he'd find work even if it was driving a milk float.

At that time, something happened that I saw as a bad omen: the canaries left Point. In those days, they kept two in every mine to warn the miners if carbon monoxide was present. Very sensitive birds, canaries and the two at Point were treated like household pets. Vincent said that all the men used to whistle and talk to them as they worked. And then, in 1986, the National Coal Board announced that all canaries would be removed from the mines and replaced by electronic detectors. It seemed prophetic to me.

Nellie

Extract from her unfinished biography, Street Life

Rudi's first reaction was to ring the newspaper and threaten to sue them. It wasn't like him but I think it showed how he was struggling under the pressure. He kept it all together for me, he kept *me* together, but there were days when I worried that he'd leave, that it would all be too much for him and he'd walk away to an easier life. He used to assure me that nothing would ever make him do that, that he was right there by my side whatever happened. But I had been left so many times the damage was done. Fear was part of my DNA.

We'd met innocently, on that wonderful snowy night in 1985 and now he must have thought he'd walked into a lion's den.

He told me not to read the article, that it would only upset me. It did. Deeply. But more because I couldn't believe that two people who'd lived under our roof, cooked our meals and shared our life, could do this. The worst thing was that none of it was true.

"Sue the ass off them," Ricky Rich suggested. "Take them to Court. They can't get away with something like this! Jeez!"

It wasn't as simple as it might have been in America where they went around suing everyone. We didn't do that in this country. Rudi spoke to a lawyer and the prices he quoted were way out of our league. I mean we weren't broke but we weren't rolling in money either despite what the papers said. Honestly they created personas of people that were completely fabricated and got away with it. How unfair was that? The most frustrating thing of all was there was nothing we could do about it.

Rudi telephoned the News of the World.

"Fuck off," they said, and put down the phone.

Chimp

Rhoswen found the lawyer who represented me in the custody case. Despite the soft promise of her name, Primrose O'Neill was a rottweiler, a woman in her forties with short blonde hair who never smiled and was probably happiest snuggled up in bed at night with a law book.

From the start she was down to earth, efficient, reliable. I don't know what her background was – we never saw a glimpse of who she was behind the immaculate business suit – but she knew her stuff.

I was even more impressed when she showed me the witnesses she had lined up for the hearing. There were statements from Mrs Bennett and that girl Cynthia who Nellie lived with when she moved down to London. I was shocked when I read a statement from someone called Toby Prince who said he'd picked Nellie up at a party in London and had sex with her against a lamp post leaving Morwenna, presumably, all on her own at home. And of course we had the statements from the police about the drugs they found in the house and the conviction for possessing heroin to support our case. All of it added up to one conclusion: that Nellie was unreliable and completely incapable of looking after a young child.

Primrose O'Neill was confident we'd win, that the Judge would be on our side. I mean how could he not be? Compared to Nellie, I was a paragon of virtue.

Nellie

Extract from her unfinished biography, Street Life

The only way I could cope with that first day of the Court case was to focus on what I would wear. I wanted to look my best. It might sound trivial compared to what was at stake but clothes were my suit of armour, my cloak of protection. If I looked good, nothing could pierce it. Or so I thought.

So I chose a soft baby blue suit. The jacket was tailored and the skirt was pencil. Underneath I wore a white blouse with a pussy bow. I completed the look with high heels and bright red lipstick. I was ready to take on the world. Almost.

We had a family solicitor called Rufus Carpenter. We met him in this miserable cubicle in the Court that had a strip light across the ceiling and plastic bucket chairs. It was optimistically called an interview room but it was stark and bleak and bare. Outside the door, kids attending the Youth Court in the same building prowled and snarled and chain smoked.

Rufus showed us the statements from Chimp's witnesses. I couldn't believe they'd got one from Mrs Bennett. There was also one from Cynthia, that boy Toby I'd driven down Pall Mall with hanging out of the sun roof in the snow and the camera man I'd had a fling with on ***Let's Talk!*** How had Chimp got hold of all these people? How had he persuaded Mrs Bennett to testify against me? To be fair you could see in her statement she was trying to be neutral but she had to agree, with whoever took the statement, that there were times when I left Morwenna alone; that there were times when I was late or forgot where I was supposed to be. She was a very truthful woman Mrs Bennett. I guess that made her a good witness.

Rudi chain smoked and paced about the room. I chain smoked and when I noticed my hands were shaking, I excused myself and dropped two Valium in the Ladies.

I cried when I read the statement Joe had written. Even after all this time, even after all that had happened, he was still right by our side. He described how he had been a solid regular figure in Morwenna's life and how I was nothing but a good mother. He described how he continued to see Morwenna at her grandparents' house in Ffynnongroyw and how he believed the right place for her was at home with me. He said that Grace was living with Chimp and Rhoswen and how Morwenna was scared of her. He described how Grace had strung Mr Boo up from the light fitting, how she had plaited Morwenna's hair so tightly it had made her cry and how she had locked her in the coal shed when Chimp and Rhoswen were upstairs.

It made me so mad. I wanted to go to Wales there and then, grab hold of that girl by the throat and shake her. How dare she do that to my daughter?!

"Are you alright Mrs Davis?" Rufus asked, wiping his perpetually runny nose.

"Don't call me that," I said coldly. "Don't ever call me that again."

Rufus looked a little taken aback.

"Well how should I address you?" he stammered.

"I'm Nellie Morgan," I said. "I've never been anyone else."

Polly

Nellie didn't do herself any favours. She came across as hostile in the witness box: a bit high and mighty to be honest. She answered back and nearly had a stand up row with Chimp's solicitor. I sat there cringing in the public gallery. Why hadn't someone told her just to answer the questions and come across as slightly more meek and mild?

In the papers they called her "Miss High and Mighty" and described her attending Court dressed like an air hostess or as if she was going to the races at Ascot instead of attending a custody hearing about her daughter. She couldn't win, not even if she'd turned up in sack cloth and ashes and as for that smug grin on Chimp's face and that hatchet faced solicitor of his, well, it was all I could do to stay in my seat. Vincent had hold of my arm in case I bolted from my seat, leapt over the balcony and caused a riot. As if I would. I am not that sort of person. I wish I was. I always wished I was more Nellie but not in that situation. In that situation she should have been more me.

I don't know what the magistrates were thinking. There were three of them: a man who looked like he was asleep and two women in pearls. To them it was just another custody battle between a man and a woman who no longer got on. Just another day's business. Before that hearing I had faith in the justice system. I should have known better. I really should. It wasn't about justice at all.

We weren't allowed to see Nellie at lunch time because she was halfway through giving her evidence and she wasn't allowed to speak to anyone but we managed to speak to Rudi. He was wearing a cream coloured suit and dark glasses. He looked so out of place, like he belonged in a casino in Monte Carlo rather than a dirty dingy magistrates court in Wrexham.

"You ok mate?" Vincent asked as we joined him in a quiet corner.

Rudi took off his glasses and rubbed his eyes. They were bloodshot and he looked exhausted. He didn't need to say anything. We knew.

Chimp

I felt quietly confident. Our witnesses did well. There was a lot of questioning about our home environment, particularly about Grace, but that didn't bother me. I could handle Grace. I explained how she was a poor orphaned child who had been through so much in her young short life and had come to live with us after her father committed suicide. Yes there was some turbulence but that was only to be expected. It was nothing more than other teenagers of her age were going through. I thought that made us look good people, that the magistrates would be impressed that we'd taken Grace in like that.

"What about the matters Mr Evans raises in his statement?"

I thought the male magistrate was asleep but he'd been listening all along. I wasn't comfortable with him, with the way he looked at me. I had the two women eating out of my hand but he was a different kettle of fish and I needed to be careful with him.

"What was it he said, "stringing up her favourite toy from the light fighting? Locking her in the coal shed"?"

I brushed it off. Mr Evans had exaggerated. Grace wouldn't do that. She loved Morwenna. She couldn't wait for her to come and live with us, for us to be a complete family. She saw her as her little sister. He annoyed me a bit going off on a tangent like that. I mean what did it have to do with Grace? Weren't we supposed to be talking about Morwenna?

He gave me the eye, he wrote something down and he didn't say anymore and despite that I was quietly confident that we had it, that it was in the bag and I looked up and gave Nellie the most triumphant smile I could as I left the witness stand.

Beat that, Nellie on the Telly.

Nellie

Extract from her unfinished biography, Street Life

It was amazing what they brought up at that trial. Rudi says I shouldn't call it a trial, but it felt like a trial, it felt like I was on trial. They even brought up the music I had been listening to when we went to stay in The Gower for the benefit concert. I'd left that tape in the bedroom and thought nothing of it. It wasn't with the things that Chimp returned to me and I just thought it had got lost. Music that said I was still living my life like an irresponsible teenager rather than as the mother of a three year old girl.

I mean can you believe it? Judging me by the music I listened to? And then there was the time we were in Las Vegas on our honeymoon and I hadn't even bothered to ring Tom and Sarah to see how Morwenna was. They even brought up the fine I received for not registering Morwenna's birth on time and how I'd posed for *Penthouse* magazine and Page Three of *The Sun.*

They also questioned us about the house Rudi and I lived in Sussex. Somehow I got the impression they thought it reckless to have a swimming pool or to live so close to the sea. Who did Morwenna stay with when I was at work, when Rudi was away touring?

"Toto and Shirley."

"The couple who sold their story to the News of the World?"

That male magistrate really got into it. I don't think he liked women. He definitely didn't like me.

"The couple who by their own admission, used to supply you with drugs? You left a three year old girl with a couple who used to supply you with drugs Mrs Davis?"

"Stop calling me that," I snapped. "I'm not Mrs Davis."

There was a gasp from the public gallery and the magistrate peeled off his glasses and held them by their limb as he looked at me.

"Not Mrs Davis? It says here that you are Mrs Davis. Would you like to tell the Bench who you are if you are not Mrs Davis?"

"I'm Nellie Morgan," I said, looking up at the public gallery. "Davis is my married name and I'm not married anymore."

"Have you and Mr Davis divorced?"

"No," I said, floundering and wondering what the hell he was going on about now. "But it's only a matter of time."

"Can we believe anything you have told us today Mrs er Miss Morgan?"

What did I say to that? And what was this? I felt like I was back in the headmistress's office or that Owen had caught me stealing money from his secret stash in the wardrobe.

"Believe what you like," I said. "I'm a good mother. I know I am."

There was another collective gasp from the public gallery, as if I'd crossed a line, as if I'd spoken out of turn and shocked everyone by answering him back like that. In the papers they called me Miss High and Mighty. I wasn't Nellie on the Telly anymore. Somehow I had become a person the public despised. A young mother who took drugs and left her young child with strangers, a woman who couldn't even tell the truth in Court. Nellie on the Telly had gone.

I'd always drawn a lot of comfort from the public adoring me and it hurt that they turned against me like that. Later, at *The Suns of Life,* I learned that I constantly looked to others for approval, for reaffirmation, for confirmation that I was ok as a person. Relying on the public to make you feel confident is a big mistake. It can turn around in the blink of an eye. That's what happened to me in that Court room. It wasn't about Morwenna. It was me and my lifestyle that were on trial.

They referred to the photographs I took, to my book of rock stars in their socks which got passed down the Bench. That caused one of the women magistrates to raise her very finely pencilled eyebrows. She probably hadn't seen a half naked man for years.

"These er *people,*" she said once her eyebrows had recovered. "They are famous people are they not? Famous people wearing socks?"

"Yes," I said. "That's why it's called *Sex in Socks.*"

There was a ripple of muffled laughter from the public gallery. I hadn't meant to sound cheeky but it seemed like everything I said in that witness box came out wrong.

She gave me a look that could cut ice.

"I realise that Mrs Davis. What I am trying to establish is when these photographs were taken. Rock stars, as you call them, are nocturnal creatures are they not?"

"Well," I said, attempting some humour (big mistake: never attempt humour with magistrates). "They don't go to many Church services let's put it that way."

I expected the audience – can you call it an audience – to laugh. They didn't.

The magistrate looked at me like I was something stuck to the bottom of her shoe.

"You do realise Mrs Davis, that this is a very serious matter. That this is about deciding who your daughter should live with?"

"Of course I do," I said. "Only I don't see what my book has got to do with it."

"Very well. In that case I'll get straight to the point. Most of these photographs look like they were taken at night. And if they were taken at night, who was looking after Morwenna?"

I tried to explain that they had been taken as and when, that they were a collection over the years but I don't think I explained it very well. I tried to explain that some of them were taken at the ***Let's Talk!*** studio and that must have been when I was living in London but I couldn't account for every single one of them. Did she expect me to?

"We heard from Letitia Bennett earlier," the woman continued. "Did you leave Morwenna alone when some of these were taken? Because if Letitia Bennett only looked after Morwenna for a few hours a week it doesn't add up does it? I mean there are an awful lot of photographs here Mrs Davis plus, by your own account, you were working every Friday night at the television studios. Mrs Davis?"

I was sure she kept calling me Mrs Davis on purpose, because she knew I'd objected to that title when her colleague questioned me earlier.

"I didn't leave Morwenna on her own all the time if that's what you're suggesting," I said.

She glared at me one more time. I had a sinking feeling I hadn't made the netball team and that I would be kept in after school.

"That will be all Mrs Davis, thank you."

Polly

It will come as no surprise to learn that the magistrates didn't award custody to Nellie and Rudi. Their lifestyle got the third degree, turned inside out and upside down. The Press gleefully reported it every day of the Court case, dreaming up more fantastical headlines as they went along.

But what did surprise me was that the Magistrates, who at times I wanted to batter, allowed Joe's application to be heard. It came out of left field, out of nowhere and I felt so proud of him as he took the stand to give evidence. He was the only one who spoke the truth that day and when, at the end, he said he also wanted to apply for custody, there was a gasp in the Court.

"We've got a nice little flat in Mostyn, not far from Llannerch -Y-Mor," he said. "It's only Council like but we keep it nice… we've even got geraniums in a window box… Lisa does the flowers… she's here, in the gallery if you want to speak to her. We don't have much but our families, mine and Chimp's, I mean, Mr Davis… our families have always been close. And if you ask me, it's not right for Morwenna to live in the same house as Grace Chappell. It's clear to me that she's jealous of Morwenna and that Morwenna's frightened of her. Only last week I found her locked in the coal shed again and that's not right. She doesn't listen, Grace, not even when I tell her off. I think she's jealous see and to be honest I wouldn't leave the two of them alone together for five minutes let alone let them live under the same roof."

There was complete silence after he'd finished. I shut my eyes. Why hadn't Chimp picked up on this? Why hadn't he stopped it?

The case went on for three days. And at the end, the Magistrates said that Joe's evidence was the most honest they had heard during the proceedings but that they had to give priority to family ties. Their final decision was that Morwenna should live with her grandparents in Ffynnongroyw. They didn't say that Grace was the reason she shouldn't live with Chimp and Rhoswen but I am sure she was.

Nellie's lawyer appealed and it went to a District Judge who upheld the Magistrates' decision and dismissed Joe's application as "spurious". He also referred to Nellie as confrontational and unreliable and shot a few warning words at Chimp about his domestic situation and how contact between Grace and Morwenna should be closely monitored.

Morwenna was to live with Tom and Sarah in Ffynnongroyw. Tom and Sarah had given good solid evidence to the Court. They came across as pillars of the community and no one mentioned the fact that Tom had a drink problem or that Joe had stopped him jumping off Cardaewar railway bridge in the middle of the night. They presented themselves to the world as honest and trustworthy Baptists who lived a law abiding lifestyle.

I might have dwelt on it more if I hadn't had other things in my life to steal my attention.

Like being pregnant, for example.

Chimp

It's not true that I tried to punch Joe Evans outside the Court. That was something the Press made up. Ok so maybe we jostled a little but that's all it was. There were so many people there was no room to move.

To be honest, I was pissed off with him. Standing up there making some stupid application for custody of Morwenna and saying I hadn't noticed what was going on with Grace and Morwenna. It was nothing to do with him. We had seen glimpses of her behaviour and I had spoken to Grace and sorted it out. He didn't need to stand up there all high and mighty and exaggerate things just so he or Nellie could get custody. He'd always had a crush on her and so he was going to say anything wasn't he? And as for him applying for custody, well that was a joke. As if the magistrates would entertain that. He was a hard drinking striking miner who'd lost his job. Did anyone mention that? Did they fuck.

So I was pissed that he'd tried it on like that and pissed that what he'd said probably persuaded the magistrates not to allow Morwenna to live with us.

"At least she'll be with your parents," Rhoswen said. "At least Nellie didn't win."

That might have been true but I was still not happy. I wanted my daughter home with me. It was where she belonged. I spoke to my dad again after the hearing and repeated what I'd said about Joe not having contact with Morwenna. I didn't want it, I didn't think a man like that was a good influence on her and I didn't understand why he was allowing it.

"She's very fond of him Emyr," he said. "You want to take that away from her as well?"

His words stung and I walked away. Mam came after me but I shrugged her off. I didn't want any platitudes. I didn't want to hear her say *he doesn't mean it, you know how he is* because that's what I'd been hearing all my life and I didn't want to hear it anymore.

Nellie

Extract from her unfinished biography, Street Life

When I walked out of Court that day, I felt numb. There were all these reporters shoving microphones in my face and shouting my name. I felt like I was in a world of strangers and that the world I lived in wasn't reliable. I mean how could anyone dictate where my daughter lived? I was the one who had brought her into this world, given birth to her and cared for her. How could anyone take her away from me?

Rudi steered me through the jostling crowds and into Ricky Rich's Opel Manta. Once inside, we were safe, the world was shut out and I closed my eyes so that I couldn't see the faces squashed up against the windows but I could still hear their fists banging on the roof.

I felt completely numb and disconnected as Rudi took my hand in the back seat.

"It doesn't mean you can't see her," he said. "We'll go see her all the time."

He was only trying to make it right I know he was but it felt like the end of the world. I couldn't see it any other way. I saw it as the Court judging me as a bad person, as a bad mother, someone who wasn't considered fit and proper. I saw it as the Court saying I couldn't be with my daughter.

We'd got her room all ready for her coming home. There was new wallpaper – pink rabbits because she loved rabbits, and a little night light that threw out star patterns across the walls. It was all waiting for her and now she wasn't coming home. I can honestly say it was the worst pain I have ever felt in my life.

So I remember that but I only remember snatches of what came afterwards and my diary doesn't help for that year – there are a lot of blank pages and where I have managed to write some words down, they don't make sense.

I didn't make sense at that time. It took a whole lot of unravelling before I would make sense again.

Polly

During the weeks after the Court case, Rudi called me several times sounding exhausted.

"I can't get through to her," he said. "It's like her heart has been broken."

Vincent and I caught the train to Sussex at Easter and what I saw shocked me. Nellie was like a skeleton with wild eyes and unkempt hair. I had never seen her like that. She had always loved hair and clothes and makeup and now she didn't seem to care what she looked like.

I knew she was on a whole lot of pills. She used to pop them in front of me, two, three, four at a time, like sweets. I tried to speak to her about it but it was hopeless.

"What do you know?" she'd say, her eyes coming in and out of focus, her voice slurred. "Leave me alone Polly. Go back to Wales and leave me alone."

I didn't tell her I was pregnant – somehow I thought that might rub salt into the wounds. She didn't notice either, she was so wrapped up in the fragmented, discombobulated world she lived in. She wasn't the Nellie I'd grown up with, the girl who'd walked into school so full of confidence, the girl with all the crazy plans and schemes and dreams. She was a wreck.

Rudi told me how she'd got in the car one night saying she was driving to Wales and he couldn't stop her. The police brought her home in her pyjamas and she lost her driving licence. In Court she laughed at the Magistrates and said "*what else are you going to take away from me?*"

There were more headlines in the paper after that; ***Nellie off the Planet!*** is one I remember accompanied by a picture of Nellie looking a complete wreck.

Rudi said that several times he had suggested they drive to Wales but in the end he gave up because she was in such a state. They arranged phonecalls but Nellie would start crying as soon as she heard Morwenna's voice. Joe offered to drive Morwenna up to Sussex but Rudi wasn't sure it was a good idea, not with the way Nellie was and then Nellie would turn on him and accuse him of being in league with everyone else who was trying to stop her seeing her daughter.

How Rudi coped with it all, I don't know. The band even cancelled their Australian tour so he could stay home with her. That's how much he loved her.

Joe stepped up his presence in Morwenna's life. He took her out as often as he could even though he was struggling with his own demons at that time. He took her to Llandudno and to the Hidden Valley and they were always going to see that rusty old rusty ship at Llannerch -Y- Mor. I had to rescue them a few times when they ran out of petrol or got lost but I was always impressed by the time he gave her. It was like he was trying to redress the balance, trying to make sure she didn't forget her mother, trying to step up for Nellie when she no longer could.

Was she his daughter? Well we'll never know that will we. Nellie never said and what was the point in rocking the boat? Where would that leave Morwenna? It would only make things worse. As Vincent said, sleeping dogs and all that.

And then, in June 1987, Margaret Thatcher was elected Prime Minister for the third time.

Polly

I gave birth to Awen on 16th October 1987. Awen means "poetic inspiration" and I can honestly say she's always been mine. Her timing though, couldn't have been worse. I went into labour on 15th October, the same day the Great Storm hit the UK.

My waters broke on the kitchen floor in the late afternoon. The power had gone off and the phone line was dead and we couldn't call an ambulance or the doctor so Vincent and I walked to the hospital. I've never known a storm like it. Trees came crashing down all around us with great cracks and groans and the roar of the wind was deafening. I kept having to stop to catch my breath, the contractions were coming so fast and it was so difficult to fight against the wind.

I was beginning to think we'd never make it to the hospital when Dai Roberts from Llinegr farm pulled up on a tractor.

I have gone down in history as only woman to arrive at Daneth General on the back of a tractor. They did a piece about it in the local paper. It was a bit of light hearted relief at the time.

It wasn't until I held Awen for the first time that I understood what Nellie was going through. That powerful, overwhelming love a mother feels for her child is like no other and I honestly don't know how Nellie coped with Morwenna being taken away from her. Well, she didn't, did she. She didn't cope at all and to be fair, I don't think I would have either.

Chimp

Looking back, could we have foreseen it? I've been asked that question a hundred times. By psychologists, by doctors, by the newspapers, by my mother, by everyone who has tried to make sense of something that didn't make sense. And every time they asked, it was like a finger being pointed at us; that somehow it was our fault for not seeing it coming.

We knew Grace was damaged. Troubled. Use all those words: they applied to her. Her story has been told so many times now it's gone down in history although as time has passed, memories have faded and it isn't a story at the forefront of everyone's mind anymore.

And when they ask me, I say no, there was nothing. We didn't see it coming. How could we? How can you look into someone's mind and know what they're going to do? And if you love someone, if they live under your roof, you never think they would be capable of doing anything like that. Not even the mothers of murderers believe their sons would kill.

When I'm on my own, I look back and try to see if there were any signs. And I wonder if one of them was after the Hungerford Massacre on 19th August 1987. It was shocking, brutal for a hundred reasons. One summer afternoon a man dressed in army gear walked down the high street of a sleepy English town and shot 15 people dead, including his mother. At the time, it was unheard of to have a shooting in the UK. We had IRA bombs and heard about shootings in Northern Ireland on the News but that was different. Hungerford was unprecedented.

Grace was fascinated by the gunman, Michael Ryan. She used to sit in front of the TV and watch the News on the BBC and then switch channels and watch it on ITV. Year later, we were clearing out her room and found a scrapbook crammed with newspaper clippings about him and the Hungerford shootings. We had no idea she'd made that scrapbook. It shocked us.

Grace was 16 at the time and had an obsession with the Gothic. She had her ears pierced multiple times, wore black lipstick and listened to a lot of weird music. We put it down to her being a teenager and thought little of it. Everyone is a little strange at 16. I know I was.

Three things stand out for me about 1987: the custody case, Nellie going to Florida and Hungerford. I wish I could say that my memory contained brighter things but that's the truth of it I'm afraid.

Nellie

Extract from her unfinished biography, Street Life

I don't know what would have happened if Rudi hadn't taken me to Florida in the summer of 1987 and booked me into *The Suns of Life*. It was Colita's suggestion and apparently she knew people high up in the organisation who could fast track my admission.

I remember a clean white building full of hushed corridors and sunshine. I remember that every day there were fresh flowers in my room. And I remember Nurse Divine because, we always say now, she was heaven sent.

If my life had been turmoil and chaos, it ended as soon as I walked through those glass doors. It was like entering a different world. Rudi says that for the first two weeks I thought I was in heaven.

They did everything. They treated mind, body and spirit as one. I had steam baths scented with rose. There were gardens full of beautiful bright flowers and on Sunday afternoons, we always had strawberry ice cream. My personal nurse was Nurse Divine and she had a smile so bright it would have lit up the Florida Keys.

Nurse Divine encouraged me to work on my mind. I was taught to let go of fear, to change my thinking, to explore some very dark places from childhood. I learned about attachment disorders, about why I didn't like being on my own at night, the basis for my disastrous relationship with Chimp and the reasons for my casual affairs. I learned so much about myself. How to feel. How to think. Who I was. And most of all I learned I wasn't a bad person. No one was a bad person. It was all about changing the relationship you had with the world and most importantly, with yourself. It was all about changing your thinking and your perception; taking yourself apart piece by piece and putting the pieces back together the right way up.

In *The Suns of Life*, I wasn't Nellie on the Telly. I'd left her behind at Heathrow airport. My hair wasn't peroxide any more: I was letting the natural colour grow back. That was a part of my therapy. Not covering up who I really was. I didn't wear tons of makeup, I didn't have my suits of armour to hide behind. I was just a girl in pyjamas who had got a bit lost.

I was a little anxious about meeting Colita. I wasn't sure how she would see me and whether she'd think I was good enough for her son.

Would she judge me for the things I'd done, for the mess I'd become?

When she came, I was sitting in my room, in the big green chair by the window. It let the light and the sun in from dawn to dusk. From there I could see palm trees and the fountain, a view I'd come to love.

She was wearing a cherry red dress and a big smile when she walked in.

"I brought you a key lime pie," she said. "You can't come to Florida and not have a key lime pie."

Not once did she berate me. Not once did she question me about anything. We just sat there talking like old friends and I felt like I'd known her for years. She told me how she was half Cuban and half American and had grown up in Havana. She told me she went on holiday to Jamaica when she was 21 and came back pregnant with Rudi. I was impressed by how open she was, how easily she told me that.

She didn't stay long on the first visit. She didn't want to tire me. She left in a cloud of gentle perfume and sunshine and I slept well that night.

Morwenna

I didn't notice her absence. I mean, not in a negative way because, although I was only five or six years old at the time, I understood that she was on holiday or away on business or whatever it was that Uncle Joe told me. I did not feel abandoned. I had this quiet, firm knowledge that her absence was only temporary. Uncle Joe made sure of that.

Five year olds have little memory and they are more resilient than we give them credit for. It certainly didn't affect me.

Now I know where she was, it does. All those days when I was probably on the beach or playing with my dolls there she was, thousands of miles away in *The Suns of Life* in Florida eating ice cream on Sundays and trying to fix her mind. I have learned so much more about absence with the passing of time.

Polly

My life was taken up with the baby and I feel a bit guilty that I took my eye off the ball with Nellie. On the other hand I knew where she was and I knew she was safe. Rudi kept me updated in brief, long distance phonecalls. He said she was doing well, he asked for the baby, he never made a drama out of anything.

I took the baby round to see Mam when she was just a few weeks old. She was their only grandchild so I had to try. Every autumn, Mam made chutney from the windfall pears up at Llinegr Farm and when she opened the back door that afternoon, the smell of vinegar and spice wafted out to greet me. That smell was home to me, it got into the carpets, it climbed the stairs and it permeated the very fabric of the house. It was the smell. of autumn, Mam's chutney – vinegar and spice and steamed up windows in the kitchen.

When Mam saw Awen wrapped up in blankets her face lit up and very gently, she leaned down and lifted her out of the pram, looking down at her face and making cooing noises.

"Her name's Awen," I said as she lifted her to her shoulder. "Isn't she beautiful Mam?"

Mam looked over at me and there was so much emotion in her face.

"I remember when I had you," she said, her eyes shining. "It was early in the morning and the birds were singing."

"I had howling wind," I said. "We got a lift on a tractor to Daneth."

"I saw that," she said, rocking Awen in her arms. "I saw it in the paper."

I was still standing at the back door. She hadn't invited me in and so I knew Da was inside.

"Da in is he?"

Mam's face changed, torn it was, between wanting us all to be this one big happy family and Da's stony disapproval of anything Joe and I did. I clung on to the hope that a baby might melt it and repair the bonds, but I should have known better really.

And then he appeared, looming behind Mam – he was a big tall man Da – and looking over her shoulder at the baby.

"Look Gordon," Mam said, half turning around. "Look at our granddaughter. Isn't she beautiful?"

I half expected Da to grunt and turn away but he didn't.

"Ah well best come in then," he said. "Best come in."

My heart lifted. It might only have been a few words but with Da, a few words was a lot compared to the silence we'd had for the past few years and I didn't wait to be asked twice. He never thawed completely Da but Awen changed things and that afternoon with the smell of chutney in the air and the kitchen windows all steamed up, my heart felt lighter than it had for months.

Nellie

Extract from her unfinished biography, Street Life

I spent nearly a year in *The Suns of Life*. Nine months of ice cream on Sundays and healing myself. I had a lot of peaceful, quiet time after the chaos. I used to worry about Rudi: that he was neglecting his music, that the band weren't touring but he reassured me that there was plenty of time for that later on. They were going to concentrate on the States and Australia and give up trying to make it in the UK.

Ricky Rich and Dragon and Perry came to visit. I am not sure what Nurse Divine made of *Powder Room*! They drank all this beer and threw the cans in my bin and when they left I got hauled into the discussion room because they thought it was me who had drunk them!

Me and Rudi, well we got closer. He truly saw me, I think, during that year. I had been stripped down and rebuilt like some old car and he stood by me through the whole process. It only made me love him more. I was amazed that he was still around and seemed to love me for what I was, for all the dark and the shade.

Best of all was the telephone contact I had with Morwenna, arranged by Joe from Tom Horse's house. It must have cost a fortune but apparently, Tom Horse knew all about it and paid the bills without question.

I was so surprised by that and it made me feel better. I am forever grateful to them for giving me the gift of Morwenna's voice. It meant the world to me.

1988

Nellie

Extract from her unfinished biography, Street Life

It was Colita's idea that we go and stay at the farm when I was released from *The Suns of Life* in April 1988. I was anxious about leaving. It had become my home and the thought of travelling eight hours on a plane back to the UK seemed overwhelming.

Going to Colita and Manford's farm seemed a better idea. A halfway house while I adjusted to being in the real world again. Half of me wanted to get back to the UK to see Morwenna but most of me was overwhelmingly anxious about the whole thing.

"You'll love the farm," Rudi said one afternoon as we sat in the gardens at *The Suns of Life*. It might have been winter but it was warm. I loved that Florida heat. I couldn't imagine going back to the wind and rain and snow of the UK.

"We can spend some time there and think about the UK after that," Rudi said. "There's no deadlines, no rush. You know you have to take it one thought at a time."

He had picked up my therapy. He knew the steps I had to take. And so on a bright morning in April, we headed off to the farm.

I imagined the farm would be like that place where the benefit concert for the miners had taken place in South Wales or maybe the farmhouse in Sussex. It wasn't like that at all. Colita's and Manford's farm in Jupiter was more like a ranch, a beautiful white house set down in acres of wide open space and fields.

Colita came to pick us up and we drove out to Jupiter in her red Ford convertible. Maybe it was the Florida sun or maybe I was in a better place; I just remember feeling happy that day and happiness wasn't something I was used to feeling. And when we got there, two beautiful white horses with blonde manes stood in the field at the front, swishing their tails.

"Well look at that," Colita smiled, catching my eye in the rear view mirror. "Charley and Burt have come out to say hello."

Their house was cool, homely, welcoming, beautiful. There were rugs on the stone floors, pictures on the walls and framed photographs of Rudi on the grand piano. The back doors opened on to a seating area with cane furniture and steps leading down to an infinity pool.

Three dogs bounded out to meet us as we walked in. Three crazy dogs that ran round in circles and chased their tails. Rudi's step dad, Manford, walked out of his study wearing orange shorts and holding a bottle of beer. Lunch was already laid out on the kitchen table.

I have never felt at home anywhere but I felt at home instantly in that beautiful house with its faded gold and red walls, the sun coming through the blinds and the soft hum of the air conditioning. After lunch, we walked round the grounds and visited the horses in the adjoining field. Manford gave me a floppy orange sun hat.

"Florida sun ain't polite like English sun," Manford said as he and the dogs followed us around the estate. "It'll burn you as soon as look at you."

Manford was older than Colita and as quiet as Colita was outgoing. He'd made a fortune setting up gas stations across the United States and fell in love with Colita when he saw her dancing in a club in New York. He wasn't worried she came with a two year old son. He took them both on and now, forty years later, they were still going strong. They'd lived in New York for most of their lives but after Manford had a health scare with his heart, they reassessed their lives and relocated to Florida.

We sat out by the pool on that first night listening to the crickets and the frogs, the nightly concert Colita calls the Florida lullaby. There seemed to be so much promise, so much hope, such a different way of looking at life in America and I fell in love with its optimism. The UK seemed bleak and depressing by comparison and I couldn't imagine going home. The trouble was Morwenna was there and I missed her more with each passing day.

Chimp

If Joe hadn't stuck his nose in where it wasn't wanted, Morwenna would have forgotten all about Nellie and in time she would have come to live with me and Rhoswen. I'm sure of it.

I was not happy when I found out that Morwenna was speaking to Nellie regularly on the phone and said so to Da.

"For God's sake Emyr," Da said. "What do you have against that woman? She's her mother for God's sake."

Other parts of my life were better. I was busy with the Charity and I'd also started copyright proceedings against Nellie to get a share of the royalties she was raking in from publishing early photographs of *The Sons*. Sometimes I missed the band but equally I enjoyed being a businessman.

I did an interview with the local paper recently for a feature called ***Where Are They Now?*** and they asked me if there was any chance of *The Sons* getting back together for a reunion tour.

"Not a chance mate," I said. "Not a chance."

George tried to get in contact after the article was published but I wasn't interested. As far as I'm concerned the days of *The Sons* are gone and they belong to a different time, a different life.

Polly

Vincent was still working at Point in 1988, Sidney was still sleeping on the shed roof and I was a mother. Margaret Thatcher became the longest serving Prime Minister of the 20th century and that continued to baffle me. Men were still struggling to find work even though the government was determined to hoodwink us by saying unemployment had fallen to its lowest level for seven years. Try telling that to the unemployed miners in South Wales and Yorkshire and Nottingham. I suppose if you lived in the South of England life was pretty good. If you lived in Wales or the North of England or the Midlands, it was completely different. It was like a divided nation.

Vincent and I lived a simple life. I was doing some voluntary work with the local drug support team. Heroin use in the mining communities had soared and I worked with kids as young as fourteen. Alot of the miners' houses were sold off and people moved into the neighbourhoods who had no sense of community spirit. Many of them brought their drug habits with them. We didn't have it as bad as some of the Northern towns but even so, it was a problem no one seemed to care about.

But in the summer of 1988, the sun came out.

In the summer, Nellie came back.

Nellie

Extract from her unfinished biography, Street Life

We spent three months at the farm in Jupiter. We used to lie in bed at night and make plans for our future. Rudi knew my number one priority was Morwenna. He knew that despite all we had, despite waking up every morning in Paradise, my life was not and could never be, complete without her.

Colita loves reminiscing about when Rudi was little and because she loves her son so much, she understood how painful it was for me to be separated from my daughter. I thought she might judge me when I told her the Court had more or less pronounced me an unfit mother, but she didn't. Instead she told me about Judy.

I'd seen the framed photographs scattered about the farm of this beautiful dark haired girl riding a horse, cuddling a dog, sitting on the beach. She'd caught my eye when I first walked in but I had this feeling I shouldn't ask.

It was just me and Colita out by the pool that night. We were drinking tequila and we had become very close.

"Seven years ago now," she said, smiling into the darkness after she told me about her adopted daughter who'd died, aged just twenty one, from a drug overdose.

"Did she spend time at *The Suns of Life?*" I asked quietly.

Colita looked out across the night.

"Yes she did," she said. "But not even they could save her."

I stood up and I went to her chair and put my arms around her and we sat like that for a long time.

When I got into bed later that night, Rudi was lying on his stomach with his face pressed into the pillow.

"You been shooting the breeze with my mom?"

I smiled at him and I kissed the back of his head.

"Honey why didn't you tell me about your sister?"

Rudi pushed his elbows behind him and sat up and stroked my hair.

"Did my Mom tell you?"

I nodded.

"I'm so sorry," I said. "I'm so sorry."

"It's ok," he said. "I've dealt with it. It's ok honey, don't cry."

I learned many things that night. The first was where the compassion and understanding he showed to me, to everyone who went wrong, came from.

The second was that I felt this new steely resolve for Morwenna. I was going to fight for her and be a proper mother. I was not going to be the sort of mother mine had been. I was going to be a mother like Colita.

We flew back to the UK in July 1988. And you know what? I finally got to watch ***Saturday Night Fever*** on the plane. They were showing it because it was the ten year anniversary of its release. It was so dated! Or maybe I had grown.

Polly

Nellie came down to Wales in the autumn of 1988. She seemed more at peace with herself than I'd ever seen her before: calm, relaxed, fatalistic even. They stayed in a hotel in Rhyl and we all spent a lot of time together. Morwenna loved Awen and asked Nellie if they could get a baby so that she could dress her up in pretty clothes. Like mother like daughter!

One afternoon Joe and Lisa came over from Mostyn and the six of us and the children spent the afternoon on the beach at Talacre. That old lighthouse loomed over us and the Castle Bay was all shut up, dark and foreboding looking.

"To think I lived there!" Nellie said as the wind whipped her hair around her face. I liked it better long and dark. I'd always thought the peroxide was too harsh.

There was a brisk wind blowing in from the sea. Lisa and I walked out across the sand while Vincent and Rudi stayed with Awen. Joe and Nellie were playing French cricket with Morwenna and their shouts and laughter followed us until they were blown away on the wind.

"How's Joe been?" I said.

"Oh you know," she said. "Still looking for work but it's hard when everyone's going for the same job. Sometimes he goes back to South Wales to see Badger Jones and the boys. I'm not sure it's good for him going over the past all over again but he likes being with them and we can't really understand what they went through in the Strike can we? It's no wonder so many of them turned to the drink. I mean he does drink quite a bit Joe," she said. "Quite a bit."

"He's always liked the drink," I said, linking my arm through hers. "I used to listen out for him coming home and I could tell by how many chairs he crashed into just how drunk he was."

We laughed a little at that and changed the subject but later, after we lost Joe, I remembered that conversation.

That was the last time we were all together, the six of us and the girls but of course we didn't know it then. It's only when you look back that you can apply these labels to the days gone by.

It had been such a lovely afternoon and then Chimp arrived, spoiling it all, stomping through the sand dunes with a storm on his face.

"You were supposed to drop her off at mum and dad's an hour ago!" he shouted at Nellie. "What the bloody hell are you playing at?"

Joe stepped in between them.

"There's no need to speak to her like that," he said.

Chimp glared at him.

"It's got nothing to do with you," he said. "Nothing to do with you at all."

Chimp

Things got difficult when Nellie came back from the States. I mean she thought she could just walk in and take Morwenna whenever she wanted to. It had been much easier when she had been thousands of miles away and yes I resented her for coming back, for swanning around like she did, for buying Morwenna all those expensive presents. It felt like she was constantly kicking sand in our faces.

She was always late bringing her back to Mam and Da's and that's why I went to the beach that day. I was sick of it. She had no respect for our lives, for what Rhoswen and I might be doing.

So there they were, one big happy family running around on the beach playing French cricket or something. Even that great big lumping idiot Joe was there. Rhoswen stayed up in the carpark in our jeep but I wasn't waiting any longer. It was a Sunday evening and I wanted to watch something on the telly and them running around like that seemed to say they didn't give a toss about me or Rhoswen; we could wait.

I think I handled it well despite how angry I was feeling. I calmly approached Morwenna and told Nellie that I was taking her because we'd been expecting her an hour ago. I do accept that Morwenna started to cry and then that big lump Joe had to stick his oar in.

I mean just exactly who did he think he was? If you ask me he deserved what he had coming to him. I'm sorry if that sounds harsh but he was always poking his nose in where it wasn't wanted. I could smell the alcohol on his breath and that pissed me off even more - the fact he was half pissed and spending time with my daughter. I just took Morwenna, lifted her up and took her and I know she was upset but she had to learn. I was the constant in her life. She couldn't rely on her mother. I didn't bank on Nellie being around for long. She was inconsistent if she was anything.

Do I have regrets? Well we all do don't we? I don't have regrets about trying to protect Morwenna from the hurt I was sure was coming to her when Nellie decided to up sticks and go somewhere else and that's just what she did later on, just as I predicted. She was her own worst enemy, the master of her own destiny in the end. I'm sorry if that sounds harsh. I'm only telling it like it was.

Nellie

Extract from her unfinished biography, Street Life

I didn't cause a scene. I just kissed Morwenna, told her to be good for her daddy and let him take her. It broke my heart to see her looking back at me over his shoulder and holding out her hands to me as Chimp marched her off across the sand. Why did he always have to ruin everything? We'd had such a lovely day. I was stronger by then, so much stronger, and I wasn't going to let Chimp get under my skin.

I don't know why he had to be so nasty to Joe. I think he's got a real issue with Joe probably because in this whole sorry affair Joe has always been on my side, if sides are to be taken.

I could see Morwenna loved Joe very much and that they had a really strong bond. He chased the incoming tide with her, patiently built sandcastles and told her stories about mermaids and sea creatures and underwater kingdoms. I remember Morwenna sitting transfixed on the sand as he spoke to her and I got up and walked over and crouched down beside him and I touched his shoulder

"Thank you Joe," I said. "Thank you for all you've done."

We spent ten days in that hotel in Rhyl and whilst I cherished every moment I spent with Morwenna, Chimp was clearly not happy that I was back. Every opportunity he got he tried to make it difficult for me. You would think that after all we had been through we could call a truce and just try to work something out between us that was best for our daughter. I still had hopes that one day she'd live with us but the way Chimp was made me despair at times that it would ever be anything other than a battle.

We looked around for a house to rent in the area and eventually found Rhamscott, a big five bedroomed house with a garden near Mostyn. I didn't particularly want to settle in North Wales, but if it meant being near to Morwenna it would do for now. I had already missed out on so much of her young life I didn't want to miss out on anymore.

We moved in just before Christmas 1988 and I couldn't wait to show Morwenna the bedroom where she'd sleep when she stayed with us. Her favourite colour is purple and so it was purple! We were there just over six months and it was a lovely, happy time. It surprised me how happy I could be in Wales. Rudi says it's all about papering over the old memories and replacing them with new ones. He says that the only reason I have such negative feelings about Wales is because I associate it with being a teenager and the times I spent on my own in that old rambling hotel.

I love that man so much. He is my heart, my soul, my strength, my *raison d'etre.* I never thought that I, Nellie Morgan, would know love like this. To have a man who walks beside me and takes me for all I am. It's unbelievable.

Polly

Nellie invited us to stay at Christmas, just after they'd moved in to Rhamscott. She had gone completely over the top with Christmas decorations and there was tinsel everywhere, even in the bathroom.

"I'll cook the Christmas lunch," she said. "You don't need to do a thing."

"You mean you've progressed from pickled eggs and toast?" I teased her.

"No," she laughed. "You know that's my signature dish."

Nellie had come so far, changed so much, learned so much. She was softer and kinder when she came back from Florida. Maybe it was *The Suns of Life* that had done it or maybe it was Rudi. Whatever it was, she laughed a lot and didn't let things get under her skin not even when the gas ran out on Christmas Eve.

"Rudi says we'll barbecue the turkey if it doesn't come back on," she said. "Like they do on the beach in Australia."

We were in high spirits and looking forward to Morwenna arriving even though that dreadful *Mistletoe and Wine* song kept coming on the radio!

And then, late in the afternoon, Chimp telephoned and Nellie went out into the hall to take the call.

I looked at Rudi and he nodded and I went out after her.

"She's not coming," she said, sitting on the stairs with the telephone receiver cradled in her hand. "Chimp says she's got a cold."

I had my suspicions that this was a deliberate ploy by Chimp to keep Morwenna at home for Christmas because it seemed that every opportunity he got, he put an obstacle in the way.

I took the receiver from her.

"Now you listen to me Chimp Davis," I said as firmly as I could. "You're to bring Morwenna over tomorrow morning and stop playing these games."

And you know what he did? He laughed. He laughed down the phone and hung up. I stared at the buzzing receiver in my hand. I had a good mind to ring him back and give him what for but my concern was more for Nellie.

Nellie wrapped her cardigan around her and hugged her knees. I sat down next to her on the stairs.

"I'm alright Poll, really I am," she said, leaning into my shoulder. "But I'm not putting up with this much longer."

I've never forgotten her saying that and yes I blame him. I blame him to this day for the chain of events he put into action. If he hadn't made things so difficult, Nellie would never have done what she did. If he'd been even a tiny bit more reasonable and stopped trying to win all the time – why did he see it as something he had to win instead of something to work out for Morwenna's sake? If he'd done that, then maybe Nellie would still be here.

Chimp

It was exhausting. Nellie was so unreasonable. I spent hours in my study brooding on it all and Grace would come in and climb up to sit on my knee. I used to tell her she was too old to sit on my knee – she was what, sixteen, seventeen by then – but she used to sulk if I said that and so I always gave in. She was very thin, very small. People were always saying she didn't look her age.

"You know what, Grace," I said to her one time. "Things would be so much easier if Nellie wasn't around."

The situation with Nellie and Morwenna was ruling our lives. I was always sounding off about something Nellie had done or hadn't done. It really stressed me out. Rhoswen used to say I had to try to calm down a little, step back, but I wasn't going to do that. I wasn't going to let Nellie win. The Court had more or less pronounced her an unfit mother. Why else had they refused to let our daughter live with her? I was only trying to uphold what the Court had said and I was quite sure they hadn't intended Morwenna to spend as much time with her as she was spending. I hadn't expected Nellie to come back to Wales and settle here. Never in a million years. I mean she always used to say how she hated the place. And then she and Rudi rented that big house near Mostyn like they were lord and lady of the manor! Our cottage, Rhoswen's cottage, was only small. I mean we loved it but I used to think that Nellie chose a five bedroomed house deliberately, to rub our noses in it, to try to entice Morwenna away. Not that she could of course. There was a Court Order in place.

There were other stresses going on in my life at the time. Richard had disappeared after irregularities in his financial affairs came to light. Financial affairs meant us and every other band he managed. Luckily the cottage was held in a trust fund so at least our accommodation was safe. I don't know how Richard got himself into that mess and I felt betrayed because instead of sticking around and riding out the storm, he legged it to France and disappeared. It turned out the contract the band had signed with him at the outset gave him 90% of royalties from all future sales. I cursed myself for being so naïve but we had been so young and I had trusted him.

We never saw a penny from ***No Milk Today*** despite it being one of the greatest hits of all time. In addition, I lost the copyright case against Nellie for the photographs and was ordered to pay her legal costs and we were still paying off the solicitor's fees from the custody case. Our financial situation was dire and I spent hours looking for more land to buy and sell. We had to release money from Rhoswen's trust fund to help us through and that didn't sit well with me. It only made me want to work harder on the Charity and find more land to buy and sell.

The pressure was on all round and I could do without Nellie and the games she played.

1989

Nellie

Extract from her unfinished biography, Street Life

In early 1989, I felt some of the old symptoms coming back and although I'd been sober for over 18 months, I started craving for something to take the edges off. I didn't like the way I was feeling. I felt tempted and for the first time, I didn't trust myself. I was losing the self confidence I'd gained in America and I began to worry I'd relapse.

At night I had dreams that I was falling off a roof or holding a still born baby and I recognised the signs and did not want to go back there. Rudi tried to reassure me by saying I was bound to feel unsettled from time to time and it didn't mean a full blown relapse was on the way. Even so we made a transatlantic call to Nurse Divine and she suggested I have a couple of weeks of r&r with them.

"I don't want to leave Morwenna," I told Rudi as we lay in bed that night. "If I go back to *The Suns,* Chimp will use it against me and do something to stop me seeing her when we get back. He'll say I'm mentally unstable or something."

Paranoia? I don't know but all I know is that I was seeing things that weren't there and waking up in the middle of the night feeling so afraid without knowing why.

"So we'll take her with us," he said.

I sat up and looked down at him. The red numbers on the radio alarm clock said it was two o'clock in the morning.

"He'll never agree to that," I said. "It's a battle getting him to agree to a day on the beach let alone taking her to Florida."

"So we don't ask him," Rudi said, reaching up and stroking my hair.

At first I didn't understand what he meant.

"You mean just take her?"

"Uh huh."

"We can't do that. Could we? Could we do that?"

He raised himself on one elbow and he put his hand gently at the back of my neck and pulled my face closer to his.

"Just think," he said. "Of the life we could live out there. No more cat and mouse. No more hit and run."

His words both scared and excited me. I had never thought of it before. We had been so intent on pleasing Chimp and not stepping on anyone's toes, I had never considered the rebel card.

When I woke up in the morning the conversation floated into my mind. Maybe he had said those words to chase away the demons in the early hours of the morning. It did seem a bit crazy.

Rudi's side of the bed was empty but within moments of my waking, the bedroom door opened and he came in with a cup of tea.

"Remember what we talked about last night?" he said, sitting down on my side of the bed and handing me the tea.

I nodded.

"Good," he said. "You just hold on to that. We've tried it his way for long enough. Now it's time to try it our way."

He left me holding my tea and feeling this new sense of excitement building up inside me. It was outrageous, ridiculous, impossible. How could we take Morwenna to Florida, just like that? No, it was madness. We'd get arrested, we'd get stopped at the border and thrown into prison. No, it was too crazy to think of. And so I put it out of my mind.

I was due to speak to Morwenna on the phone that night. It didn't happen. When I rang, Rhoswen answered and said that Morwenna had gone out with Chimp for a walk. Morwenna never missed my Sunday calls. I was convinced they were trying to keep her away from me but I was too scared to say anything. Scared that if I did, they'd say I was paranoid, mentally unstable and not fit to even have contact with her and they'd go back to Court and stop me seeing her.

This carried on for about six weeks. I'd ring the house and there'd be no answer. She wasn't there when we went to pick her up. When it was their turn to bring her over, the car broke down. There was always an excuse and I was climbing the walls. And then, early in the Spring, when the daffodils and primroses were coming out, Chimp told me they were taking her away to Spain for a week.

"No," I said. "No. You are not taking her to Spain."

I didn't trust Grace and I'd never forgotten how she'd stuck Morwenna's mouth together with Sellotape.

Chimp laughed.

"Oh?" he said. "Try and stop me." and he put down the phone.

Rudi called Joe. They had this low voiced conversation and afterwards he came into the room where I was lying on the couch trying to concentrate on the TV.

"Not much longer now babe," he said, leaning down and kissing my forehead. "Not much longer."

Polly

I didn't know they were planning it. The police came to see us after they'd left the country and that was the first I knew about it. The police didn't believe me. I was her best friend wasn't I? Surely she'd confided in me? No I said, truthfully, she hadn't. What about helping her get Morwenna away? they said. Had I helped my brother arrange that?

Joe. With a sinking heart I learned about his involvement. He hadn't told me. None of them had told me.

"But I only spoke to Nellie yesterday," I said to Vincent after the police had gone.

"She's protecting you," he said. "This way you can't get into trouble."

After the police left, I was in a state of shock and disbelief. They had Joe down at the police station and unusually, Da telephoned me demanding to know what the bloody hell was going on now because he'd had the police banging on his door.

I had a lot of phone calls that night including a particularly abusive one from Chimp accusing me of all sorts of things. When he hung up Rhoswen rang back trying a different tack.

"Tell us where she is Polly," she pleaded. "Chimp's going out of his mind. It's not good for a little girl to be torn away from her family like this."

I'd had enough of them, I really had.

"For your information," I said, my heart pounding. "Morwenna hasn't been torn away from her family. For your information, Nellie is her mother and if you and Chimp hadn't made things so difficult, this wouldn't have happened."

There was a moment's silence.

"You'll get your come uppance one day," she said in a low, controlled voice. "You and that brother of yours. You'll get your come uppance."

I was stunned by the vitriol coming down the phone that night. Chimp's mum was the next to ring, promising eternal hell fire and damnation for the wicked things I'd done.

After that, Vincent pulled the phone out of the wall. I tried to get Awen to settle but she was fractious: probably picking up on all the negativity in the house. After I finally got her to sleep, I went downstairs to join Vincent and on the TV there were these dreadful pictures of football fans trying to get out of a football stadium.

"Whatever's happened now?" I said to Vincent who, by then, had lost himself in a few bottles of beer.

"No idea," he said. "But I don't think we're going to forget this day in a hurry."

We didn't know it at the time but what we'd seen on the telly was Hillsborough. And that's another story altogether.

Nellie

Extract from her unfinished biography, Street Life

I still don't know how we managed to pull it off. All I know is we did and she's here and we are living in Florida as one happy little family.

We couldn't have done it without Joe. He picked Morwenna up to take her out for the day, just as he usually did but instead of taking her to the beach, he drove her straight to Heathrow airport where we were waiting. I laughed and I cried. I told her we were going on a wonderful adventure to a place where mummies and daughters lived happily ever after.

She had no spare clothes, nothing, but does that matter when you're five years old? Rudi had bought her this gigantic pink teddy that they nearly refused to let on the plane and as for the rest, well, she'd have all she wanted when we got to the States. And she has. Colita and Manford treat her like she's their granddaughter. She goes out riding with Colita – I was a little nervous at first until she said "honey I first rode a horse when I was in diapers. The younger you start the better."

I sit on the porch sometimes and I watch Morwenna with Rudi in the pool and I pinch myself because never in a million years did I dream we'd all be in Florida together. It's like a dream come true.

I spent a couple of weeks at *The Suns of Life* when we got back here and that put me back on track. Ice cream on Sundays and Nurse Divine were just what I needed.

We've been here six months now and there is nothing Chimp can do about it. He knows we are somewhere in Florida but he doesn't know exactly where. We are beyond the jurisdiction of the English Courts and beyond his controlling grasp. I know it means we can never go back to England but that's not the end of the world is it? Polly and Vincent can always come out here for a holiday.

Joe got into a bit of trouble about it all. I was sorry about that because his intentions were truly good. The Court didn't see it that way – it doesn't like people assisting others to abduct children – that's what they called it apparently – and he got a suspended sentence. Polly said he was lucky because in Court, they'd brought up the fact he'd been a flying picket during the Miners' Strike although what that's got to do with anything, I don't know.

Anyway Polly was a bit upset that we didn't tell her our plans but she got over it and Joe took it all in his stride like Joe does. One day I will thank him properly for what he has done. As for Chimp, Polly says he's pretty pissed off.

"You know what he's like Nellie," she said to me on the phone. "He stews on things. I'm worried he won't let it rest. That he might do something."

As far as I'm concerned he can stew all he likes. He likes to think he can control everything but this time he can't. Morwenna is with me and that is where she's staying so stick that in your pipe and smoke it Mr Emyr Davis.

Nothing will ever separate me from my daughter again.

Morwenna

Those were the last words Mum ever wrote. Words written in black pen on cream paper, words about me. From then on the pages are empty. I look at them and wonder what else she was going to write in her autobiography; what the rest of her life might have looked like.

I remember it vaguely. Coming back to England, shadowy people buzzing around me; sitting on a plane with the air hostesses fussing round me and that great big pink teddy bear strapped in by my side. I didn't know what it all meant. I didn't have a clue. I didn't think it meant anything, I was just going back to England. I didn't question where Mum or Rudi or Colita or Manford were. I was only six years old. I didn't know that a terrible tragedy had just happened but I do remember mum crying and holding on to me and pleading with someone not to let me go and how they pulled her away. I remember I started crying too although I didn't really know why. I had no concept of what it all meant. I had no idea my life had just changed for ever. I had no idea that would be the last time I saw her.

When Auntie Polly gave me the autobiography, there was a photograph album with it. I was only in Florida for six months but mum took so many photographs you'd think I'd been there a lifetime. There was me on a horse, me in the pool, me everywhere. Rudi laughing in the sun, pushing his hair back with his hand, Mum wearing pink shorts and big black sunglasses, crouched down by the barbecue and smiling up at the camera. We look like any other normal family. We didn't know what was just around the corner. Maybe it's best we don't know or how would we ever get out of bed in the morning?

From what I know now, Colita and Manford did all they could to keep me with them in Florida but it was never going to happen. There were no blood ties. Rudi was not my father. Dad was.

I went back to live with my grandparents in Wales. I remember people speaking in quiet voices, tiptoeing around me. I remember a long car journey and being given ice cream in a motorway service station which is odd because it was autumn. I remember Auntie Polly hugging me like she'd never let me go. It was all a mystery to me. I remember being confused when they said I couldn't speak to Mum on the phone. How they said she'd gone away for a while. And when I asked when she was coming back Granpy took me out in the garden to see the hedgehogs. I was the only one living in oblivion. The rest of them were living with the knowledge of something that was too horrific to comprehend.

Chimp

We have been asked so many times, by journalists, TV reporters, everyone we know and everyone we meet: were there any signs? Did we see it coming?

It's thirty years ago now and people have largely forgotten unless they run some anniversary special or documentary about Nellie on the TV and then all the questions start again. I wish they wouldn't. I wish they'd leave it alone. We've had to live with it for so long now we just want to live a peaceful life and put it all behind us.

When Nellie abducted Morwenna and took her to the States, I was beside myself. I couldn't believe what she'd done and my brain picked and picked and picked over how to get Morwenna back home. We spent a fortune we didn't have consulting lawyers in the hope they'd go to Court to get an Order forcing Nellie to bring her back. None of them could help. Morwenna was outside the jurisdiction and no Court could order Nellie to bring her home.

I couldn't let it rest. Couldn't they get the United States to extradite her? Nellie had committed a criminal offence. Not in the United States they said. As far as they were concerned it was a UK matter and they didn't extradite anyone except the most serious of offenders.

It seemed breath taking that Nellie could get away with it; that she could take my daughter to the States and no one could get her back.

It was all I thought about. I didn't sleep, I paced the house, I ranted and I raved. Rhoswen says it was like living with a monster. As for Grace, well yes she absorbed it all. My anger at Nellie, my fury. In the end I decided that there was only one thing I could do. I would go out there and bring her home. There was nothing anyone could do to stop me. Rhoswen tried to talk me out of it but I shut her out, I shut them all out: the voices of reason, the voices of good intention. If I didn't do something I'd lose my mind. And if no one else could help, I was going to take matters into my own hands.

Rhoswen refused to come with me. We had a great big row and she told me I was on my way to a nervous breakdown and what was more I'd go through it on my own because she wasn't putting up with it much longer. I told her to go to hell and went to the study, slamming the door.

A few moments later, Grace opened it.

"I'll come with you," she said. "I'll help you find her."

It seemed to me that Grace was the only one at that time who understood what I was going through. Maybe I confided in her too much, leaned on her more than I should have done I don't know. Maybe I wasn't thinking straight. But she was an adult, seventeen years old and when I felt like no one was listening and no one understood, she did.

I thought her intentions were good; that she was coming with me to offer support and I was truly grateful. It was a long flight to Miami and I didn't even know where Nellie and Morwenna were. All I knew was that I had to find and reclaim my daughter and that drove me on. It never seemed impossible to me. I had to do it, I had no choice and having someone with me took the edges off a bit.

Rhoswen tried to stop us but I was past listening, past caring. She's never thrown it back at me. She's never pointed the finger like so many others have. She says that although she didn't like me much at that time she always loved me. And somehow, she still does.

Polly

As far as I know this is what happened. At the time we reeled from the shock, the horror and the disbelief and then gradually, the whole horrible picture got pieced together. There are still pieces missing but after thirty years, most of the jigsaw is complete. The only thing still missing is the *why*. Grace has never really explained it and I have never truly understood her motives.

What did we know about Grace really? More after it happened because the papers filled pages and pages with her story, but before that we knew very little.

Afterwards, the papers reported her as saying she was glad she'd done it. That it wasn't the first time she'd shot someone. She said her father hadn't had the gun that day he holed them up in The Gower. She had. She said it was her who had shot him, to put him out of his misery like she'd done with a fox in the woods once when it broke a leg. She said it hadn't been suicide at all. She'd pulled the trigger. She'd killed her father.

I mean can you believe it? It still makes my head spin. There was so much to take in at the time. Over the years I've learned to live with it but if I stop and think about it too much it still overwhelms me. Back then, so much was said and written about her I didn't know what to believe in the end.

Chimp

I agreed to write this down because I wanted to set the record straight. I hope it might even improve my relationship with Morwenna because we have never been as close as we once were. I've tried, but there's obstacles all along the way and she won't walk over them, she won't cross the river. She's a grown woman now but these things run deep. So I agreed, when she said she wanted to do this, to write down what happened from my point of view. I have never gone into it before. Not even when the tabloid reporters banged on our door all day and all night. Not even years later when they asked me to appear on documentaries or rang me up to get my comment on something. I never wanted to speak about it. It was too horrific, too unreal to tell to strangers.

Sometimes I get asked to do an interview about the band, about ***No Milk Today***. I gave up doing those interviews years ago because they were never about the music. They always came back to the same thing: Grace and what happened that day in Jupiter. It was like the band, the records, the Charity, came second. I suppose it makes for a good story: how I rescued Grace only for her to end up shooting my partner's new boyfriend but someone died here and it's not just a story. It's a tragedy and it should never have happened.

Anyway. We landed in Miami and stayed in this cheap budget hotel. It wasn't a nice area and I told Grace that she wasn't to go out without me. Miami was a dangerous place in those days. It probably still is if you wander into the wrong area.

Anyway somehow she'd done her homework and was way ahead of me. It came out later that she'd rung *The Suns of Life* where we knew Nellie had been a patient and got her address. It was as easy as that. There was an enquiry into it afterwards but as far as the unwitting woman on the other end of the phone was concerned, she was just helping a girl who had come out to Florida to visit her auntie.

That morning, I woke up in the hotel room to find Grace was missing. I called reception but that was only manned from time to time by this big black guy who kept a gun behind the desk and he was going crazy because that gun had gone missing and he didn't have time to listen to a guest who didn't know where his step daughter – that's how I described her – was.

I was in a strange country. I didn't know the area. I spoke to the police but they weren't interested. They had much bigger fish to fry in Miami than looking for an 18 year old girl. They had shootings and drugs and gangs and a missing English girl was not high on their list of priorities.

"So she'll come back when she's hungry," the officer I spoke to said and hung up. Honestly. That's what he said. I remember it to this day.

All I could do was wait. I was holed up in that tiny little hotel room with its yellow walls and pathetic excuse for a shower. It didn't even have MTV! Outside, police sirens wailed constantly. The air conditioning was broken and the windows were nailed shut. It was hot, so bloody hot. I remember there was this fly buzzing around driving me crazy and I couldn't even open a window to let it out. I called Rhoswen and she said perhaps Grace had just gone out for a walk. In Miami? In a place she didn't know? I thought about going out to look for her but I was cautious about Miami and I'd probably end up getting robbed or worse. I told myself it was best to stay put and wait for her and tear her off a strip about going off on her own when she came back.

We only had three days. Three days to get Morwenna back. That was what the trip was supposed to be about but somehow it had, yet again, become about Grace. I was angry with her for turning it around like that. Whenever Morwenna was involved that is what Grace did. At the time I thought it was just another of her tactics to turn the spotlight back on her and away from Morwenna. I suppose I should have questioned why she was so keen to go with me to Florida. I mean she was always so jealous of my relationship with Morwenna. Why would she want to help me find her?

So I was waiting for her in that claustrophobic hot little hotel room watching the News to pass the time when this red headline flashed BREAKING and the newsreader on CNN said they were getting reports about a shooting in Florida. My heart sank because I had this horrible feeling Grace was involved and I couldn't shake it. I mean Florida is a big State and anything could have happened to anyone but somehow I knew Grace was involved and my first thought was that she'd got caught up in it and been hurt.

It never crossed my mind that she might be responsible for the shooting. Grace with a gun? Too far fetched. Never in a million years would I have believed she would steal a gun and hitch a ride to the farm in Jupiter where Nellie and Rudi and Morwenna were living with Rudi's parents. The man who gave her a ride was interviewed later by the police and said she seemed like a nice kid who was looking for her English auntie. No there was nothing out of the ordinary about her. Skinny kid, English. About 15. He'd dropped her off and thought nothing more of it. Until he turned on the TV later and recognised her.

How long was that journey? From Miami to Jupiter? About an hour and a half. And he said if he'd known for one moment that the kid had a gun he would have called the cops and kicked her out. But he didn't, he hadn't, it was all quite a shock. He'd mixed with some tough guys in his time, seen some things on the mean streets of Miami but this? A seemingly innocent English kid getting into his Ford with a gun hidden someplace? Unbelievable. Completely unbelievable.

The police say she must have waited for some time outside the house, hiding behind the barn maybe or one of the outbuildings. Colita and Manford, Rudi's parents, were out that day at a horse show although it was pure chance that they were. Grace couldn't have known that. And she just waited and waited and then Rudi came out.

I still wonder if she planned it; if, sitting beside me on the plane reading some blood thirsty horror novel, it was all swimming around her head or whether it was done on impulse. She has never gone into great detail. All she's told those parole hearings is what she's been saying for years. That she thought she was doing me a favour. That she was trying to help me. That Nellie needed to be taught a lesson.

No wonder she never got parole.

Morwenna

Grace didn't mean to kill Rudi. She meant to kill my mum. Well, she did that anyway didn't she? By shooting Rudi she effectively took away mum's life too.

When I look back at the photographs, when I read her autobiography, I can see they were a young couple very much in love with the rest of their lives to look forward to.

Grace took that away from them when she hitched a ride to the farm, hid outside and pulled the trigger. I don't know how my mum coped with seeing Rudi like that. I mean one moment it was a sunny afternoon in Paradise, the next Rudi was bleeding out in her arms. If the man hadn't come to deliver hay for the horses and overpowered Grace and disarmed her, she would have killed Nellie too. I can't imagine what my mum went through. I'm not surprised she checked out not long afterwards. It may be yesterday's news to most people but it's still today's headlines for me.

Grace has never acknowledged what she did. She has never said sorry or given a proper explanation for why she did it. All she has said is that Rudi got in the way and that Nellie deserved to die because all she did was cause trouble for my dad.

Where was I? I didn't see it. I don't remember it. I've met with psychiatrists and psychologists who have assessed me to see if I suffered trauma, damage, repressed memory, long term effects. And I have told them all the same thing.

I was playing out back in the pool and I don't remember a thing.

Polly

I could not get my head around Rudi being shot. He wasn't shot by a random stranger, it wasn't some American crazy kid who did it. It was Grace. Rudi never hurt her, he hardly knew her.

I can't imagine how Rudi's parents coped with it. They never appeared on TV or in the papers. They just withdrew and maintained a quiet dignity. I'd never met them until Morwenna went to live over there years later.

Powder Room's records stormed the charts after it happened. It's always the way isn't it? No one had really heard of them in the UK before the shooting and then ***Mesmerise*** got to number one. I used to listen to Rudi's voice coming out of the radio and think *that's all that's left of him now. Just his voice.*

Nellie was completely broken by it. She was admitted into *The Suns of Life* and when I rang they wouldn't discuss anything with me because I wasn't a relative. I used to stay up all night, too shocked to sleep. The world seemed so unpredictable, so fragile.

Grace was eventually found guilty in 1991. She stalled the process for two years: sacking her lawyers, objecting to the Jury. Apparently you can do that in the States. When she did eventually stand trial, she ran the Florida stand your ground defence which apparently is the same as self defence in this country. She said that Rudi had come out of the house with a gun and she had to shoot first to protect herself. I mean unbelievable. Bloody unbelievable.

Nellie never knew that Grace ended up with a life sentence with no parole because by then, Nellie had checked out. It happened on a sunny winter's day on 1st February 1990, four months after Rudi was killed and two days before her twenty seventh birthday. There was a big inquiry at *The Suns of Life* afterwards and a lot of questions were asked about how someone could get their hands on so many drugs when they were already identified as a suicide risk.

I felt empty when I heard. Hollow. Lost. Sick. Angry. Angry that it had all come to this. I used to close my eyes and see Nellie walking into school tossing her long brown hair and giving the girls her death stare. I remember her climbing down the ladder at the benefit concert in that ridiculous ballgown. There are so many things I remember. It seems incredible, impossible, unreal that she isn't here anymore. I used to cry every time I saw Morwenna. That poor poor child.

We couldn't afford to fly to the States and there was no one here willing to bring her home. Nellie's mother had disappeared years ago. Colita and Manford made all the arrangements but it was Tom Horse who paid for Nellie to be brought back to Wales, God rest his soul.

Chimp insisted on the funeral taking place at Craesor Chapel in Ffynnongroyw. It wouldn't have been what Nellie wanted, not at all. She would have wanted black horses with feathered plumes on their heads and a full State ceremony! She definitely wouldn't have wanted a quiet ceremony in Wales.

"That's the point see," Joe said. "If it happens anywhere else, London for example, it's going to be overrun by Press and reporters. I can understand Chimp's reasoning. For once."

I think Nellie would have preferred a bit of a fuss, I think she would have wanted fireworks and reporters hostling and jostling and letting off flashbulbs rather than the sedate, quiet flower strewn service that it was. But what could I say? What influence did I have? No one had any influence. Chimp was still her husband, even if it was in name only, and he had the final say.

That day was dark, wet and stormy as if the world was reluctant to relinquish one of its brightest sparks. Halfway through the service, the chapel door opened and Ricky Rich, Perry and Dragon from *Powder Room* came in very quietly and shuffled into a pew at the back. They were all in black, wearing shades and they didn't stay long, disappearing into the rain and damp afterwards in a shiny black limousine.

I couldn't believe the hymns Chimp had chosen. I mean *All Things Bright and Beautiful?* When we sang that in Assembly at school, Nellie would change the words and sing

I have lost my padded bra

I left it in his car

I should have stayed at home last night

And now we've gone too far

The only time I ever got into trouble at school was when I giggled at Nellie singing that and we got hauled out of Assembly. Our form tutor suggested I might want to re-think the company I was keeping but I didn't and I'm glad I didn't.

I could hear her, that day, standing beside me singing those words to that hymn and despite the day, despite the bleakness of it all, in some peculiar way, it brought the spirit of Nellie back to me in all her fiery, rebellious glory and it made me smile.

We had a bit of a do down at the Welfare afterwards but it wasn't very well attended. Ffynnongroyw wasn't Nellie's home and some people thought she'd got a bit above herself. Joe and Chimp nearly had a punch up and Mam attempted to separate them by brandishing her umbrella.

"You ought to be ashamed of yourself, both of you! At her funeral too! Can't you just let things lie for just one day? For just one day?"

Nellie's ashes were flown out to Florida. Chimp didn't discuss these things with me of course he didn't but Joe had an ear to the ground and Tom Horse insisted that Chimp agree to Colita's suggestion.

She wanted, you see, for Nellie and Rudi to be returned to the earth together. She wanted their joint ashes to be scattered over the Pacific Ocean. And in the end, that's what they did.

The only good thing about 1990 is that in November, Margaret Thatcher resigned, putting an end to her eleven year reign of terror. There was a big bonfire down the Welfare that night.

Chimp

There had been bad feeling between me and Nellie but I still loved her. She was a big part of my life and we had a daughter together. It broke my heart when she committed suicide. I withdrew from everyone, even Rhoswen. I just couldn't get my head around how a chain of events could lead to such tragedy. All I had wanted to do was get access to my daughter. How could it have gone so wrong and end up with two people dying?

For two years I walked around in a daze. Yes I had Morwenna but the price was too high. As for Grace, well, she was sent to the correctional facility where she stayed for two years until she was found guilty of murder although she fought the process all the way.

I never wanted to see or hear from her again. She tried to contact me but I told the prison I didn't want contact with her. There was nothing to say. She used to write letters, send cards covered in primitive, hand drawn lovehearts. She used to write weird things like "now we can be together" and say how she'd done it for me because she loved me.

I found it all quite sickening. That she could think that shooting one man and causing the death of a woman didn't mean anything apart from clearing the way for her stupid fantasies. I hated hearing ***No Milk Today*** and I still turn it off when it comes on the radio.

How did I explain it all to Morwenna? Well I didn't, not until she was older. I never wanted to tell her at all but Rhoswen said we had to, that at some stage she was bound to start asking questions about her mother. Maybe I should have told her earlier because by the time I finally got the courage to do it, she already knew. And that caused a big rift between us, one that could never heal because I hadn't told her, her dad who was supposed to protect her and keep her safe and always be honest with her.

Grace got 25 years life in 1991 and her first parole was in 2004. In 2011 she came up for parole again and got a ten year denial. She can't be considered for parole again until 2021. Megan and Paul keep us updated and sometimes it's mentioned fleetingly on the News. It's an old story now and it doesn't get much coverage over here.

Apparently she's as good as gold in prison. Megan and Paul continue to support her. Megan says Grace is different now. She says she's turned into a lovely woman who just wants to get out and start a family before it's too late. She says she's got a poster of the band in our younger days pinned up on her cell wall.

Rhoswen talks about leopards and spots and I have to say that what she says makes far more sense to me than what Megan says despite the fact that Grace is a dab hand at cross stitch cushions and a convert to Creationism.

I mean it's all words and spin isn't it? What lies underneath? I suspect it's as dark and as deep as it's always been.

Morwenna

It was Uncle Joe who told me. It was autumn 1995 and I was twelve years old.

"So you see," he said, as we sat on the beach at Talacre. "There was once this beautiful princess who was very sad and decided she didn't want to live in this world anymore. So she went to live in a kingdom under the sea instead. People couldn't see her anymore but she was always near them, especially her daughter who she loved very much."

"Are you talking about my mum?" I said.

A cold wind blew in from the sea. I was bundled up in a coat and scarf and bobble hat and the old red and white lighthouse stood solid and firm in the distance.

"Did she do that?" I said when he didn't speak. "Did she decide she didn't want to live in this world anymore?"

Uncle Joe stood up.

"She did," he said. "But you must always remember how much she loved you Morwenna. You were the shining light in what had become a very dark world."

I was puzzled.

"Why was it so dark?" I said. "Didn't she live in the sunshine?"

Uncle Joe reached out his hand and I took it and stood up.

"Aye," he said. "She did. But sometimes the darkness can come from within however bright the sun might be. Come on now. Let's go and get some chips shall we?"

"Did mum get too sad to live in this world anymore?" I asked my dad when I saw him the next day.

Dad stared at me.

"Who told you that?" he said.

"Uncle Joe," I said. "He said sometimes the world can become dark even if the sun is shining."

I saw him exchange a look with Rhoswen above my head.

"He had no right to tell you that," he said. I could see he was angry but I didn't understand why. "He's spent his whole life meddling and interfering in our business."

"So is it true then?"

"We'll have this conversation again when you're older," he said. "Now get your things or we'll be late for Nanny and Granpy."

"I only want to know about my mum," I persisted. "About Nellie."

"That's enough Morwenna," he said. "Get your coat."

Dad has never liked me calling her Nellie. He says it sounds disrespectful. Why does it? I like calling her Nellie. That's who she was isn't it? Nellie on the Telly? I've watched some of her old clips on You Tube. She makes me laugh. She wore some pretty weird clothes but back in the Eighties I guess they all did.

Calling her Nellie was just one of the things Dad and I argued about. Another thing was when I played *Powder Room* records. As I got older, we didn't seem able to have a conversation without disagreeing about something. It wasn't deliberate. Even if someone's your dad it doesn't mean you're going to get on with them and although I feel a bit disloyal for saying this, Uncle Joe felt more of a dad to me than he did.

I will never forget Auntie Polly coming round to tell me that Uncle Joe had died. In my head I imagined he'd gone to live in the underwater kingdom with Nellie. Even though I was sixteen by then, that story gave me comfort. We still remain children at heart.

Polly

Joe died at Christmas 1999. It's twenty years ago and I miss him every day. We may not have lived in each other's pockets but you always know someone's around don't you, that someone's there and has your back. He always had mine. And Nellie's too. He always had her back.

It wasn't dramatic. It was stupid. Stupid because it was such a waste of life. He was only 41 and we were teetering on the edge of a new century. He went out. He drank too much. He had a fight and he fell and hit his head on the pavement. He spent 7 days in intensive care before we had the conversation about turning things off. You know it had to get to that point before Da would speak to him. And by that time, Joe couldn't hear the regret and the love and the sadness in the words Da spoke to him.

Lisa was in pieces, my mum was in pieces, I kept it together but I don't know how. He was my brother and he'd always been there, strong and tall and protective. I might have been a grown woman by then with a husband and child of my own but losing Joe made me feel like a lost and lonely child. My brother was no longer there to protect me from the hooded claw.

One dark evening, Lisa and I were in the hospital and went to get coffee from the machine in the canteen. It was empty and bright with harsh, artificial light.

"I think his drinking got worse when Nellie died," she said. "Oh I know, I know he's always been in love with her. I don't mind. He loved me too. It might have been easier for him if he'd had a job, something to focus on, but as soon as he started one, they'd find out he'd been a striking miner and a picket and ask him to leave. Some of the South Wales boys went over to England to work on that Channel Tunnel because they couldn't get work. He was thinking about it but wasn't sure he wanted to go to England."

I knew Joe had struggled but until that point, I hadn't realised just how much. I felt overwhelmingly sad about it all.

"It was Morwenna who got him through," Lisa smiled, batting her tears away with her finger tips. "Morwenna."

My heart sank. We hadn't told her he was in hospital. I didn't think she should see him like this and Lisa agreed.

"It's hard enough for us," she said.

Two days later, the machines were turned off and I walked away from my brother for the last time. I didn't want to leave him there all on his own.

"That's the most peaceful I've seen him in a long time," Lisa said, taking my arm at the door as we looked back at him. Mam was quietly weeping in a chair by the bed and Da stood with his arm around her shoulders.

"Best leave them to it," Lisa said quietly as we left the room.

Outside in the corridor, nurses with tinsel round their hats were going off shift and heading home for Christmas.

"Will you be alright?" I asked Lisa as we walked out into the cold night air.

"Joe's still with me," she smiled. "I hear his voice all the time."

When I got to Tom and Sarah's house, the Christmas tree blinked happily through the window.

"How's Joe?" Tom Horse said when he opened the front door. I shook my head and looked down at my feet, not trusting myself to speak.

"Oh no," he said. "No love, no."

For the first time in my life he hugged me and for a moment, we stood there in the hall with the carols floating out from the kitchen radio.

"Do you want me to tell Morwenna?" he said. There were tears on his face but he tried to pretend there weren't. Men of his generation didn't cry. Not even when the man you'd treated like a son had left this world.

"No," I said. "I'll do it. It might be better if she hears it from me."

He nodded.

At that moment, Morwenna appeared at the top of the stairs.

"Auntie Polly!" she said, her face lighting up. "Happy Christmas!"

She looked so grown up in a red velvet dress with her long dark hair tied back with a red ribbon but also, so young.

"What's wrong?" she said when she got to the bottom of the stairs. "You look really sad."

"Go in the kitchen with Auntie Polly," Tom said. "She's got

something to tell you."

How did I tell her? It was hard enough for me to believe it was true let alone put it into words.

"Is Uncle Joe alright?" she said when we were in the kitchen with the door closed. "It's Christmas Eve and he didn't come. He always comes on Christmas Eve."

We sat at the table and I put my hands over hers and told her in simple words.

"When?" she said, raising her head, tears shining brightly in her eyes. "When will people stop leaving me?"

I went to her and held her head close to my heart and the clock ticked and ***In the Bleak Mid Winter*** came on the radio. It was five minutes of a lifetime that we spent, just the two of us, a moment of closeness I'll never forget. I didn't know how to make it right. My heart broke for her and for Joe and all over again for Nellie and Rudi.

It was a nice funeral if you can call any funeral nice. The Colliery band from Point marched down the High Street with the band from Cwm beside them. Men from Mostyn, who had worked with Joe at Bersham, brought up the rear.

It was a grey January day and their banners and flags flew defiantly in the gloom. Their mines may have gone but they were still proud men, men who held their heads up high in a world that had crashed and burned around them.

Badger Jones came up from Merthyr, still with that white streak running through his black hair although it was more grey than black now.

"I can't believe it," he said to me as we stood outside the chapel. "I can't. I can't believe it. If there's anything I can do Polly, anything…"

"You did enough all those years ago," I managed to smile despite myself. "You always left more coal outside Alison and Frank's house than anyone else's."

He smiled and drifted away.

Craesor Chapel was packed, absolutely packed but despite the occasion, the divisions were still there. Some of the miners refused to sit next to each other and some preferred to stand rather than sit next to men they still called Scabs.

Mam was so shocked by what had happened to Joe even her sharp tongue was silenced. She left most of the arrangements to me and Lisa and the only thing she asked for was that we sing ***Abide With Me.*** Despite their differences, the voices of the men from North and South Wales came together and soared up into the Clwydian Hills, all their divisions and differences and words and anger forgotten for a moment. Beautiful it was. It made the hairs on the back of my neck stand up and it made Mam cry all over again.

The last song we played, as everyone was filing out into the January drizzle, was ***Harvest for the World*** by The Christians. The words in that song say a lot about hopes and dreams and divisions and Joe had loved it. As we were standing outside, Da took both of my hands in his and squeezed them tight. I don't think I'd ever seen tears in his eyes before but they were there. He couldn't speak but that look, well. Da.

At the Wake, they drank the Welfare dry and there was a bit of a punch up apparently when the South Wales lot – who were the last to leave – started singing old picketing songs. Well, there'd have to be a punch up at Joe's funeral wouldn't there? He wouldn't have wanted anything else.

Me and Vincent left early with Mam and Da because Vincent thought there might be trouble but it was a good send off. Joe would have been amazed at how many people came, how many people loved him.

The next morning, we couldn't find Sidney anywhere. He was an old cat by then and Vincent used to say he'd had 999 lives not 9. Anyway I left his food out for him and kept an eye on the shed roof and that night we went out looking for him in the fields with torches. I'd had a feeling something wasn't right for a while and I kept meaning to take him to the vet but what with all that was going on with Joe I never got round to it.

We never found him and he never came home. Vincent said old cats always go away to die and it was just his time but even so, it broke my heart all over again. It was all mixed up with the loss of Joe. Joe and Sidney, the half blind, tail less cat he'd brought home from Point all those years ago and now he'd gone, too.

Polly

Afterwards, in the days that follow a funeral, in the days when you try to adjust to the absence of someone you love, Morwenna spent a lot of time at our house. There can't have been much comfort at her house with Sarah praying all over the place and Tom Horse rolling in drunk all the time. That's how she described it, anyway.

Having her there gave me something to focus on and I was glad of her company. She loved cooking with me in the kitchen and sometimes she just sat at the kitchen table drawing. Awen was four years younger than her and Morwenna treated her like a little sister. Sometimes I'd look at them and think how amazing it was that I had a daughter and Nellie had a daughter and there they were, sitting at the kitchen table, right in front of me.

Morwenna had a lot of questions. We answered them as best as we could. I got out the photo albums and showed her pictures of Joe and me shivering on the beach when we were little and me and Nellie in our school uniforms. I had also kept a little book Morwenna created after Nellie died.

"I remember that," she said, touching the dresses she'd drawn and filled in with oddments of material from Sarah's sewing basket. "When I missed mum I used to design her a dress so she could wear it when she came home."

"You're good at it," I said. "Have you thought any more about going to art college?"

She shrugged.

"No," she said. "I'm not sure what to do yet."

"What are Colita and Manford like?" she asked me as we looked at the photographs of Florida. "Rudi's parents? Have you got any photos of them?"

I hadn't because I'd never met them but I'd kept in touch by letter.

"I'd like to meet them one day," she said.

It's fair to say that at that time, Morwenna was still looking for her place in the world but even I was surprised when, just after her nineteenth birthday, she announced she was going to Florida.

Morwennna

Dad tried to talk me out of going to America. He wanted me to be a doctor or something, go to University and get letters after my name. He put a lot of store by that sort of stuff and as for Rhoswen, she was all for women being highly educated because, she said, women had to prove they were better than men.

Did they?

What did Wales mean to me? I was always someone else's shadow while I lived there. Someone's daughter, someone's legacy, the daughter of an ill fated television presenter and a famous rock star. Auntie Polly told me that after Rudi and Nellie died, the Press camped out in the garden trying to get photographs of me for the papers. I mean what sort of behaviour is that? I was only a kid.

And then, about a month before I went to America, the story about my mum and Rudi got re-kindled when Toto and Shirley sold another story to the papers.

"They used to work at the farmhouse in Sussex," Auntie Polly sighed. "When Nellie and Rudi were living there. They've already sold their story to the papers once. You'd think they'd made enough money out of misery."

This time there was a twist. This time they said they'd been paid by my dad to plant drugs in Nellie and Rudi's kitchen drawer.

Vincent turned white and threw the paper in the sink.

"I knew it," he said. "I bloody knew it."

Within twenty four hours, photographers were camping outside Tom and Sarah's house hoping to catch a shot of me or anyone who might look good splashed all over the front page. I was alarmed, I'd never experienced anything like it before and I had a taste of what Nellie must have experienced in her lifetime. Men jumped out of shop doorways and flashed cameras in my face or called out my name on the street, asking how I felt now I knew the truth.

How did I feel? How did I feel?

"Is it true dad?" I asked him on the phone. "Is it true you paid these people to plant drugs in Nellie's house so you could get custody of me?"

"Don't call her that," he said.

"I'm nineteen now," I said. "I can call her what I like. That's not the issue here dad. Did you pay them? Did you?"

He drew in a breath and there was silence for a moment.

"They're pond life Morwenna," he said calmly, trying to play it down. "Those sort of people are only ever interested in one thing and that's money. It's such a long time ago anyway. Everyone has moved on since then. How are you getting on applying for St. Andrews?"

I felt hot, mad and frustrated that he wasn't answering the question – dad is good at that.

"For once in my life tell me the bloody truth!" I shouted and this woman passing the phone box gave me quite a look.

He went sort of quiet on me for a moment.

"I don't know what to say Morwenna," he said. "I don't know what to say."

I came off the phone and I knew what I was going to do with more certainty than ever. Four weeks later, I landed at Miami airport.

I didn't speak to dad again for years.

Chimp

Yes she went and I had a blazing row with Polly on the phone when I found out Morwenna was going to America.

"You knew about this didn't you?" I said. "You knew."

Polly was irritatingly calm.

"I didn't know," she said. "I only found out a few days ago."

"Put her on the phone," I said. "I want to speak to her."

Polly paused.

"She doesn't want to speak to you Chimp," she said. "You know that."

I was infuriated. All her life I had tried to protect her and do the right thing and she was acting as headstrong as her mother. She was only nineteen years old! I felt so frustrated but worst of all, I had this hollow feeling that I'd lost her, that I'd lost Morwenna forever.

"She'll be back," Rhoswen said. "It's only a holiday. She'll be back in a few weeks and you can try to speak to her then."

"But what if she doesn't come back?" I said, pacing the kitchen. "What if she decides to stay out there?"

Rhoswen looked at me.

"Well then you have to let her go."

It's true she was back in a few weeks. I went to Polly's house and caught a glimpse of her out in the garden reading a magazine on the sun lounger, sun tanned and long legged and lovely but when she saw me, she went inside and refused to come out again. Sometimes I could hardly believe that Nellie and I, with all our faults and foibles, had created something as perfect, as beautiful as Morwenna.

Two weeks later, she left England for good. Polly says Colita and Manford treat her like family, like she's their granddaughter. She isn't, she's my daughter but what can I do?

You set out in life to do the right thing. You follow your dreams and you follow your heart and you try to keep the things you love safe. I have learned you can't control everything, you can't keep everything safe: there are some things you just have to let go and Morwenna was one of them.

That was 2002. It seems a long time ago now. It *was* a long time ago.

Seventeen years to be precise.

Rhoswen and I are in our sixties now and Mam is in her eighties. Da didn't make it, not with all that drinking. He had a stroke and died two years ago. I had always hoped that one day we might make up and have a decent father/son relationship but suddenly you realise that it's over, that the chance has gone.

Richard went to prison for false accounting. He's out now but I've never seen a penny of our royalties. He hasn't even contacted Rhoswen and that hurt her a lot. By all accounts he went to the Far East, Cambodia or somewhere and that's the last we heard of him.

As for us, we still live in the little cottage with the apple orchard in Wrexham. I've never wanted to go anywhere else. I like the quiet life. Sometimes I get asked to do an interview but I always decline. I want to put those days of *The Sons* behind me. I'd erase them completely if I could. I'm not a rock star anymore. It's funny to look back at your younger self and wonder why you wanted the ambitions you almost killed yourself for.

I did agree that ***No Milk Today*** could be used in that advert, you know the one where the man has the pregnant wife and every morning he comes out of the house to see the milkfloat driving away and he can't run fast enough to catch up with it. Until he gets his Nike trainers and then he catches up. It made us a bit of money at the time.

The Hope Centres are probably the thing I'm most proud of, apart from Morwenna of course. Over the years, things have thawed a little between us to the point where we speak at Christmas and on birthdays but we've never been close since she found out about the drugs. It still hurts but I'm more used to it these days. She has her own life now.

Rhoswen has been my rock. There was a little dodgy patch when the police started investigating the fires *Meibion Glyndwr* set between 1979 and 1995 but they never managed to pin anything on us.

I have told the truth just like Morwenna asked me to. These words haven't been easy to write and have stirred up a lot of memories; many of them painful and difficult.

I'd like to close by saying that everything I did, I did for my daughter.

Everything.

Polly

Morwenna left for Florida in 2002 and she has made her home out there. Vincent and I have been out there for a few holidays although since Vincent had his hip operation and I developed diabetes we're not as flexible as we used to be. That's what age brings. Awen says 56 is young these days but some days when I get out of bed in the morning, I don't share her optimism.

Colita and Manford welcomed Morwenna like she was part of the family and they welcomed her so well she stayed. Morwenna has found her place in the world.

I always hoped she and Awen would be life long friends but after Morwenna went to the States they drifted apart. Awen turned out the wilder of the two especially during her teenage years. Vincent used to lock her in her bedroom to stop her going out! Ironic isn't it, that Nellie's child was the more studious, quiet one and my child was the rebel! Awen's settled now: she's a lovely woman in her early thirties who works as a travel agent and lives in a flat in Cardiff with a view across the bay. I wish she'd get a proper boyfriend but she doesn't seem to stay with them long. Vincent says young women don't want anything permanent these days.

I don't know if Morwenna knows that Nellie was pregnant when she died. I didn't tell her. I didn't tell anyone apart from Vincent and I can't remember who told me. It must have been Colita. I often wonder what she would have had, a little boy or a little girl and whether the baby would have been coffee coloured like Rudi or fair and pale like Nellie.

So much has happened since those dark distant days of the 1980s when we used to spray ourselves with *Chic* by Yardley and rinse colours into our hair with Toners and Shaders; when we did quizzes in magazines to find out who we'd marry; when we lay on the hotel beds eating crisps pilfered from the downstairs bar: Nellie was always salt and vinegar, I was always cheese and onion.

Sometimes I play my old records and remember how she tried to teach me to dance to *Saturday Night Fever* in her bedroom and some nights, if Vincent is out, I light the candles and I sit quietly and I listen to all the old songs and Nellie comes alive for me again.

She was my best friend and I still miss her. It's nearly thirty years since she died and I often wonder how she would be at 56. Would she have grown old gracefully? I doubt it. I suspect she'd still be going around in mini skirts and ridiculous shoes well into her nineties.

She cast a spell, Nellie, and she's still out there, somewhere. You can see her old broadcasts on You Tube and you can still buy *Sex in Socks* on Amazon. It's classed as vintage now. Does that mean we're old?

As time goes on, things get less raw. We could have done without Nellie's mum selling her story to the paper after she died but to be honest, I wouldn't have expected anything less. And that isn't all she did. After Nellie died, she found out Chimp's address and went knocking on his door asking if she'd left her any money. Breath taking isn't it? Chimp sent her away with a flea in her ear but he's hardly whiter than white.

Nellie and Chimp never got divorced. I don't know why when they were probably the ideal candidates for it! That meant that when she died, everything went to Chimp. Everything. The royalties from her books, the royalties from her photographs. The savings she'd squirrelled away. Chimp never mentioned it but he did well, oh yes I think he did quite well out of it. What Nellie would have thought about that, well, you can guess. But the one thing I did get because Colita sent it over to me was the sash. The sash Nellie was given for being Miss Sunshine Queen when we were in our teens.

And then there was Toto and Shirley. I don't know if what they wrote in the paper was true but again I wouldn't be surprised. Chimp didn't always play fair. And look at him now. He's made a fortune out of the old mine sites. Ok yes so he's helped a lot of people but he's made a lot of money too. It's no coincidence that a lot of storage warehouses and supermarkets have been built on the old mining land he bought. No prizes for guessing who got the profit from selling the land.

Anyway I said I wouldn't be bitter when I wrote this. I said I'd tell the truth just like Morwenna asked us to do and I believe I've done that.

Morwenna is a dress designer now. She definitely has Nellie's style, her love of clothes. She's just designed a collection of period clothes for a film set in Regency times. They love that sort of stuff in America. We're going to visit her when Vincent gets over his hip operation. I'm looking forward to going to Florida again.

As for Wales, well, the scars from the miners strike are still here, etched deep into the soil and the mountains and the valleys. The last deep mine in the UK, Kellingley, in, South Yorkshire, closed in 2015. On that day, two of the miners' wives organised a march through Knottingley, led by a miner dressed as the Grim Reaper and behind him, the miners marched proudly, holding their colliery banners as the brass band played.

Point closed in 1996. The liquidation plant came to nothing but we were lucky the mine stayed open so long. When it closed, Da retired and Vincent became a driving instructor.

I still get a Christmas card from Badger Jones. He prefers to be called Mark these days and he's settled with his own tyre business and five step children. As for Lisa, she's married to a boy who drives lorries for Hotpoint. At first, she was all tied up with guilt about it and thought I'd be upset in case it was doing a disservice to Joe's memory. I told her he'd be happy for her, he'd want her to find love.

Mary Williams is in a nursing home in Yorkshire. She still writes letters. She still blames Margaret Thatcher for changing our world. When Thatcher died in 2013, there were celebrations in all the old mining communities. In Goldthorpe, Yorkshire, they burnt an effigy of her and a man dressed as the devil brandished a placard which said "*The devil has come for Thatcher, the children's milk snatcher.*" The miners and their children have never forgotten her legacy. To us, it is a different legacy from the one the Tories might want us to remember. She divided this country, she destroyed the mining communities and she crucified the working class.

Mam and Da are still going strong. They've got central heating and a bathroom extension now. Mam got into that remake of *Poldark* a few years ago and when I first saw Aidan Turner I did a double take and caught my breath because he's a dead ringer for Rudi, he really is.

Da and Tom Horse never reconciled. When Tom died a few years ago, Da didn't even go to the funeral. I mean how sad is that? They'd known each other since they were young boys.

Every year on Joe's birthday, I walk up to *Moel Y Gamelin*. Sometimes Lisa comes with me. That's where we scattered Joe's ashes, on the highest point of his beloved Clwydian Hills. He's still there, in the hills and the valleys and the call of the wind.

There's always loss in a life time but there's love too. I've been lucky. I have Vincent and Awen and at the end of the day, that's all I ever wanted.

Morwenna

It was strange at first, arriving at the house in Florida and knowing that Nellie had woken up there in the morning, cleaned her teeth in the bathroom and walked out the front door into the sunlight. I didn't find it difficult, I found it comforting. I felt closer to her there. I couldn't find her in Wales but I found her in Florida. The first thing I saw when I walked in was a framed photograph in the hall of Nellie and Rudi sitting on a tractor in the snow. It was like she was there to welcome me.

Colita and Manford hadn't seen me since I was a kid and now I was a grown woman. They made me so welcome despite the fact they hadn't seen me for so many years. I stayed for two weeks and then I went home again but by then I knew. I knew where I wanted to be and where I belonged.

So I went back. I was excited about starting a new life. I didn't feel scared. I didn't question it. I just knew where I wanted to be.

Colita and Manford treated me like a long lost granddaughter. I will always be grateful to them for that. Nellie brought a whole lot of trouble to their door but despite that, they clearly loved her. I didn't know if I should acknowledge what had happened to Rudi or how I might do that but Colita approached it head on by getting out a photo album and showing me photos she'd taken over his lifetime.

One of the demons I wanted to lay to rest was Grace. It wasn't easy arranging to visit her in prison but Manford seemed to know just about everyone there was to know and it got sorted.

I dressed down on Colita's advice. For a Florida day I looked like I was going to a funeral in my black trousers and white shirt. Manford dropped me off at the gate and waited outside in his truck.

"Be strong," he said. "She can't hurt you no more."

I looked at him and wondered how he knew. Manford was not a man who said much but when he did, his insight often surprised me.

Grace had put her hair up in a ponytail and was wearing a white dress printed with yellow daisies. She hadn't dressed down. She'd dressed like she was sixteen years old on a summer day. It was weird.

It was 2008, just after her first parole and before her second in 2011. The way she talked was like she was coming home soon, like nothing had changed, like she hadn't killed a man. I was 25 and she was 37 and yet she seemed suspended in time, stuck at the same age she'd been when she was convicted in 1991. Does prison do that? Does it keep you stuck in a timewarp?

All I know is I found her breath-taking. The last time I'd seen her was when I was a child and the shady memories I had of her were tinged with darkness and fear. That's why I did it. That's why I went to see her. I had to put the ghosts to rest.

She held up photographs against the glass of the cats she was looking after on the Cat Care Programme. She told me their names and how one of them was deaf and another had been shot on a farm and she'd nursed it back to health. The irony was lost on her.

I didn't want to talk about cats or the industrial cleaning course she was doing or the girl in the cell next door who had suffocated her mother with a feather pillow. I was acutely aware that time was running out and so I just came out with it. I cut through her and I said "Why did you do it Grace? Why did you shoot Rudi?"

She stared at me with this strange smile on her face.

"He sent you didn't he? Chimp. He sent you. I knew he still loved me. I knew it."

I wasn't sure I'd heard her correctly. I mean we were talking down a phone through a glass panel. Was she really talking about *my dad?*

"You didn't know did you," she sighed. "Well I guess you had to find out sometime."

"I'm talking about Rudi," I said, feeling hot and bothered despite the cool of the air conditioning.

"So am I," she said. "Why did I do it? So I could be with Chimp. So it would just be the two of us with no one else causing problems. And you know what Morticia? One day we will be together. Just you wait and see."

Did I learn anything from her? From that visit? All I know is that when I walked back out into the sunlight, into freedom, I took great big gulps of fresh air like I wanted to get the real world back inside me. All I can think of is that she was trying to shock me, trying to have the upper hand like she'd always done. And so what she said, how she was, was disturbing, but I wasn't five years old anymore and I could handle it.

"Ok?" Manford asked, searching my face as I got into the truck and he started the engine.

I don't know how he felt about me going to see the person who had killed his stepson.

"I don't think I'll come again," I said.

Manford nodded and looked straight ahead as he pushed the truck into gear.

"At least you done it," he said. "At least you done it."

When I got home I spent twenty minutes in the shower trying to get the stench of that place out of my nose and hair and mind.

"Well honey?" Colita said, coming out poolside, her hair wrapped in a towel. "How'd it go?"

I looked up at her, this graceful elegant woman whose strength shines in her face, whose dignity holds up her shoulders and I didn't know what to say. How could I say all I felt about Grace? She had changed our lives and yet she didn't seem to know it. Or maybe she did. Maybe that was what made her look so smug, so sixteen, so removed.

That was eleven years ago, in 2008. Time moves on. Grace got a ten year denial at her parole in 2011 so she won't be coming up again until 2021. I doubt she's changed much. I expect she's still stuck in that timewarp, still stuck in the mind that lets her believe in a parallel universe, in the yellow brick road, in some crazy relationship with my dad.

Colita volunteers at *The Suns of Life*. She gives the residents ice cream on Sundays and takes them for walks round the grounds. She even persuaded the management to put up some of Nellie's photographs in the foyer and they're good! She captured a time and a place that has long gone now.

One day I went along with her to see where Nellie spent her last days. I was anxious about it but I felt the need to do these things: I had to put the past to rest before I could move on. On that day I met Vivien, a tough old New Yorker who took a liking to the dress I was wearing and put me in touch with a designer in Boca Raton. So now, I design clothes for film sets and on Sundays I go over to Colita's and eat Key Lime Pie and lie in the sun.

Manford's not so good since his stroke but he still keeps his eye on the price of a barrel of oil. I have an apartment in West Palm and Colita gave me the photo from the hallway when I moved in. Nellie and Rudi are sitting on the back of a tractor surrounded by snow. Nellie is wearing a ballgown and shades and Rudi has his arm around her and they are laughing, freeze framed in that happy moment for ever.

It took me years to finish *No Milk Today*. I stole the title from dad's most famous song because I think that is when it all changed. They didn't know how significant it was at the time but what if dad had turned the car around and driven away from that house in The Gower? What if they'd never met Grace? I found some of the things difficult to read and difficult to transcribe: that's why it took so long. Some of mum's words gave me sleepless and tearful nights. Dad said it might not be pretty and he was right but on the other hand, I'm glad I stuck at it. I know my mum now, I know who she was in all her flawed beauty and that is what it was all about. It is my tribute to her and Uncle Joe and I hope I have done them proud.

Polly

When I walk on the beach at Talacre, I feel it the most: the longing, the *hiraeth*.

I stand on that beach and I hear the wind in my ears and I look at that old lighthouse – it's been restored now – and I think back to the days when we were young and carefree and desperate to catch a glimpse of the lighthouse ghost.

Mam says the *hiraeth* can play tricks on you, that it can make you long for something that never really was, but I'm sure it was real, I'm sure.

Ffynnongroyw and Talacre have changed so much in my lifetime. The Castle Bay Hotel has gone, Nanny Gwyn's bungalow on the dunes has gone, the pit has gone and the mining community has gone.

In 2017, the National Lottery paid for Point's winding wheel to be restored and given to the Shropshire Mining Trust. Vincent and I went along when they unveiled it and watched as they placed a statue of a pit pony where the mine shaft used to be. Da couldn't go, he can hardly walk these days, but we took photographs and showed him afterwards and his face lit up.

Change is not all doom and gloom. When Vincent and I went down to see Arwen in Cardiff, we diverted briefly to Merthyr Vale and I was amazed to find that Cwm has become a nature reserve with rivers and streams and native wildlife. Joe would have loved it.

Sometimes when I walk on the beach at Talacre, I think about all the coal under the ground, stretching for miles out to sea. There's wind turbines out there now and the coal sleeps beneath my feet. Vincent says it's new energy for new times.

If I close my eyes, I can hear Nellie's laughter and imagine that at any minute, Joe will come striding over the sand dunes saying "*what the blazing armpits are you doing out here without a coat?*"

The old lighthouse has seen it all. It stands there, haunting and eternal, watching over us like a silent witness to all that has been and all that is yet to come.

And so, I walk on.

Author's Note

On 9th January 1972, a pay dispute led to the first miners' strike taking place since 1926. Miners' wages had not increased in line with other industries since the 1960s and the NUM were locked into a dispute with the Tory government.

On 9th February 1972, the government declared a State of emergency and introduced the 3 day working week to save electricity. Television stations closed down early and powercuts were a frequent occurrence. Miners returned to work on 28th February after the Executive Committee of the NUM and the government came to an agreement. This was a 21% increase in wages, making the miners the highest paid group of the working classes.

By 1973, the miners had slipped down to 18th place. Britain was in the grip of an economic crisis which had seen the cost of imported heating oil skyrocket as a result of the Arab Israeli war. Britain needed coal to fire the power stations, make iron and steel and heat homes. The miners were in a strong position to negotiate for another pay increase.

The Ted Heath government refused their demand for a 7% pay rise and on 4th February, the miners voted for all out strike. The prime minister called a snap election in which he asked the public to decide who was in charge of running Britain: the government or the miners. A hung parliament resulted and as the Tories were unable to form an agreement with the Liberals, Labour swept into power. The new Labour government under Harold Wilson agreed to the NUM's demands and the National Coal Board drafted The Plan For Coal, calling for a £600 million investment to stabilise and expand the UK coal mining industry over the next ten years. At the time, Britain had vast reserves of coal estimated to last for over a hundred years.

In 1979, the conservatives were voted back into Whitehall with Margaret Thatcher as Prime Minister. Her biographer, Charles Moore, records how shortly after coming to power, she summonsed her Home Secretary Willie Whitelaw and told him: "The last conservative government was destroyed by the miners strike. We'll have another and we'll win."

In 1977, conservative MP Nicholas Ridley drafted a secret plan which reported on nationalised industries and proposed strategies for how any national strike should be dealt with in the future. Proposals included stockpiling coal, increasing power station capacity to switch from coal to oil, the use of non union haulage drivers, cuts in supplementary benefits to the families of those on strike and training and equipping a large mobile squad of police who could be deployed to any area under threat of mass picketing.

In 1979, The Whitehall Civil Contingencies Unit reported it best to have a strike that began in the Spring and that it should be over pit closures which tended to divide the National Union of Mineworkers rather than pay, which tended to unite it.

In 1981, Margaret Thatcher threatened to break with The Plan for Coal and close 23 working pits. A ballot for a strike was held with 87% in favour. The NUM Executive had a clear mandate for strike action if the government breached the plan. The government backed down. Some miners went out on strike but Joe Gormley rejected a call for a national strike and persuaded the miners to accept a 9.3% pay rise and return to work.

Margaret Thatcher referred to the miners as "the enemy within" and disliked the relationship the NUM had with the NCB. In March 1983, she appointed 70 year old Ian McGregor as the new Chairman of the NCB, replacing Joe Gormley. He was an American industrialist who had successfully challenged Unions in America and been appointed to the Board of nationalised car maker British Leyland. He succeeded in ousting one of the most militant Union leaders, "Red Robbo" and his success resulted in him being appointed leader of the British Steel Corporation where he had turned the industry around – largely by slashing 80,000 jobs.

McGregor was tasked with finding new markets for British coal and revising the industry. He was also given covert instructions to exact revenge for the 1972 and 1974 miners strikes and break Arthur Scargill. When the Miners' Strike began in 1984, it was only expected to last a matter of weeks but the emergence of the flying pickets was unexpected. McGregor demanded a massive police crackdown and Thatcher agreed. The Miners Strike of 1984/5 was the first time police were sent in to an industrial dispute. The police became an instrument of the State.

The Miners Strike was not something that came out of the blue. It had been cleverly orchestrated for years. The government knew that by threatening to close pits, the miners would strike and Thatcher would show them who was in charge. She would make the rules, reduce the power of the unions, destroy the relationship the NUM had with the NCB and defeat Arthur Scargill.

The mainstream news and national newspapers were heavily prejudiced in the government's favour, portraying the miners as a group of violent men determined to overturn the status quo of Britain.

After the strike, the British economy changed. National industries were privatised and organised labour defeated. Working class communities were fractured and there was a steady increase in social inequality in Britain. It was the end of twentieth century Britain as a new order came in: one that focused on the individual, speculative capitalism, the de-regulation of the financial markets, the dismantling of protection for workers and the rise of the gig economy and zero hour contracts. Some communities have never recovered.

There has never been an investigation into what happened at the Orgreave coking plant on 18th June 1984. The Orgreave Truth and Justice Campaign (otjc.org.uk) continues to fight for a full and independent enquiry into policing and State involvement.

Research Credits

National Justice for Mineworkers website: njfm.org.uk

BBC Archives

Queen Coal: Women of the Miners' Strike by Triona Holden

The HLF Funded Project "Point of Ayr Then and Now" (POACH)

The men and women who recorded their memories of the Miners' Strike including John Lowe from Nottingham whose diaries were referenced by the Daily Mirror.

The fabulous Wikipedia

New Statesman

Guardian: 7th March 2009 article: Arthur Scargill: "We could surrender or stand and fight"

www.rhostyllen.info/bersham

The Yorkshire Post

Black Gold: Jeremy Paxman

The Orgreave Truth and Justice Campaign: otcj.org.uk

Available worldwide from
Amazon

---

www.mtp.agency

www.facebook.com/mtp.agency

@mtp_agency